HOSEA

Hosea

A THEOLOGICAL COMMENTARY

by James M. Ward

Perkins School of Theology
Southern Methodist University

HARPER & ROW, PUBLISHERS

NEW YORK

To my parents,
Dorothy R. Ward
and
Merrill W. Ward

CONTENTS

ABBREVIATIONS

The standard commentaries have been referred to throughout the book by the surnames of their authors. They are listed in the Bibliography.

The following abbreviations of *versions of the Bible* have been used:

ASV   *The Holy Bible. American Standard Revised Version.* New York, 1901.

BH   Kittel, R., ed. *Biblia Hebraica.* 3rd ed. Stuttgart, 1951.

Chicago   Smith, J. M. P., Goodspeed, E. J., and others. *The Complete Bible: An American Translation.* Chicago, 1939.

Jerusalem   Osty, E. *Amos, Osee (La Sainte Bible de Jerusalem).* 2nd ed. Paris, 1960.

JPS   *The Holy Scriptures According to the Masoretic Text.* The Jewish Publication Society of America. Philadelphia, 1917.

KJV   *The Westminster Study Edition of the Holy Bible. Authorized (King James) Version.* Philadelphia, 1948.

Knox   Knox, Ronald. *The Holy Bible. A Translation from the Latin Vulgate in the Light of the Hebrew and Greek Originals.* London, 1955.

LXX   Ziegler, Joseph, ed. *Duodecim prophetae. Septuaginta* XIII. Göttingen, 1943.

Moffatt   Moffatt, James. *A New Translation of the Bible.* New York, 1935.

MT   The Masoretic Text. References are to the 3rd ed. of Kittel; see BH, above.

RSV   *The Holy Bible. Revised Standard Version.* New York, 1952.

OTHER ABBREVIATIONS

AJSL	*American Journal of Semitic Languages and Literatures.*
BDB	Brown, Frances, Driver, S. R., and Briggs, C. A. *A Hebrew and English Lexicon of the Old Testament.* Oxford, 1907.
BJRL	*Bulletin of the John Rylands Library*
BZ	*Biblische Zeitschrift*
(B)ZAW	*(Beihefte zur) Zeitschrift für die Alttestamentliche Wissenschaft*
CBQ	*Catholic Biblical Quarterly*
Ev. Theol.	*Evangelische Theologie*
G.K.	Kautzsch, E. *Gesenius' Hebrew Grammar.* 2nd English ed. by A. E. Cowley. Oxford, 1910. References are to paragraph numbers.
HTR	*Harvard Theological Review*
HUCA	*Hebrew Union College Annual*
IDB	*The Interpreter's Dictionary of the Bible*
JBL	*Journal of Biblical Literature*
JNES	*Journal of Near Eastern Studies*
JPOS	*Journal of the Palestine Oriental Society*
JTS	*Journal of Theological Studies*
Köhler	Köhler, Ludwig, and Baumgartner, Walter. *Lexicon in Veteris Testamenti Libros.* Leiden, 1953. *Supplementum,* Leiden, 1958.
TZ	*Theologische Zeitschrift*
VT	*Vetus Testamentum*
ZKT	*Zeitschrift für katholische Theologie*

PREFACE

An explanation of the method and manner of presentation in the book is given at the end of the Introduction. Therefore, it is only necessary here to acknowledge the debts that I have incurred in writing it.

Professor Samuel Terrien, of Union Theological Seminary in New York, read the first draft of Part One and made suggestions that had a fundamental influence on the ultimate shape and scope of the book. His encouragement was invaluable to me. It is appropriate here also to acknowledge gratefully my larger debt to him and to Professor James Muilenburg, now of San Francisco Theological Seminary, who were my teachers in the Old Testament.

It is a pleasure to record my thanks to several people in the Perkins School of Theology. My Old Testament colleagues, Professors Kermit Schoonover and William Power, read portions of the manuscript and made numerous, helpful comments. Mrs. Nadell Lightfoot typed two drafts of the book, and countless minor revisions, with cheerful and boundless patience. Professor Decherd Turner, Librarian of Bridwell Library, and his staff, provided unexcelled bibliographic services.

Finally, I must express my gratitude to Dean Joseph Quillian, who supports in numerous ways the scholarly work of the Perkins faculty, and to my wife, Elaine, who is a constant source of encouragement and help to all the scholars in the Ward household.

J. M. W.

January, 1966

INTRODUCTION

Israel's literary monuments cluster around the salient events of her history. The social and political upheaval of the eleventh and tenth centuries B.C. produced not only a new monarchial state but also the major collections of narrative material in Genesis, Exodus, Numbers, Joshua, Judges, and Samuel. The other terminus of the Davidic kingship, in the sixth century, was marked by Jeremiah, Ezekiel, Deuteronomy, and the great Deuteronomistic history (Joshua–2 Kings); and the restoration of Jerusalem and the temple at the end of that century was celebrated in various ways by a similar cluster of writings. These are the most obvious illustrations of the thesis. An equally notable though less obvious case is that of the Assyrian crisis in the eighth century and the Books of Hosea, Amos, Micah, and First Isaiah.

One is likely to think of these books as having been produced "along the way" between the rise and fall of the Hebrew monarchy, because the Old Testament as a whole now reflects the Judean viewpoint, according to which the decisive events of Israel's history after the Mosaic era were the conquest, the establishment of the Davidic kingdom, the Babylonian exile, and the return of the Judean exiles to Jerusalem. In this framework, the Assyrian crisis of the eighth century appears as an important but not truly decisive event. This appearance has been heightened by the writer of the Books of Kings, who has consigned the northern kingdom of Israel, from its beginning, to a status outside the true Israel of God, and who has therefore been able to interpret its fall as having no radical effect upon the destiny of the covenant-people. A similar though more subtle impression has been created by the Judean editor of Hos. 1–3, whose comments (e.g., Hos. 1:7) imply that Judah will go on forever as the bearer of Yahwistic religion, undisturbed by the collapse of Israel.

A moment's reflection will serve to correct this picture of covenantal history. The Assyrian crisis of the eighth century issued in the dissolution of the Israelite state and the consequent loss of political unity and self-determination for the majority of the people who were conscious heirs of the Yahwistic tradition. For them, the exile came in 721 B.C., when Samaria fell. Moreover, Judah did not escape the crisis unscathed. She was shaken to the foundations and never regained her former equilibrium. She did manage to maintain her political and geographical unity, on a reduced scale, but she lost her self-determination. The final destruction of the Judean state took place in the sixth century B.C., but its fate was sealed in the Assyrian crisis of the eighth century, as Micah and Isaiah knew. At that time, the great Israelite experiment with kingship as the instrument of divine rule in history was effectively finished, even though some faithful Judean Yahwists of the seventh century, especially king Josiah, tried to prove that it was not.

Thus, the prophets of the eighth century were the theological contemporaries of the sixth-century prophets. Their oracles were produced in response to the final crisis in the history of the Israelite state. Those of Amos and Hosea were apparently made public in the northern kingdom. Since Amos was from Judah, the Book of Hosea is presumably the only extant collection of oracles from a northern Israelite prophet. I say presumably, because the book says nothing explicitly about Hosea's place of origin or residence. We merely assume from the actual northern setting of his oracles that he was a native of that kingdom. In any case, the book is unique as an internal witness to the religious situation in northern Israel.

It is an astonishing fact of Israel's literary history that the first collections of prophetic oracles were not made until two hundred years after the birth of a written national literature which, according to the current scholarly consensus, is to be dated in the tenth century B.C. There may have been none worthy of permanent preservation before the eighth century, although the narratives about Elijah lead us to doubt that this was actually the case. It is entirely possible that other collections were made but, by the accidents of transmission, they failed to survive. Whatever the cause may have been, the fact remains that the first collections of prophetic oracles to be preserved in ancient Israel, and the only one in the northern kingdom, were a response to one of the few major crises in the cultural history of the people of the covenant. Indeed, if we bear in mind what has just been said about the fundamental contemporaneity of the eighth- and sixth-century prophets, we may say that the bulk of the prophetic literature of the

Old Testament was a word spoken in and above the event of the nation's destruction. From the perspective of the heirs of the covenant, that word, when understood in relationship to that event, is one that reveals the purpose and demand of God and is therefore redemptive.

Hosea's words, contributory to that word, are easily the richest in theological significance among those of the eighth-century prophets and are second to none in the entire Old Testament. The exposition of their theological significance is the aim of this book.

Because the Book of Hosea is a theological document and not a personal memoir or chronicle of Israel's history, I have been concerned with the personal and historical allusions in the book only in so far as they are important to the theological meaning, but I have not tried to provide full clarification of these matters for their own sake. They are not unimportant in their own right, and many of them pose interesting problems for historical research. However, I have chosen to deal with the oracles only on their own terms, that is, as theological statements.[1]

This designation of the oracles might seem to require no justification. An explanation is probably desirable, however, because of the many possible meanings of the term "theology" and the widespread debate over the nature of biblical theology. I mean by theology nothing more than a deliberate discourse about God and the world, which gives evidence of careful evaluation of alternative views of the nature and purpose of existence. Put another way, it is an explicit interpretation of human existence in the light of conscious convictions about God.

"Religion" is often used instead of "theology" in connection with the prophets, and frequently it has been denied that there is any theology in the prophetic books. As a matter of fact, there is very little else. It is true, of course, that if theology be defined as a highly abstract, systematic form of reasoning in which a particular set of technical terms, especially terms that have been formulated in non-biblical languages and times, is employed, then the prophetic writings are not theology. This definition is often implied in current discussions of the problem, especially in the United States, but not all theology is of that kind.

Even in the broader sense, not all of the Old Testament is explicitly

---

[1] For an excellent survey of Hosea's allusions to contemporary events, and their implications for his view of Israel's place among the nations, see the new book by Norman K. Gottwald, *All the Kingdoms of the Earth* (New York, 1964), pp. 119–46.

theological. Some of the narrative and legal materials are only implicitly so, as are the prayers of the Psalter. Prayers, of course, are addressed *to* God and are not third-person statements about him. The prophetic books, on the other hand, are largely made up of explicit affirmations about God, his actions, and their consequences. Even though many of these are presented as oracles from God himself, they are nevertheless statements about his purposes, actions, and the like, all presupposing considerable theological reflection. These statements are often extremely compact in form, especially when the form is poetry; but they are always theological.

Religion is more than theology. The "religion" of the prophets involved more than the composing of theological utterances. Undoubtedly, they participated in rituals and prayed, and obviously they made ethical judgments, acted in various ways on the basis of their convictions, and experienced a variety of feelings in conjunction with these acts. What they have left us in the Bible, however, is theological utterance. Faith is more than words, but the Bible is not. It is a verbalization of the implications of faith and of certain convictions about God. The student of the prophets may wish to debate with the systematic theologian about the adequacy of any particular restatement of prophetic affirmations, but he cannot define either the terms or the materials of the debate as untheological.

Many of the prophetic oracles were "received" by the prophets in states of ecstasy or, at the least, of heightened inspiration. They were in this sense "revelations," and can be formally distinguished from the calm, deliberate argumentations of, say, the sermonic monologue in Deut. 1–11, or the treatise of a modern systematic theologian. However, neither the literary form of the prophetic utterance nor the psychological state of the prophet while he formulated it determines whether it is a theological statement. This is wholly a question of the meaning of his words.[2]

The foregoing issue is primarily one of terminology. Another, more serious issue, which goes well beyond the level of definitions, is that of

[2] The whole question of the nature of prophetic experience in its relationship to the forms of prophetic utterance is admirably discussed in J. Lindblom, *Prophecy in Ancient Israel* (Oxford and Philadelphia, 1962). Lindblom rightly declines to judge the ultimate origin of the prophetic oracles on the basis of the psychic experience of the prophet or of his presentation of them as words of God. They are "revelations" from God in the sense that this is what they appear to be to the prophet. The implication and validity of such a conviction are themselves subjects for theological analysis.

the proper object of an Old Testament theology. Is it, for instance, the systematic ordering of biblical statements along the lines of Christian dogmatics: revelation, God, creation, man, sin, salvation?[3] Is it the systematic ordering of biblical statements according to other categories that may be considered more regulative of the Old Testament itself, such as the covenant or the kingship of God?[4] Far from consisting of a systematic ordering at all, is it not rather a serial explication of the various parts of the Old Testament, each of which, though taken singly, is always considered in relation to the whole?[5]

Since I have not written here a theology of the Old Testament, it is not appropriate for me to enter this debate fully in these pages. One need not take sides in the discussion in order to interpret the theology of one part of the Old Testament. Nevertheless, the very writing of such an interpretation, in this case of the Book of Hosea, implies a commitment to the third position mentioned, and I do in fact believe that the most adequate *approach* to biblical theology is the exposition of its theologies. To begin the exposition of biblical theology in this way, however, is not to deny that there is *a* theology of the Old Testament. Perhaps there is. If one contrasts any of its parts theologically with any other ancient literature, he is impressed by the close community of conviction shared by the Old Testament writers. Yet, there are dangers connected with a premature effort to write a theology of the Old Testament. One is that an extraneous norm be employed in judging which among conflicting affirmations is finally endorsed by the Old Testament. This danger always exists, but it is likely to be heightened by the search for unity before one has thoroughly mastered the diversity of theological perspectives. Another danger is that the interpreter will concentrate upon the common *assumptions* of the biblical writers rather than upon their particular assertions, and thereby neglect what was most important to each of the writers individually.[6] There may be actually more unity among the tacit as-

[3] See, e.g., L. Köhler, *Old Testament Theology* (London, 1957), and the concluding remarks in R. C. Dentan, *Preface to Old Testament Theology* (New Haven, 1950).

[4] Cf., W. Eichrodt, *Theology of the Old Testament*, (London, 1961) Vol. I, and O. Procksch, *Theologie des Alten Testaments* (Gütersloh, 1950).

[5] Cf., G. von Rad, *Theology of the Old Testament* (London, 1962) Vol. I.

[6] The Old Testament writers, for example, shared the common, ancient conviction that the world was flat, three stories high (underworld, earth, heaven), and surrounded by a cosmic ocean. They rarely attached much importance to this conviction, however.

sumptions of the biblical writers than among their explicit declarations. Therefore, the seeker after unity must beware of a premature concentration upon these assumptions.

It may be that one man cannot write an adequate theology of the Old Testament if first he must write (though not necessarily publish) theologies of all its components. Nevertheless, I believe that the proper means to an adequate theology of the whole is a full collection of theologies of its parts.

My principal interest, then, is in the theological significance of the Book of Hosea. Strictly speaking, it is not the theology of Hosea, although I will use this phrase frequently because it is less cumbersome than the other. The theology of the *book* presumably derives from that of the *prophet,* but it is impossible for us to determine the precise relationship between the two. Too little is known about the manner of composition and transmission of the prophetic writings for anyone to be dogmatic about his solution of the problem.

There are actually two issues involved here. The first is the question as to which of the parts of the Book of Hosea were composed by Hosea himself, a problem usually referred to as that of "authenticity." This issue, more than any other, has occupied the attention of modern critics of the prophetic literature. Furthermore, this concern has often been accompanied by a tendency to exclude from theological consideration those portions of the literature that were believed to have been composed by anyone other than the prophet himself. In other words, it has frequently been assumed that only the *ipsissima verba* of the prophet whose name is associated with a given book of the canon carry canonical authority. All editorial expansions and additions are likely to be neglected as lacking religious interest for the modern user of the Bible. Even though this disinterest, together with what it implies concerning the authority of the canon, is theoretically denied, the practical effect of the critical process is often to focus attention exclusively upon the "authentic" words of the prophets, relegating the rest to the critical waste basket. Amos 9:8b–15 is a good case in point. The vast majority of those modern works on the prophets that present this passage as a post-exilic addition to the Book of Amos (and this would comprise the majority of standard works) discuss this passage only to show that it is not attributable to Amos, and do not seek to interpret it sympathetically as a positive contribution to theology, either for its own time or for ours.

Thus, the second major issue arising out of the investigation of the authorship of the prophetic books is the status of the so-called in-authentic portions of these writings. Several possibilities suggest themselves. We can simply correct the recent inattention to these materials by making a more adequate historical appraisal of them as theological documents. Another possibility is to disregard the authenticity of the components of the prophetic books, as a merely historical question, and take the books of the canon in their present form as the proper objects of theological concern. According to this method, we would be interested only in the theology of the present books, that is to say, of their final compilers, and not in that of the "original" writers, whose theology is presumably irrecoverable.

By contrast with the older neglect of the "spurious" segments of the prophetic books, this second approach has a considerable appeal to those who consider the Bible in its present form as the starting point for interpretation. In the bald form described here, however, this method has important deficiencies. It abstracts the prophetic words from their relationship to the concrete events and institutions of Israel's life; and this interrelationship is widely, and I believe rightly, regarded as the primary medium of revelation. Furthermore, this method disregards the differences among the kinds of unity discernible in the present books of the Bible. On any but the most dogmatic assumption of the theological unity of the extant books of the Bible, the problem of the relationship between Amos 9:8b–15 and the rest of Amos is different from that of the relationship between Hab. 3 and Hab. 1–2, for example, or that between Zech. 9–14 and Zech. 1–8. In short, the nature of the literary and theological unity of each of the prophetic books must be regarded as a special problem that cannot be solved on a priori grounds. We cannot assume that, because the Book of Hosea is quantitatively dominated by threats, the promises are inauthentic. Nor can we judge Hosea's promises to be spurious if we find those of Amos to be so. On the other hand, we cannot assume that everything in the present Book of Hosea must be from Hosea himself merely because it is in the collection headed by his name. What we seek first of all is a knowledge of the internal coherence or incoherence of the collected oracles themselves. We can decide how many theological perspectives are present only on the basis of the most rigorous scrutiny of the principal units of the collection.[7]

[7] A different perspective from that of the older literary criticism has been gained in recent decades in the study of the prophets, especially in Scandinavia. The previous effort exerted on separating the authentic words of the

It must be acknowledged at the outset that the total task before us is beset with difficulties. The Book of Hosea is often exceedingly hard to interpret. The Hebrew text abounds with unusual words and unexplained allusions to events and social conditions. Furthermore, these uncertainties seem to have been compounded in the process of transmission by scribes who were as puzzled by the text as we are. Moreover, the paucity of extant information about Hosea's life and its enigmatic character add to the interpreter's perplexity. The brevity of most of the poems, their impassioned, oracular nature, and the fact that they are tightly constructed poetry and not expansive prose, must also give us pause.

The interpretation of ancient Hebrew poetry goes hand in hand with translation, and so a full translation of Hosea's oracles is necessary. Since a final translation is impossible, a final theological interpretation of Hosea is also out of the question. I hope, however, that the present translation, and the interpretation that accompanies it, are not merely eccentric, but faithful to the text and to the tradition of biblical criticism.

In my translation, I have not attempted to put everything in an entirely new way. Where the traditional English renderings have been found fully adequate I have simply followed them in one or another of their forms. Some of my departures from the English tradition have been dictated by purely poetic considerations, that is, the wish to preserve as much as possible of the Hebrew poetic form. Other changes are substantive, of course. The latter are explained in the textual notes, as are some of the former. Unexplained departures may be assumed to belong to the first type.

The chapters of this book follow for the most part the chapter divisions of the Hebrew Bible. I have dealt with Hos. 5–7 differently

---

prophet from the inauthentic additions of later scribes is now widely believed to have been based upon an erroneous assumption concerning the transmission of prophetic oracles, namely that they were written down by the prophet himself or by one of his hearers and that the transcript was subsequently edited with considerable freedom by later scribes. Today, the critic is likely to treat a collection of oracles as the final product of a dynamic process of proclamation and writing carried on by the prophet, together with a group of disciples, over a period of time, often a long time. The disciples are presumed to have been faithful students of the master, who expanded his oracles, if at all, only in conformity with his "authentic" teaching. This new attitude toward the traditionary process is a welcome one. Unfortunately, it does not provide precise means by which to decide where the faithful disciples' work leaves off and where that of the scribal glossators begins. Once again, for a summary of recent work on this subject, see Lindblom, *op. cit.*, pp. 220–291.

because the traditional chapter divisions do not do justice to the literary units, or to their peculiar settings, or to both. Often the biblical chapters seem to have been compiled out of several originally self-contained poems. On the other hand, the editor, either Hosea or someone else, has almost as often succeeded in uniting these into a new creation that manifests considerable integrity. I have concentrated upon the present coherence, where it exists, as the basis of theological exposition.

The textual notes contain many references to the Hebrew text. These will usually be inaccessible to the reader without knowledge of Hebrew. Unfortunately, no interpretation that is not a mere representation of universally accepted scholarly conclusions can stand without this effort at textual justification. Many of the textual notes, however, are accessible to those without a background in Hebrew. Most of the critical discussion of the poems is carried in these notes.

Explanations of statements in the biblical text that are apt to be confusing but are not of direct theological importance themselves have been included among the notes on the text. Items that are neither confusing nor theologically important have been omitted from the discussion altogether. Further information about them will be readily found in any good dictionary of the Bible. Undoubtedly, an infallible separation of items into these three categories has not been achieved, but this comment will explain the principle that has been followed.

Brackets in the translation enclose material that I believe to be secondary. The words put in *parentheses* are tacit in the original, or have been added to bring out what I consider to be a nuance, or represent a proposed emendation. Explanations of the particular enclosures are given in the textual notes.

Chapter and verse references are to the English Bible, unless designated otherwise. These are identical with those of the Hebrew Bible, except in the following instances:

ENGLISH		HEBREW
1:10–11	=	2:1–2
2:1–23	=	2:3–25
11:12	=	12:1
12:1–14	=	12:2–15
13:16	=	14:1
14:1–9	=	14:2–10

Where confusion might result both designations are given, e.g., 1:10 (Heb. 2:1).

PART ONE

───────────────────────────────

ISRAEL, THE BRIDE OF YAHWEH

1 A TRACT FOR THE TIMES: HOSEA 1

Superscription to the Book of Hosea (1:1)

1   The word of Yahweh that came to Hosea the son of Beeri in the days of Uzziah, Jotham, Ahaz, and Hezekiah, kings of Judah, and in the days of Jeroboam the son of Joash, king of Israel.

A Tract for the Times (1:2–9)

2   When Yahweh first spoke through Hosea,

then Yahweh said to Hosea:
"Go, take for yourself
    a whorish wife
        and whorish children;
For the land is utterly prostituted,
    away from Yahweh."

3   So he went and took Gomer, daughter of Diblaim, and she conceived and bore him a son.

4   *And Yahweh said to him:*
"Call his name Jezreel,
    for yet a little while
And I will avenge the bloodshed of Jezreel
    upon the house of Jehu,"
["And put an end to the sovereignty of the House of Israel."]

5   ["And in that day
I will break the bow of Israel
    in the valley of Jezreel."]

6   Then she conceived again and bore a daughter.
And He Said to him:
"Call her name Not-Pitied,
    for I will never again

> Have pity on the House of Israel
> to show them any favor at all."

7
> ["Yet the House of Judah will I pity
> and rescue them by Yahweh their God.
> I will not rescue them by bow, or sword,
> by warfare, or horses, or horsemen."]

8   When she had weaned Not-Pitied she conceived and bore a son.

9
> *And He said:*
> "Call his name Not-My-People,
> for you are not my people,
> and I am not your *'Ehyeh.*"

NOTES ON THE TEXT

Verse 1. A Judean editor has synchronized Hosea's ministry in Israel with Isaiah's ministry "in the days of Uzziah, Jotham, Ahaz, and Hezekiah, kings of Judah" (Isa. 1:1). The minimum period thus designated (from the last year of Uzziah to the first of Hezekiah) is 742–715 B.C., and the maximum (from the first year of Uzziah to the last of Hezekiah), 783–687 B.C. This notice tells us only that Hosea's ministry was believed by some Judeans, at the (unknown) time when the book was edited, to have occurred in the eighth century B.C.[1] Jeroboam II's reign was *ca.* 786–746 B.C. Since portions of Hosea seem to reflect powerfully the crisis that centered on the Syro–Ephraimitic invasion of Judah in 735 B.C. (see the discussion of 5:8–15, below) as well as the period of dynastic chaos between the death of Zechariah (746 B.C.) and the accession of Hoshea (732 B.C.; see the discussion of 7:3–7), the reference to

[1] The year 727 B.C. has been taken as the date of Hezekiah's accession by some scholars, on the basis of the notice in 2 Kings 18:10 that he became king in the fourth year of Hoshea of Israel. Thus, for example, Lindblom believes that Hezekiah was born in 735 B.C. (as the child dubbed "Immanuel" by Isaiah in Isa. 7:14; 8:8) and that he may have become king in 727 B.C., either as coregent with Ahaz, his father, until the latter's death a decade later (cf., 2 Kings 18:13), or under the actual rule of his mother until the attainment of his majority. See, *A Study of the Immanuel Section of Isaiah, Isa. vii, 1–ix, 6* (Lund, 1958), p. 25, note 3. If this judgment is correct, the editorial date in Hos. 1:1 is more accurate than is usually supposed.

Jeroboam in 1:1 may have been merely for the purpose of dating the beginning of Hosea's ministry (1:2; cf., Isa. 6:1 and Ezek. 1:1). It probably antedates the expanded, Judean version of the synchronism.

We know nothing whatever about Hosea's father, his place of origin, his means of livelihood, or any other outward circumstances of his life. Also, it is futile to speculate about such matters on the basis of "internal evidence." It has become common practice to suppose, for example, that Hosea was a farmer, because he used so many agricultural images. One might equally well conclude that he was a priest, or courtier, or lawyer, because he was so familiar with cultic practices, royal policies, and legal procedures. If chapters 1 and 3 report events of Hosea's life, as most scholars now believe that they do, we have only these fragments of Hosea's biography and nothing more. And even these have given rise to widely divergent inferences.

Verse 2. Critics are evenly divided over the question whether בהושע means "through Hosea" or "to Hosea." The former is the correct meaning of the preposition ב, however.

According to the MT, ילדי is a plural noun, "children" (it is so taken by *KJV, ASV, JPS, Chicago, LXX, Jerusalem,* Wellhausen, Wolff, and others).[2] Some scholars emend the text and translate "have children" (*RSV, Moffatt,* Weiser, Nötscher, and others). There is no justification for the change, however. An important point in the debate over Hosea's marital history is at stake, namely whether or not Gomer had "whorish" children before she married Hosea and whether she was therefore already a "whorish" woman. The MT, if taken literally, seems to support the conclusion that Gomer brought children with her into the marriage. The obvious connotation of such a statement may be misleading, however, and the command of God as reported here may be meant merely to cover the whole series of experiences described in vss. 3–9. The whorish children of vs. 2, then, would be none other than the three mentioned in what follows.

Verses 4d–5, 7. I believe these lines to be editorial expansions and not parts of the original tract. (1) The explanations of the first and fourth signs each consist of a single line, matching the one-line command. The second and third explanations were probably once form-

---

[2] The standard commentaries listed in the Bibliography are cited throughout merely by the surnames of their authors, and it may be assumed, unless stated otherwise, that the reference is to the discussion of the relevant chapter and verse of the Book of Hosea. The abbreviations of the versions of the Bible will be found in the List of Abbreviations.

ally identical to these. The unity and elegance of these sections are spoiled by the intrusive comments. (2) The first and fourth signs are "explained" just enough to provoke curiosity, reflection, perhaps discussion, and surely a wondering anticipation. They are vague and provocative rather than descriptive. So are the second and third signs, once the secondary lines are removed. The latter, on the other hand, are specific and descriptive. Vs. 7 presupposes the tradition about Jerusalem's miraculous deliverance from the Assyrian army in 701 B.C. (2 Kings 19:35-7), and is therefore a later Judean addition. This is the opinion of virtually all modern scholars. Vs. 5 probably suggests the Assyrian defeat of Pekah and the annexation of the Israelite territories north of the Valley of Jezreel and east of the Jordan River in 733-32 B.C. (2 Kings 15:29-30), or the final defeat of Hoshea's forces in 722-21 B.C. (2 Kings 17:3-6). Wolff, Sellin, Weiser, and others treat also vs. 5 as a later addition. In both vs. 5 and vs. 7 the *manner* of fulfilment of the sign is described. The first and the fourth sign as well as the first (Israelite) section of the third sign are silent about this irrelevant factor. (3) The third sign is a negative one: "Not-Pitied." How could it possibly suggest something positive? No one would have thought of construing it backwards as a prediction of salvation. Only one who knew that Israel had already fallen but not yet Judah (in spite of the desperate crisis of 701 B.C.) could have composed vs. 7. The argument of Wellhausen and others that vs. 5 must have been a genuine prediction by Hosea, because it proved wrong, is unconvincing. The three statements in vss. 4b-5 do not necessarily refer to a single disaster that had three, simultaneous consequences. Whether we read them as genuine predictions or *vaticinia ex eventu,* they may be taken as allusions to distinct events, though all transpired within a "little while" (whatever that means). If the third section could have acquired an historical comment as ill-suited to the original sign as vs. 7, the second section could as easily have acquired such additional notations as vss. 4d and 5. These are not integral aspects of the prediction concerning Jehu's dynasty, details of which were not fulfilled. They are historical allusions to events that actually took place within twenty years of the death of Jeroboam II, and that were naturally called to mind by the vague but suggestive sign of "Jezreel." (4) Neither vs. 4d nor vs. 5 fits comfortably into the poetic scheme. Each sounds like a clumsy afterthought. "And in that day" is especially intrusive.

ממלכות בית ישראל ("sovereignty of the House of Israel") means either the sovereignty of the House of Israel or the territory to which the royal house claimed title. ממלכות means a king's territory in Josh. 13:12, 21, 27, 30, 31, and "reign" in Jer. 26:1. In 1 Sam. 15:28 and 2 Sam. 16:3, either "sovereignty" or "royal territory" makes good sense. These are all the occurrences of the word in the OT. The statement in Hos. 1:4 could refer either to the Israelite loss of Galilee and Gilead to Assyria in 732 B.C. or to the Assyrian reduction of the Israelite kings to vassalage. Genuine sovereignty was surrendered by Menahem (2 Kings 15:19) and was not successfully recovered by any subsequent Israelite king. Whether or not this clause in vs. 4 is genuine, it does not denote the total destruction of the Israelite state, which is implied only by the third sign.

בית ישראל ("House of Israel") denotes the northern Israelite state, in the Book of Hosea (1:6; 5:1; 6:10 [?]; and 11:12), in distinction to the "House of Judah" (1:7; 5:12, 14; 6:11 [here and in the following passage simply, "Judah"]; 11:12). It is the monarchial institution of Israel, which is also designated "Ephraim" in contradistinction to Judah (cf., especially 6:10; 11:12; 5:12–14; 6:4; 10:11). It is not synonymous with the people, which is variously designated "my people" (i.e., God's; 1:9; 1:10; 2:1, 23; 4:6, 8, 12; 6:11; 11:7; and cf., 4:9, 14), "sons of Israel" (1:10; 3:1, 4, 5; 4:1), and "Israel" (9:10; 11:1, 8; 13:1; 14:1, 5; and possibly 8:2, 3 and 9:7). As one might expect, "Israel" is ambiguous. It is also used to denote the northern kingdom, as distinct from Judah (4:15, 16; 8:5, 14; 10:1 [?], 15; 13:9), and often in conjunction with "Ephraim" (5:3, 5; 6:10; 7:10; 8:8; 9:1; 10:6, 8, 9). The sequence in 6:11–7:1 is noteworthy: "My people," "Israel," "Ephraim," and "Samaria." These are not synonymous but overlapping. The focus is progressively reduced from the covenantal people to the northern state and its political center. See, further, Additional Note A: Designations of Hosea's Audience.

Verse 6. The phrase נשא אשא להם ("show them any favor at all") seems to me to be an ellipsis for נשא אשא פני להם, and, therefore, to carry the usual meaning of נשא פנים, namely, "to show consideration, kindness, partiality, etc."

Verse 9. The translation follows the MT (ואנכי לא־אהיה לכם), which has been defended as an illusion to Exod. 3:12 ff. by W. R. Smith (cited by Brown), Peters (*Osee und die Geschichte*, 1924, p. 19), van Hoonacker (cited by Buck, *Die Liebe Gottes beim Propheten*

Osee, 1953, p. 8), Buber (*The Prophetic Faith,* 1949, p. 116), and Wolff; cf., *LXX* and *JPS.* In that passage, God says, אהיה עמך ("I am [shall be] with you"), to Moses, in connection with the revelation of the divine name אהיה אשר אהיה ("I am [shall be] what I am"). He then adds, "Thus you shall speak to the Israelites, ''*Ehyeh* ("I am") has sent me to you.' " The tacit verb in the parallel member, and אלהי in 2:23 (Heb. 2:25), in connection with the reversal of the name לא־עמי, admittedly support the emendation to ואנכי לא אלהיכם ("and I am not your God"), which many scholars adopt. Yet these factors are not decisive, and the MT should be retained.

Verses 10 and 11 (*Heb. 2:1–2*). These have been placed after 2:25 (Heb. 2:23). See the next chapter.

God's RELATIONSHIP TO ISRAEL is at once communal and intimately personal. It comprehends the interior dimensions of human existence—man's reason, will, and affections—as well as the social dimensions of his corporate life. God is the Lord of Israel, the people of the covenant, and he is the Lord of each man's personal destiny. He can be Lord of each only by being Lord of both. This is a fundamental conviction of the biblical writers. Nowhere in the Bible is this twofold nature of man's relationship to God more memorably celebrated than in the oracular poems of Hosea.

Among Hosea's many contributions to the language of faith are the two powerful metaphors of God as father and husband of Israel. These symbols convey both the intimacy and the social implications of faith, and they provide a remarkably suitable vehicle for the dramatic representation of Israel's history as the people of God. Chapter 11 is built around the parental image and chapters 1–3 around the image of God's marriage to Israel. Neither of these metaphors was invented by Hosea for use in religious utterance, but their creative use by Hosea was so effective that these portions of his recorded oracles have become the classical Old Testament texts on the fatherhood and love of God.

The first three chapters of Hosea have long occupied a special place in Old Testament criticism. They have probably provoked more discussion than any other segments of the prophetic literature, except perhaps the oracles concerning Immanuel and the Suffering Servant in the Book of Isaiah (7:10–16 and 52:13–53:12). One of the reasons for this massive interest is the theological importance of the material. Another is the perplexing character of the story of Hosea's marriage to Gomer, which seems to lie in the background of these chapters. This story is one of the most interesting mysteries in the Bible, and interpreters of Hosea have shown an understandable compulsion to solve it. I believe that the mystery is insoluble and that scholarly preoccupation with the enigma of Gomer has distracted attention from the primary task of interpreting what these chapters actually say. Indeed, I would say that this preoccupation has led to a distorted view of Hosea's theology that is widely held among students of the Bible. Therefore, our first objective will be not to trace the story of Gomer but to discover the logic of Hosea's oracles.

When this primary task has been done, it will be necessary to discuss the problem of Hosea's marital history, not because a solution of the mystery can be found, but because there are important theological implications in the major theories that are currently held to explain the marriage and its bearing on Hosea's message. This is not to say that the effort to explain it is unjustified. On the contrary, no efforts of historical criticism are unjustified in themselves and all new proposals resulting therefrom are welcome. At the present time, however, the data are so meager that reconstruction is almost futile. No reconstruction is sufficiently probable to be useful in interpreting the oracles of Hosea. The meaning of these oracles and their implications for biblical theology must be discovered solely in the words themselves and not in any alleged marital history of the prophet. I will not engage in any serious discussion of that history, therefore, until dealing with Hos. 3, where the identity of Hosea's women has a direct bearing upon the meaning of the oracle itself. In treating chapters 1 and 2, it is best to keep away as much as possible from the question of Hosea's domestic affairs.

Chapter 1 is a small prophetic tract in four parts. It may never have been circulated as an ordinary tract. The Old Testament does not report any public distributions of written prophetic oracles, although the placards of Isaiah and Habakkuk show that short, written pronouncements were occasionally made (Isa. 8:1–2 and Hab. 2:2). My main reason for calling Hos. 1 a tract, however, is that it does not fit into any of the usual categories of prophetic literature. It is not a simple poetic oracle, or a prose sermon, or a personal chronicle. It is not even an ordinary sign-narrative, such as the reports of symbolic actions in Isa. 20 and Jer. 27. It resembles the catalogue of signs in Ezek. 4–5 in some respects; but it is a carefully organized document, which has internal, formal coherence, whereas Ezek. 4–5 is merely a collection of separate reports. The word "tract" will therefore serve to designate this unique prophetic creation.

The tract consists of four declarations of God, which are in poetic form, set within a brief narrative framework, which is in prose. The formula "and he said" is used in all four introductions. In the Hebrew text, the first introduction contains four words, the second, three, the third, two, and the fourth, one. By this device, the reader's attention is focused more and more closely upon the divine commands themselves.[3] This feature is one of the marks of the literary unity of the chapter. The occasions for the four words of God are stated in the sparsest prose and provide the narrative setting that is holding the oracles together. This rigid economy of language is matched by the brevity of the poetic oracles themselves. A command of God to Hosea to perform a symbolic action is given in a single sentence, and its meaning is explained in a second. This original form is preserved in the received text of the first and fourth oracles. It has been expanded editorially in the case of the second and third. The critical justification of this last opinion is presented in the Notes on the Text.

The four oracles in the little tract contain four different, though related, denunciations of Israel. Two are predictions of coming disaster and two are observations of contemporary conditions. The series of four is a minute replica of the whole corpus of Hosea's oracles of judgment. The objects of the four divine pronouncements are not identical to each other, and a proper grasp of Hosea's message requires that the differences be discerned and fully weighed. The object of the first is the land of Israel, of the second, the dynasty of Jehu, of the third, the northern kingdom itself, and of the fourth, the people of God.

According to the first part of the tract, Hosea married Gomer, daughter of Diblaim (a man who is otherwise unknown) as a symbol of the whorishness of the land, which had been devoted to strange gods. The land's condition was borne by the woman, who was a woman of "whorishness" (or "fornication"). This symbol does not threaten a future divine punishment but declares the present fact of the land's corruption. It does not say whether Gomer's "whorishness"

[3] Cf., Wolff.

was sexual or religious, since the word may mean either. Actually it could have been both, since the popular worship of nature in ancient Palestine, and elsewhere, included sexual rites. The sign is clearly explained, however, as pointing to these cults of alien gods.

The "land" included its populace, of course. It may even be that the land and the people are represented by the "whorish woman" and the "whorish children," respectively. This distinction is apparently made in 2:2, where the "children" are exhorted to plead with their "mother" on account of her infidelity to God. Whether or not this is a correct inference, however, the land in 1:2 must not be identified merely with the population. Such an identification is perhaps made in 4:1, but elsewhere in the book the land is set over against the people and assigned a status independent of them. It is "the Lord's land" (9:3), which has been made to languish by an irresponsible populace (4:3, cf., 10:1), and from which they will be expelled (9:3; cf., 11:5 and 7:16).

Hosea says that the land is utterly prostituted by forsaking Yahweh, the Lord of Israel. He thus implies that the Lord is "married" to the land. This is an astonishing use of the metaphor. We take no offense at Hosea's suggestion that God's relationship to the *people* be compared to a marriage, because it is clear in this application that a moral and not a physical bond is meant. The implication that God is married to the *land* is quite different, however, for this is an idea that belongs to Baalism and other ancient cults of nature. There, the god of rain and sky was believed to be mated to the mother goddess, the earth. Hosea's use of the marriage metaphor, therefore, entailed the bold risk of popular misunderstanding. However, Hosea never alluded to the land, or to the earth, as to a divine power. Nothing he said suggests that God was actually mated to a goddess. God possessed the land as its creator, not as its husband.

Hosea's use of the metaphor was not an accommodation to the worship of fertility gods. It was part of his polemic against it. He described the "divine wife," that is, the land, as a mundane prostitute and, in so doing, he negated the baalistic theology and emptied it of its power. He might have devised a safer polemic than this, of course, but it is hard to imagine a more powerful or memorable one.

The decisive factor in the relationship between the soil, as God's gift to man, and the religious community, was not the people's exploitation of a physical marriage between two deities, but their obedience to a moral bond between themselves and God. Hosea made this perfectly clear in chapter 4, for example, and especially in the magnificent promise of a future renewal of God's gift of the land, in 2:16–23. There, the relationship to the land is set directly in the midst of a covenantal bond with God. Thus the order of redemption, which is symbolized by the covenant, takes precedence in the oracles of Hosea over the order of creation, as it does in the Old Testament generally. The order of creation was not disregarded by Hosea, however, even though his contemporaries were led by the urgency of its problems to neglect the peculiarly human problems of existence and to corrupt their ethical understanding. A mere denial of the Canaanite or Babylonian solution of the theological problem of man's relation to the earth did not remove the problem. Hosea did not provide a full solution of his own, but he disclosed his conviction that Yahwism had to come to terms with it, positively, if it was to provide an adequate theological basis for human action, that is, an adequate ethic.

The second sign in chapter 1 is the symbolic name "Jezreel." It condemns the dynasty of Jehu, which was represented in Hosea's time by Jeroboam II. "The blood of Jezreel," for which Hosea blamed the dynasty, was probably Jehu's annihilation of the house (dynasty) of Omri, by which he established himself in power in 842 B.C. (2 Kings 9–10). Hosea may also have had in mind Jezebel's murder of Naboth the Jezeelite (1 Kings 21),[4] or other crimes of which we have no record. Danell has suggested that Hosea chose this name because it was symbolic of the nationalistic pretensions of the northern kingdom.[5] Jehu had murdered the Judean king Ahaziah, as well as the Israelite king Joram, in the Valley of Jezreel (2 Kings 9:27–28). He may have been seeking control of a reunited kingdom of the twelve tribes. Jezreel was also a place of residence for the Jehu dynasty (1 Kings 18:45 f.; 2 Kings 9:15 ff.) Consequently, the name was representative of the ruling house.

These associations make it appear likely that Hosea's indictment was political in nature, pointing especially to the pretentious exercise of power that characterized Jehu and his line. The writer of 2 Kings 10:28 f. considered Jehu less than an ardent Yahwist, but the cultic accusation he made against him amounts to little more than that he

---

[4] Cf., Y. Kaufmann, *The Religion of Israel* (Chicago, 1960), p. 370.
[5] *Studies in the Name Israel in the Old Testament* (Uppsala, 1946), pp. 146 ff.

perpetuated the schism of Jeroboam I. It cannot be taken as evidence of overt Baalism.[6] The only evidence that Hosea was thinking of the fertility cult when he chose this name is the meaning of the word itself, namely " *'El* sows." *'El* was an important Canaanite deity, and the agricultural image was well suited to the Canaanite fertility rites. It is not impossible, therefore, that the name "Jezreel" had a cultic origin.[7] There is no evidence that it was used in the fertility rites of Hosea's time, however, and it is unlikely that his indictment was meant to be cultic.

Nothing is said about the proximate cause of the disaster and whether it was to be a foreign invasion or an internal revolt. Even the editorial expansion in 1:5 is vague, although it probably points to a foreign invasion. The ultimate cause of the disaster was, of course, God (1:4b). The time of the event announced by this second sign was future. The sword had not yet begun to fall. This proclamation must have been made therefore before Shallum murdered Zechariah, the son of Jeroboam II, in 745 B.C., and brought the dynasty of Jehu to an end (2 Kings 15:8–10).

Hosea's third prophetic sign promised the dissolution of the "House of Israel," that is, the north Israelite kingdom, as a political institution. In the previous sign he had condemned only one particular dynasty, but in this sign of "Not-Pitied" he tolled the knell for the monarchial state as such. He did not predict the manner of the kingdom's fall, but he did say that it lay in the future. This announcement was therefore made before 722–21 B.C., but it is impossible to say more than this about its date. If the oracular names were actually publicized at the times of the children's births, as the narrative of chapter 1 declares, a period of at least one year transpired between the publication of the second and the third sign. No clues are provided, however, to explain the extension of Hosea's condemnation from the dynasty to the kingdom itself.

The explanation of the second name (1:6) is not an explanation

[6] Wolff interprets the association of the sign (1:4) with the command (1:2) to mean that Hosea indicted Jehu for failure to eradicate the inner baalization of Yahwism. This is a reasonable hypothesis; yet it is dangerous to force the evidence for the baalization of Yahwism in Hosea's day to do service for a reconstruction of the situation a century earlier. On the other hand, Kaufmann's denial that there was any Baalism in Israel after Jehu involves too narrow a definition of the term (*op. cit.*, p. 369).

[7] See, H. G. May, "An Interpretation of the Names of Hosea's Children," *JBL* 55 (1936), 285–91.

of the reason why God wished to destroy the kingdom. It merely tells that the name "Not-Pitied" pointed to his intended action. It is, therefore, different from the first two signs, which describe the crimes that had called them forth. It is like the fourth sign, for that one also omits any indication why the people were no longer God's people. The fourth sign is much closer to the first than it is to the third in its scope, however, and it seems quit justified to take the worship of alien gods as the basis of both the first and the fourth sign.

The first and the fourth sign are alike in two other respects. Neither is directed at the political institution of the Israelite kingdom. The first concerns the land and, by implication, also the people who have corrupted the land, whereas the fourth explicitly mentions the people themselves. Secondly, the corruption of the land and the rejection of the people as God's people are described as having come to pass already. By contrast, the destruction of Jehu's dynasty and of the north Israelite state, in the second and third signs, are placed in the future.

It is especially important to distinguish the intentions of the third and the fourth sign. In the third, a future judgment of God upon the state is predicted. In the fourth, the present destruction of the people is proclaimed. Their dissolution as the people of God is not the final disaster in a chronological series. It is a present fact. The people are already "Not-My-People." God is now no longer the one who is with them. This is not a coming divine destruction but a self-destruction that has already been fulfilled. It is a worse evil than the fall of the state, but it is not an evil to which the other is a prelude. If there is a relationship between the two, it is that God's destruction of the kingdom is the sequel to the people's destruction of itself. The latter is not to take place simultaneously with the former; it is already accomplished.

In the light of the differences among these four signs it is impossible to take them as repetitions of a single word of judgment, phrased in slightly different terms. There is a temptation that constantly attends the reading of prophetic oracles to think of them as variations on a single theme. Especially if one reads quickly, the reader is likely to miss the distinctions made in the judgmental oracles and might reduce them in his mind to a mass of pronouncements of "destruction" upon "Israel" as a "divine punishment" for "sin." There is admittedly a certain amount of repetition and imitation in the prophetic literature, especially in its latest portions. In the oracles of such prophets as Isaiah, Jeremiah, and Hosea, however, there is a profusion of images and a diversity of ideas, rather than redundancy. Yet, their oracles are compact, sometimes almost cryptic, and yield their nuances only to the careful reader.

There is another factor that has influenced recent interpretation of the Old Testament and that may have prevented commentators on Hosea from taking full account of the distinction he made between the people and the state. According to a widely heralded conception of Hebrew social psychology, a fundamental feature of Israelite mentality was the tacit understanding of the group as a psychological entity, a kind of corporate personality.[8] The individual man and the small group were felt to be particular manifestations of the tribe or nation. Correspondingly, all secondary institutions of the group would be psychologically identical with the group as it was primarily imagined ("imaged"), in Israel's case as the "family" of "Jacob." The members and institutions would thus be functional embodiments of the common "soul" of the primary group.[9]

Following this line of interpretation, it would be possible to view the Israelite monarchy as an agency of the corporate entity "Israel," a kind of functional extension of a non-differentiated psychic whole. This group-consciousness may indeed have existed during the early, tribal period of Hebrew history. The ancient custom of blood vengeance may illustrate this phenomenon. That custom presupposed a psychic community that took precedence over the individual. The latter was not the unit given chief consideration. Injury to a tribesman was first of all injury to the tribe and only secondarily injury to the man. Furthermore, guilt borne by one was necessarily borne by all, since all were particular embodiments of the same tribal "soul."

What may have been true of the pastoral Hebrew tribe, however, ceased to be true of the Israelite nation as it became more complex and differentiated. The older consciousness of corporate unity had already been modified by the time the earliest compilations of laws were made, as shown by the *lex talionis* (e.g., Exod. 21:23–24). In cases of manslaughter and bodily injury, this law presupposes the individual man and not the tribe or family as the unit of considera-

---

[8] Cf., H. W. Robinson, "The Hebrew Conception of Corporate Personality," in J. Hempel, ed., *Werden und Wesen des Alten Testaments* (*BZAW* 66, [1936]), pp. 49 ff.

[9] J. Pedersen, *Israel: Its Life and Culture* (Copenhagen and London, 1926/1940), is the basic work.

tion. To be sure, this is the first point at which one would expect the imagined "corporate personality" to break down. At other points it broke down only gradually or not at all. Yet, this illustration shows the tendency of the old psychology of giving way to new forms of thought under the pressures of advancing civilization. Although Israel continued to be described in traditional fashion as the "sons of Jacob," she was no longer a family in any meaningful sense of the term.

Some of the new institutions adopted after the settlement were capable of assimilation into the older patterns of behavior, so that no discontinuity was felt between them and the people. The priesthood of the Palestinian sanctuary was one. It was so completely absorbed into the old tribal structure of the community that the priestly "tribe" of Levi actually appropriated the place of the secular tribe of Levi. The assimilation took place before the emergence of a written literature and there are therefore no adequate historical sources to enable us to trace the process. However, the situation was quite different with the monarchy. Kingship came late into Israel and was never thoroughly assimilated.

David was a man of the people, a shepherd according to tradition, and their savior from Philistine oppression. In the royal rituals of Judah, an effort was made to establish the Davidic office as a permanent vicegerency of Yahweh. The king was designated son of God and was thus exalted as the incarnation of Israel,[10] who alone is called "son of God" in the other Old Testament traditions.[11] However, this royal theology failed to capture the minds of all Israelites, because it lacked the sanctity of immemorial antiquity and, for many, stood in opposition, not only to popular rights, but also to the right of Yahweh to rule Israel through the charismatic leader (the ancient "judge"). The narratives in Judg. 8–9 and 1 Sam. 8 vividly reflect the struggle between the two orders.[12]

In the light of the perennial tension between the idea of a monarchial state and that of a tribal theocracy in Israel, it is impossible to assume that the royal institutions were synonymous with the people in the minds of the Old Testament writers. We must beware lest a

[10] 2 Sam. 7:14; 1 Chron. 17:13; 22:10; 28:6; and especially Ps. 2:7.

[11] Exod. 4:22 f.; Deut. 14:1; 32:5, 20; Isa. 1:2, 4; 30:1, 9; Jer. 3:14, 22; 31:20; Hos. 2:1; 11:1; and Ps. 82:6.

[12] See, further, A. R. Johnson, *Sacral Kingship in Ancient Israel* (Cardiff, 1955), and S. Mowinckel, *He That Cometh* (Oxford and New York, 1956), pp. 56–95.

search for the psychological common denominator among a group of terms designating institutions of the nation, or aspects of its life, obscure the objective differences among them and the terms used to denote them. Hosea's terms in chapter 1 denote related entities, but there is no reason to suppose that he or his audience considered them merely interchangeable. The differences among them are great, and the writer was doubtless as aware of this as we are.

Hos. 1:2–9 is not a static series of signs, each repeating the same word of judgment in slightly different terms. Each part is essentially different from the other three. These differences do not consist merely in a heightening of finality in the announcement of doom. The chapter has frequently been interpreted in this way.[13] According to this theory, Hosea became more and more certain that Israel was going to be destroyed and, as he gradually lost hope, his oracular signs became gradually more absolute. The theory is false, however. There is no heightening of finality in the series. The first signs are not tentative or conditional. Each of the four is absolute, unconditional, and irrevocable. The movement of thought in the series does not consist of a progressive certainty over the coming doom. It consists of shifts in the scope and the times of judgment.[14]

In the midst of this massive utterance of condemnation, there lies a curious possibility for hope. It is nothing more than a possibility, to be sure, and one that is only implicit in the situation described here. Hos. 1:2–9 declares the covenant people to be self-destroyed and the land of their habitation to be corrupted. It also predicts the coming divine destruction of the ruling house and the future dissolution of the northern kingdom. The inner destruction has already taken place; the outer is yet to come. The little tract itself does not assert that God has a further intention for Israel beyond the annihilation of her institutions; yet, the end of the dynasty and the state, together with that of the official cultus, need not be conceived as merely punitive. It might be the opportunity for renewal, especially if these structures were partly responsible for the community's corruption. Their destruction would then be the removal of obstacles to new life. It might be the creation of those outward conditions requisite to an in-

---

[13] See, e.g., Mauchline and Brown.
[14] The difference between the term "House of Israel" and the various designations of the people is discussed in the Note on the Text of 1:4d–5, 7, and in Additional Note A: Designations of Hosea's Audience.

ner transformation. At least, we may say that the divine judgments uttered in the book of signs would be fully consistent with a promise of covenantal renewal to follow the national disasters, which Hosea believed to be imminent. Such a promise is explicitly made in later chapters of Hosea, but these have been frequently denied to Hosea himself because of their alleged incompatibility with the oracles of destruction. My concern at the moment is to show the actual basis for hope that is provided in the very oracles of destruction. This is not a sufficient basis, but it is nevertheless a real one.

There are other ways than the one I have taken to explain the relationship between the negative and positive portions of the book, in order to secure the Hosean authorship of both; but I believe they are incorrect. Some scholars have supposed that the oracles of hope came at a time when Hosea believed the people capable of repentance. According to this theory, the earlier oracles of destruction are to be interpreted conditionally. The oracles that seem absolute, on the other hand, are to be viewed as the later judgments of the prophet, uttered after he had lost hope in a national change of heart. Such an interpretation was offered by George Adam Smith.[15] It has the merit of recognizing the Hosean origin of the hopeful portions of the book, but it necessitates dating chapter 14 before chapter 13. The latter, according to Smith, is Hosea's last, despairing word.

Unfortunately for this view, however, there are no oracles in the book that may be called genuinely conditional. Nowhere is there a serious suggestion made that the disaster will be averted by repentance. Hos. 2:2–3 ("Plead with your mother . . . lest . . .") seems to be an exception, but even this passage is ambiguous. It is cast in the form of an appeal to witnesses at a trial. It becomes clear, as one reads the entire indictment against the "mother," that the conditionality is only theoretical. The plaintiff is convinced that the defendant is beyond repentance and that her condemnation is inevitable; but, a fair trial must be held. Elsewhere in Hosea, the pronouncement of disaster is unconditional.

An interesting variation on this theory has been proposed by Georg Fohrer. Hosea first preached that Israel's acceptance by God was conditional upon her repentance but later realized the impossibility of repentance apart from some prior action of God. In his later oracles, therefore, he preached the priority of divine acceptance as the

15 See pp. 303–07 and 330–54 of his commentary.

precondition of repentance.[16] The difficulty with this interpretation is that the conditional message is not explicitly presented in Hosea's oracles. As they come to us, they all presuppose the second view of the relationship between grace and repentance described by Fohrer.

Another possible approach would be to date the hopeful oracles after the Assyrian destruction of Israel (722–21 B.C.), on the assumption that the prophet changed his message to fit a changed situation, that is, preaching consolation to a thoroughly punished nation. This theory cannot be dismissed on a priori grounds. If a similar change in Judean prophecy took place after 587 B.C. (Jeremiah, Deutero-Isaiah), there is no reason why it could not have happened in Israel, even in the ministry of a single man (compare Jeremiah). Yet this theory must remain a mere possibility, because the oracles of Hosea cannot be dated. We have no way of knowing which ones were composed first, or whether the hopeful ones were published after the fall of the Israelite monarchy.

All these interpretations, then, have serious shortcomings. None of them is essential, however, in order to establish the Hosean authorship of both the destructive and the constructive oracles. Indeed, the situation described by these oracles is quite different from what the above theories, especially the first, presuppose. Survival of the state was not made conditional upon the moral renewal of the people, but the transformation of the people was made conditional upon the removal of the state. The oracles do not begin with the hope that the state could be saved and then reluctantly narrow the basis of hope to a remnant of the nation, in the manner of Amos 5:14–15. Hosea's consolation of the people was not a second-best hope, to which he was reduced by his disillusionment, but a best hope, without illusions.

To be sure, chapter 1 does not positively affirm that God proposed to make possible a covenantal renewal by destroying the kingdom, but it opens the way for such an affirmation. The affirmation itself is made in chapters 2, 3, 11, and 14. We should not expect the little tract to say everything. It deals with the present situation and its immediate outcome. It also says something about the causes of judgment; but it says nothing about the ultimate purpose of God or the ultimate future of the people. The doom of the House of Israel is sealed, but the question remains open how the Lord may use that disaster in his work with the people.

[16] "Umkehr und Erlösung beim Propheten Hosea," *TZ* 11 (1955), 161–85.

The little prophetic tract in chapter 1 does not tell us much explicitly about Hosea's theology, but it states in a highly provocative fashion several of the most important themes of his critique of Israel's life and his interpretation of her history. These themes are more fully expounded in the chapters that follow. Israel, the people of God, created for himself through the ancient religious institutions associated with the Mosaic tradition (the Book of Exodus) and through the events that led to the tribal settlement in Palestine, have ceased to be God's people, by her own action. She has inwardly renounced the ancient commitment to her God who wills to be present redemptively with his people (Exod. 3:11–18; Hos. 1:9). Her relationship to him, which can exist fully and effectively only when it is mutually acknowledged and sustained, like all relationships among persons, has thus been broken. Israel is now the self-destroyed people, the non-people, the ex-people of God. This is the meaning of the fourth sign. She has destroyed that relationship to God by religious infidelity, as is stated but not explained in the first sign. These are events in the inner history of Israel that have taken place already, for which she herself is responsible.

Two future events in her outer history are predicted in the second and in the third sign. These are acts for which God is ultimately responsible. They are the extinction of the dynastic line of king Jehu and the destruction of the monarchial state in Israel. They are closely related causally to the other, inner events, indeed they may be viewed as the final, visible outcome of those events, the divine judgments that are the conclusion of the logic of Israel's social history. The relationship between the state and Israel's religious infidelity is not explained here, as it is elsewhere in the book, but is merely implied by the combination of signs into a single tract.

Hosea's interpretation of Israel's earlier story, prior to these accomplished, inner events, and his expectation for Israel after the accomplishment of the coming, outer events, are matters that we encounter first in chapter 2. The little tract is a sharp incision into the diseased and dying body of God's people. What follows is a diagnosis of the cause of sickness and a description of its symptoms, as well as a declaration of the basis for future health, if not of the probability of recovery. In this we will discover the fundamental features of Hosea's understanding of God.

CHAPTER

2 AN ALLEGORY OF COVENANTAL HISTORY: HOSEA 2

I

2 Plead with your mother, plead
    —for she is not my wife,
    and I am not her husband—
So that she may remove her harlotries from her face
    and her adulteries from between her breasts;
3 Lest I strip her naked,
    expose her as when she was newborn,
Make her like the wilderness,
    leave her like parched ground,
      and slay her with thirst.

4 And her children I'll not pity,
    for whorish children are they;
5 For their mother played the harlot;
    shamefully she conceived them.
For she said,
    "Let me hurry after my lovers,
Who give me my bread and my water,
    my wool and my flax,
      my oil and my drink."

6 Therefore, behold, I am hedging in
    her way with thorns
And bricking up a wall against her,
    so she cannot find her paths.
7 She will chase her lovers
    but never catch them,
      seek them but never find them.
And then she will say,
    "Let me go back to my former husband,
    for I was better off then than now."

II

8   She knew not
        that it was I who gave her
            the grain, new wine, and oil,
    And lavished silver upon her,
        and gold that they fashioned for Baal.

9   Therefore, I will take back
        my grain in its time
        and my wine in its season.
    And I will seize my wool and my flax
        which cover her nakedness.

10   Now will I expose her bare loins
        in the sight of her lovers,
            and no man will save her from my hand.

11   I will put a stop to her festival gaiety:
        new moon, and sabbath, and every special feast.

12   And I will lay waste her vines and her fig trees:
        "These are my wages," said she.
        "My lovers gave them to me."
    But I will make them a thicket;
        beasts of the field will devour them.

13   And I will punish her for the festivals of the Baals,
        when she burned offerings to them,
        and displayed her rings and bracelets.
    Lovers she chased,
        but me she forgot.   [Oracle of Yahweh]

14   Therefore, behold, I am abducting her,
        and I will take her to the wilderness,
            and speak to her heart.

15   And there I will give her her vineyards,
        and make the Valley of Achor a gateway of hope.
    And there she will respond as she did in her youth,
        at the time she came up from the land of Egypt.

16   And in that day,   [Oracle of Yahweh]
    She will call me "My husband";
        never again will she call me "My Baal."

17   And I will remove from her lips the names of the Baals,
        and their names will be remembered no more.

III

18   I will make a covenant for them in that day,
        with the beasts of the field,
        with the birds of the air,
        and the reptiles of the ground.
    And bows, and swords, and warfare
        I will abolish from the land,
            and I will make them dwell in safety.
19   And I will betroth you to me forever,
        in righteousness and justice,
        in love and compassion.
20   I will betroth you to me in faithfulness,
        and you shall know Yahweh.

21   And in that day,   [Oracle of Yahweh]
    I will answer the heavens,
        and they will answer the earth.
22   And the earth will answer
        the grain, the wine, and the oil;
            and they will answer Jezreel;
23   And I will plant her for myself in the land;
        and I will pity Not-Pitied.
    And to Not-My-People I will say, "You are My people";
        and he shall say, "My God."

IV

1:10   Then the number of the sons of Israel
        will be like the sand of the sea,
            which cannot be measured or counted.
    And instead of their being called,
        "You are Not-My-People,"
    They will be called,
        "Sons of the living God."

1:11   And the sons of Judah
        and the sons of Israel will be gathered together,
            and they will appoint for themselves one head.
    And they will go up from the land;
        for great will be the day of Jezreel.
2:1   (So) say to your brothers, "My People,"
        and to your sisters, "Pitied."

NOTES ON THE TEXT

Verses 1:10–2:1 (Heb. 2:1–3). The transposition of these lines to the end of the chapter may seem arbitrary, but it is probably no more so than their placement by the editor at the beginning. Formally, the poem is distinct both from 1:2–9 and from 2:2 ff. The English versions link 1:10–2:1 with the former, not only by means of the versification, but by translating the initial conjunction as "yet," and (in the case of the *RSV*) printing the whole in a prose format distinct from the poem that follows. However, the opening word may be taken more naturally to express continuity than discontinuity. Furthermore, the piece is poetry and has no formal link to chapter 1, except for the children's names. Yet, these provide an equally close association with 2:22 f., with which it also shares poetic form. Among those who have associated 1:10–2:1 with the close of chapter 2 are *Moffatt,* Cheyne, Wolff, and Procksch (*Theologie,* p. 160). One might call 1:10–2:1 a logical conclusion to the vision of the new age (2:18–23). Yet there are good grounds for concluding that the piece is not Hosea's at all (see pp. 45–46). This is the opinion of Knight, Sellin, Robinson, Hölscher (*Die Propheten,* p. 425), Lindblom (*Hosea,* p. 56), Welch (*Kings and Prophets,* pp. 136 f.), and Cheyne (in W. R. Smith, *The Prophets,* 1895; p. xvii), all of whom accept the authenticity of 2:14–23. I disagree heartily with those who simply deny any hopeful passages to Hosea. My objection to 1:10–2:1 is precisely that it is so unlike the other promises, which I believe to be genuine.

Verse 2 (Heb. 4). The verb ריב suggests judicial argument (cf., 4:1, 4), and I retain the standard English translation ("plead"), with this in mind.[1]

Many commentators regard vs. 2b as a reference to cosmetics and jewelry as trademarks of the prostitute. Kaufmann (*The Religion of Israel,* p. 370) thinks of a mask and ornaments worn by the wife in a mock drama put on by Hosea, Gomer, and their children. Jer. 3:3 ("you have a harlot's brow") once again implies that the prostitute's

---

[1] See, B. Gemser, "The *rib-* or controversy-pattern in Hebrew mentality," in M. Noth and D. W. Thomas, eds., *Wisdom in Israel and the Ancient Near East* (*Supplements to Vetus Testamentum* Vol. III, Leiden, 1955), pp. 130–37.

face was marked in some way to make her recognizable as such. In the Middle Assyrian Laws, harlots were required to go unveiled in public.[2] If they were caught violating this law, their clothing was given to the prosecutor, and they were flogged, although they were allowed to keep their jewelry. We must beware of inferring too much from this law regarding the "badge" of prostitutes in Assyria (let alone the Near East generally), because the same law prescribes similar treatment of female slaves.

The phrase "she is not my wife" has often been interpreted as a technical formula of divorce, but Nötscher cautions against making this a critical dogma, since such usage has not yet been established for Palestine, as it has for Mesopotamia.

Verse 6 (Heb. 8). MT has "*your* way," but I have followed the *LXX,* with most commentators. It is fairly common practice to move 2:6–7 after 2:13 (*Moffatt,* Weiser, Mauchline, Wolff, and others). Vss. 8–17, however, comprise three five-line strophes, while 6–7 forms the climax to 2–7, which consists of four-line strophes. There are notable links between 6–7 and 2–13, to be sure, but they simply show that the whole chapter is a thematic unity and not that 6–7 has been displaced.

Here and in vs. 7 (Heb. 9) the verb אלכה ("let me go") should be translated as a cohortative (cf., *Moffatt,* Cheyne, Harper, and Brown).

Verse 12 (Heb. 14). The *LXX*'s addition of birds and reptiles here is accepted by Sellin as necessary to make full sense of the antithesis in vs. 18. The strophe will support a tristich here; so, this judgment may be correct.

Verse 13 (Heb. 15). The exact nature of the objects worn here is uncertain.

Verse 14 (Heb. 16). The verb connotes an element of coercion; so, "abduct" is better than "allure" (cf., the English versions). The wife has no freedom not to go into the wilderness. The wooing takes place *after* the abduction, and the betrothal is made *in* the wilderness.

Verse 15 (Heb. 17). I have taken the verb in the first clause (ונתתי) to govern the second also. The old Valley of Achor ("Trouble") is the scene of Achan's disobedience on the occasion of the first settle-

---

[2] See, Pritchard, *Ancient Near Eastern Texts* (2nd ed.; Princeton, 1955), p. 183.

ment in Palestine (Josh. 7, esp. vs. 26). In the new settlement it will be remembered quite differently, as the Valley of Hope.

Verse 18 (Heb. 20). "Warfare" can hardly be "broken" (this is what the verb actually means) as the bow and the sword can, and perhaps it should be deleted as an expansionist gloss (though, cf. Ps. 76:4 [Eng. 76:3]). Cf., also, 1:7.

Verse 19 (Heb. 21). The MT repeats "I will betroth you to me" in the second line, perhaps by mistake.

Verse 21 (Heb. 23). I have deleted a second "I will answer" from the MT. There seems to be no adequate explanation of the curious "Oracle of Yahweh" in vss. 13, 16, and 21. This formula, common elsewhere in the prophetic literature, is not characteristic of Hosea, occurring only once more, in 11:11. To say that it is editorial does not really explain it, of course.

Verse 23 (Heb. 25). Many translators change "plant her" to "plant him" (e.g., *RSV*, Robinson, and Nötscher). It is possible that an original masculine pronoun has been changed into a feminine under the influence of the feminine name "Not-Pitied" in the next clause. The *LXX* supports the MT in reading "her," however, and I take this to mean the bride, who is the subject in the rest of the poem.

Verse 1:11 (Heb. 2:2). "Jezreel" is taken with 2:1 (Heb. 2:3) ("Jezreel, say to . . .") by Procksch (*BH*), who supposes that the Masoretes reconstructed "day of Jezreel" after "Yahweh" in an original "day of Yahweh" had dropped out, and by Mauchline, who supposes that the text originally contained "Jezreel" both at the end of vs. 11 and at the beginning of 2:1. But the verb in vs. 1a and the pronouns ("your") in vss. 1a and 1b are plural, so Jezreel can hardly be the one addressed here (though, see next note).

Verse 2:1 (Heb. 2:3). The verb "say," the pronouns "your," and the nouns "brothers" and "sisters" are all plural in the MT. *LXX* translates the nouns in the singular, as do many commentators. But I regard this as a tendentious translation based on the unwarranted assumption that the dramatis personae of chapter 1 are carried over into chapter 2. The names in chapter 2 are designations of the restored Israelites.

This verse is linked to 2:2 by Procksch (*BH*) and the *KJV*, but the commentators are all agreed that it belongs with 1:10–11 (thus, *ASV, RSV, Moffatt, Chicago,* and *Jerusalem*). The plural imperative verbs are a basis for joining vss. 1 and 2, of course, as is the similarity between the metaphors ("mother," and "brothers and sisters"). When 1:10–2:1 is placed at the *end* of the chapter, these features of vs. 1 make it a superb climax to the whole poem, echoing the beginning line in the closing one. Indeed, if 1:10–2:1 originally stood after 2:23, the stylistic affinity between vs. 1 and vs. 2 might well have given rise to the transposition of these lines to the beginning of the chapter.

Hosea 1:2 compares the land of Israel to an unchaste wife and Israel's relationship with God to a wilfully broken marriage. Chapter 2 is a commentary on this text. The simple analogy is extended to an allegory illuminating the whole history of Israel's life under God.

We discover in this poem the pattern that dominates the Book of Hosea: a criticism of Israel's contemporary existence and an announcement of the imminent dissolution of her institutions, brought about by her apostasy; a recollection of the past and its manifestations of God's grace and Israel's blindness; the promise of a renewal of covenantal life, viewed as a recapitulation of the story of God's love; and the hope of Israel's faithful response in the new era. When we add chapter 1, as a tract dealing with Israel's present and immediate future, and chapter 3, as a symbol of the coming era, the pattern is extended to the whole of Hos. 1–3. Virtually the same sequence of themes is found also in chapters 4–14. Chapters 4–10 correspond to chapter 1 and the first half of chapter 2; and chapters 11–14 take up the themes of the second half of chapter 2, and those of chapter 3.

Hosea's allegory of infidelity and renewal opens with a husband's appeal to the children of his estranged wife to intercede with their mother for the sake of them all (2:2–4). The hypothetical children are her hearers and their mother is Israel, who is at once their nation and themselves. The appeal is an indirect, conditional threat, which ostensibly invites the wife's repentance as the means of preventing her severe punishment. Quickly, the conditional threat gives way to a recollection of the wife's follies (2:5, 8, 12, 13). On the assumption that she is incorrigible by ordinary means of discipline, the husband (God) sets forth his design for extraordinary discipline (2:6–7a, 9–13) and his hope for a reconciliation (2:7, 14 ff.).

The idolatrous nature of Israel's popular religion is the clear object of Hosea's passionate attack. Yet the reader may mistake the precise character of the crime. It was not simply the adoption of Canaanite deities in place of or alongside the worship of the Lord, and still less was it the mere introduction of images into Israel's imageless cult, although both of these were involved (cf., 2:7, 12, 14, 15, 19, and 2:10, respectively.) The chief perversion of which the cult is accused in this poem is the idolatrous preoccupation with economic goals and sensual experiences, to the exclusion of other aspects of life. We infer that the popular cult was little concerned with problems of justice and social responsibility, or with guilt and forgiveness (cf., 4:1 ff.). Although Hosea hoped for these qualities in the religion of the future (2:14–23), there is every indication that he missed them in the religion of the present. The most obvious needs of life dominated the people's attention.

It is no wonder that this temptation was strong in ancient Israel, in the face of continual economic hardship and in a time when the production of crops and the powers of the gods were inseparably linked in the imaginations of men. It is a wonder that the prophets of Israel were able to discover another way of understanding.

Israel's quest for aesthetic experience in the public worship of God was perfectly justifiable. The Yahwistic teaching about creation did not foster an ascetic attitude toward worship or life. Genuine Yahwism gave full play to the emotions, both dark and light, in lamentation, thanksgiving, and the other moods of man. Song and dance were both worthy vehicles of worship. But the legitimate quest for emotional catharsis and exultation and for the subtler modes of aesthetic experience was unfortunately corrupted by the sexual theology of popular religion. Since the order of nature was explained by analogy to the process of animal procreation, it was inevitable that both the celebration of the need for physical survival and the quest for emotional fulfilment should become occasions for sexual license in both its subtler and grosser forms.

Any ritual celebration may bring into play the male–female polarity. The emotions awakened in worship are frequently influenced by sexual impulses and charged with sexual energy. In the popular worship of ancient Palestine, however, the use of sexual energies was deliberate and culminated in the sanctification of fornication and in sensual ecstasy. Also, of course, the rites were believed to be magically effective for achieving the economic goals of the community. Thus, they fostered self-idolatry and obscured the Yahwistic belief in the sole sovereignty of God, beyond all human efforts at dominion through magical rites. Needless to say, the cult led to the deterioration of Israelite sexual mores and thus contributed to the dissolution of normative family bonds. Another, even more basic evil was the dehumanization of all life by a cult preoccupied in a peculiarly narrow way with physical and sensual needs.

It may be that some such degradation of persons and relationships inevitably results from the idolizing of a part of the natural order and, further, that the idolatry of nature is the necessary concomitant of the pluralizing of the One. It is impossible to have more than One who is absolute. Looked at in this way, the crime of Israel may be interpreted as the adoption of other gods beside the Lord. But it is important to discern the peculiar nature of the people's polytheism and its specific corollaries for worship and ethics. It was one particular form of idolatry, for no two are exactly alike.

The children's appeal to their mother in 2:4 implies an invitation to avert the penalty for apostasy by a turnabout in behavior. Some commentators have held that chapter 2 is a miscellany of originally independent poems, loosely joined by an editor.[3] If this were true, 2:2–5 could perhaps be interpreted as an expression of Hosea's hope for a reformation. Yet 2:2–13 is so well integrated in its present form that it is impossible to deal with portions of it as if they stood alone. As it is, the poem does not express the speaker's expectation of the wife's reformation. Rather, it contains his public declaration of his intention to cast off his faithless wife. The children are called as witnesses to this declaration. When the wife's punishment is accomplished, the justice and propriety of the husband's treatment will be acknowledged by all. This legal action insures fair treatment of the wife, and since it is open to public scrutiny, it protects the husband against public misunderstanding. The entire scene is, of course, allegorical and not real.

The prophets' conviction that God would do nothing "without revealing his secret to his servants the prophets" (Amos 3:7) does not imply that their preaching was always intended to bring immediate national repentance. They were too keenly aware of the hardness of men's hearts to embrace such a rationalistic notion of sin and repentance. They also knew the corporate nature of evil and the relative helplessness of one generation to eradicate the consequences of its predecessors' follies. We distort the messages of the prophets if we take them merely as exhortations to the religious community to transform itself. While moral reformation was undoubtedly an im-

---

[3] Cf., e.g., Sellin, Robinson, Weiser, and Wolff.

portant objective of their proclamation, they seem to have been principally concerned with the declaration of what God was doing in the world. The reader of their oracles is often left uninstructed as to the concrete effects that they hoped they would have upon their hearers. Surely they themselves did not know what the immediate results of their work would be.

Amos seems to have preached a conditional threat at one period in his ministry (Amos 4:6–12; 7:1–6), hoping for social reformation (Amos 5:14–15); but he did not stop declaring the impending judgment of God after he became convinced that the hope was futile (Amos 8:1–9:8a). Even the damned had to be instructed about their fate and its causes. Was this done merely out of spite? Or did the prophet wish to exalt the sovereignty and justice of God, even in the face of inevitable disaster? Over and over again Ezekiel proposes this last motive as the ultimate rationale for his proclamation (Ezek. 36:38; 39:21–24, 28 f.; 6:7, 14; 7:4, 9, 27). He may have been convinced that God's resources for redemption would finally prevail over man's resistance, but he was also convinced of his own obligation to proclaim the divine word whatever the immediate result might be (cf., Ezek. 3:16–21). Isaiah denied altogether that his direct objective was to secure moral reform and avert the judgment of God. The preliminary aim of his preaching was the opposite of that, namely to harden the people's hearts (Isa. 6:9 ff.).

The prophets were hardheaded analysts of the human condition. They wasted no time with the sentimentality of an "if only . . ." viewpoint. They sought to describe the world as it was and God as he is, however frightful the vision might be. The victory of grace over evil would be won at the cost of great pain. The exilic prophets taught this eloquently, and Hosea, before them, was no less discerning or eloquent. This understanding pervades his entire book. Nowhere does he offer redemption apart from national disaster.

On the other hand, Hosea does not predict the fall of the nation as a mere disaster. He interprets it as a necessary phase in the reconstruction of a faithful, covenantal community. Because Israel had misappropriated the cultus and the economy of Canaan, losing their soul in trying to gain the world, God would have to take these people back to the point where they had begun, so that their life could be remade in obedience.

The aberrations condemned in chapter 2 were essentially cultic and not political. Yet the two realms were inseparable. The cultus of Baalism provided motives for the exploitation of all the resources of natural and social life and a point of view that inevitably shaped the people's attitude and behavior in economic and political affairs, as well as in such personal spheres as health and the protection of life and property. The conjunction of the political and cultic aspects of Israel's predicament is a constant feature of the oracles in Hos. 4–14. Nevertheless, chapter 2 focuses upon the heart of the problem, namely national worship and belief. As these were, so was the nation.

The traditional Israelite rites provided the means by which new generations were educated into the covenant (Deut. 31:10–13) and by which the faith of the community as a whole was renewed. Thus, continuity with the past was maintained and the historic convictions of Yahwism continually reaffirmed. The great pilgrimage festivals, especially Tabernacles, were the chief occasions of the sacred year.[4] Here the sovereignty of the God of the fathers over the royal establishment and the processes of nature was confirmed. In the harvest celebration and the periodic renewal of the "covenant with David," the economic and political institutions were subjected to the impulse and criticism of traditional Yahwism. No other vehicle had an equal opportunity of providing a Yahwistic motivation for national affairs and of preventing the displacement of covenantal theology by a rival interpretation of life. When these festivals were modified by local, Palestinian, liturgical practices, the ultimate consequence was a modification of the whole communal perspective and, therefore, of the Israelite way of life. No institution of modern public life occupies a comparable role as a molder of human behavior. The functions analogous to those of church, school, press, and theatre resided in the single instrumentality of the annual covenantal celebration. It was the cultural heart of the commonwealth. According to Hosea, the heart had been corrupted by Baalism. Therefore, the entire organism had become perverse.

[4] Covenant-renewal may have taken place every year at the feast of Tabernacles and not merely every seven years. In any case, the great fall festival, and perhaps the other pilgrimage festivals, provided the occasion for a ritual dramatization of the story of Israel's redemption and for a reaffirmation of the historic faith of Yahwism. See, H.-J. Kraus, *Gottesdienst in Israel* (Munich, 1954); A. Weiser, *Die Psalmen* (Göttingen, 1950), pp. 11–28 (English tr., *The Psalms*. Philadelphia and London, 1962, pp. 23–52); G. von Rad, *Das formgeschichtliche Problem des Hexateuchs* (Stuttgart, 1938), reprinted in *Gesammelte Studien zum Alten Testament* (Munich, 1958), pp. 9–86.

As a remedy for the disease, Hosea prescribed the abolition of the national rites. The cure was to be forcibly administered by means of military conquest and political exile. After a convalescence in the "desert," the patient would be reinstated in the community of peoples. In this way, the course of Israel's cultural history would be reversed. The external gains in political and economic affairs that had been achieved since the days of the tribal confederacy were to be surrendered in the interest of a rebirth of Yahwism. The form in which the future destiny of Israel was presented is a recapitulation of the past. The events of Israel's former redemption—Egyptian captivity, deliverance, covenant-establishment in the desert, settlement in the sown land, and creation of a unified society—were to be repeated. The shape of the future was discovered in the shape of the past.

Israel's history is conceived by Hosea as divided into two eras. The first is drawing to a close and the second is breaking in. The final event of the old era is a return to the point of beginning, which thus completes the pattern of Israel's life. At the same time, it is the first event of the new era, which is characterized symbolically in terms of the decisive events of the old. This representation of the future epoch by means of the salient features of the past is frequently encountered in other parts of the Book of Hosea, as well as in chapter 2, and a synopsis of these materials presented here will strengthen the reader's appreciation of the underlying pattern of thought in the prophet's oracles.

The pattern of Israel's history described in chapter 2 is sketched most concisely, and chronologically, in chapter 11. It is presented somewhat loosely again in chapters 12–14. It may be outlined as follows:

1. *The Exodus from Egypt.* The Lord redeemed Israel from slavery and anonymity in Egypt and led him providentially in the wilderness.

> "When Israel was a child I loved him,
>   and out of Egypt I called my son." (11:1)

> "I am Yahweh your God
>   from the land of Egypt." (12:9)

> "By a prophet Yahweh brought up
>   Israel from Egypt. . . ." (12:13)

"I am Yahweh your God
  from the land of Egypt;
And you know no God but me;
  for besides me there is no savior." (13:4)

"Like grapes in the wilderness
  I found Israel." (9:10)

"I led them with cords of devotion,
  with bonds of love. . . ." (11:4)

"I shepherded you in the wilderness,
  in a land of drought." (13:5)

"She will respond as she did in her youth,
  at the time she came up from the land of Egypt."
  (2:15)

The frequent shifts in gender in references to Israel correspond
to shifts in metaphor. In chapters 4–14 the masculine is usually
employed, in conformity with standard Hebrew usage, especially
since Israel is often personified as Jacob or Ephraim. The bridal
metaphor dictates the use of the feminine in chapters 1–3 and
occasionally elsewhere (e.g., 4:16, 19).

2. *The Settlement in Palestine.* This was the next major event of
the history of salvation, according to biblical tradition. Hosea accepts
this conviction to the extent that he regards Israel's enjoyment of the
land as a gift from God (2:8; 13:6). But the conquest marked for
him the beginning of Israel's apostasy from God, and it is represented
in his oracles chiefly in that light. The receipt of the gift of the land
from God's hand is proclaimed in positive terms only as a feature
of the second story of redemption (2:21–23; 14:4–8).

In the old era, Israel had failed to acknowledge the source of his
blessing and to accept his true destiny as the son of God, but had
turned instead to Baalism.

"As I called them,
  so they left me.
To Baals they sacrificed;
  to idols they burned offerings." (11:2)

"As they were pastured, so they were satisfied;
  (as) they were satisfied, so they were arrogant.
    Thus they forgot me." (13:6; cf., 13:1)

"They came to Baal-Peor
    and consecrated themselves to Baal." (9:10)

"All their evil was in Gilgal;
    Yea, there I learned to hate them." (9:15)

Israel's apostasy, which had begun already in the wilderness and
the earliest days of settlement, continued into the present and was
marked by moral, cultic, and political evils of various sorts. The
relevant passages need not be quoted here. This theme dominates
the whole of chapters 4–10 and much of chapters 12–13.

One special feature of the present (old) era is the institution of
the monarchy, whose inception "in the days of Gibeah," under Saul,
Hosea recalls as a dark event in Israel's history (9:9; 10:9).

3. *The Fall of the State and the Exile.* The internal decay and
the foolhardy diplomacy of Israel are leading to the imminent fall
of the kingdom and to the exile of the people from the land. These
events are symbolized as a "return to Egypt" and a second wandering
in the "wilderness."

"He will return to the land of Egypt,
    and Asshur will be his king,
        because they refused to return." (11:5)

". . . they will be derided in the land of Egypt." (7:16)

"He will remember their guilt
    and punish them for their sin:
        they will return to Egypt." (8:13)

"They will not remain in Yahweh's land;
    but Ephraim will return to Egypt,
    and in Assyria they will eat unclean food." (9:3)

"Though they flee from the desolation,
    Egypt will gather them up;
    Memphis will bury them." (9:6)

". . . they will be fugitives among the nations." (9:17)

"I will again make you dwell in tents,
    as in the days of assembly." (12:9; cf., 12:6)

"Therefore, behold, I am abducting her,
    and I will take her to the wilderness. . . ." (2:14)

4. *The New Exodus and Settlement in the Land.* As in the old exodus — wilderness era, God will redeem Israel once more, as an expression of his transcendent love.

> "When he roars, the children
>   will come trembling from the sea.
> They will hurry like birds out of Egypt,
>   like doves from the land of Asshur;
>   and I will restore them to their homes." (11:10–11)

> "I will heal their apostasy;
>   I will love them willingly. . . .
>   I will be like dew to Israel. . . .
> Those who would live in his shade will return;
>   they will thrive like the corn. . . ." (14:4–7)

> "And the sons of Judah
>   and the sons of Israel will be gathered together,
>   and they will appoint for themselves one head.
> And they will go up from the land;
>   for great will be the day of Jezreel." (1:11)

> "Afterward the sons of Israel will return
>   and seek Yahweh their God. . . .
> They will come in fear to Yahweh and his goodness
>   in the latter days." (3:5)

> "And I will take her to the wilderness,
>   and speak to her heart.
> And there I will give her her vineyards
>   and make the Valley of Achor a gateway of hope.
> And there she will respond as she did in her youth,
>   at the time she came up from the land of Egypt. . . .
> I will make a covenant for them in that day, . . .
>   and you shall know Yahweh. . . .
> And I will plant her for myself in the land." (2:14–23)

This proclamation of the new exodus, of the covenant-making in the wilderness, and of the new settlement is, of course, the burden of the entire chapter 14, as well as of 2:15–23, and 1:10–2:1, and the symbolic action of chapter 3. Unlike the present era, the new one will be marked by Israel's faithful response to God. It is not, therefore, a mere repetition of the calamitous, old era.

We may note, finally, that chapters 1–3 and 4–14 are arranged according to the same chronological scheme. The first part of each group of chapters is concerned with Israel's present situation and its immediate consequences (1:2–9; 2:2–14; 4:1–10:15). The second part of each group is dominated by an interest in the past and the future (2:15–23 + 1:10–2:1; 3:1–5; 11–12; 14).

There is much to be said in later pages about Hosea's interpretation of Israel's history and many additional allusions to be discussed that have not been cited here. This summary is meant only to show in bold strokes the fundamental pattern of thought that we will encounter over and over again in various ways throughout Hosea's oracles.

Hosea's use of the idea of repetition, or recapitulation, was new in Israelite literature. We find it again in Deutero-Isaiah, where the notion of a second exodus and settlement is powerfully used (Isa. 40), and again in Jeremiah's picture of a new covenant (Jer. 31:31–34). Nothing comparable to Hosea's scheme appears, however, in other pre-exilic books of the Old Testament. The story of Israel's past was continually retold in the liturgies of the annual festivals, to be sure,[5] but Hosea proclaimed more than a cult-dramatic rehearsal of the past. He predicted the enactment of a similar drama in the historic life of the Israelite people, on the stage of western Asia. The idea of cosmic, or natural, repetition was universal in ancient times and was effectively enacted in the agricultural and civil ceremonies of various peoples. We have no way of knowing whether Hosea's use of the motif of recapitulation was a conscious adaptation of this idea. Yet the actual result of his preaching of a coming renewal was the transformation of a central theme of popular belief into a vehicle of genuinely prophetic Yahwism. This renewal was not bred out of nature by necessity, but out of a historic community of free men by the free grace of God.

Some of the features of the allegory of covenantal history are not fully transparent and require, therefore, further comment. Chief among these are the references to impending chastisement in 2:3, 6–7a, 9–13. Is the discipline described in 2:3, 6 f., identical with that in 2:9–13? Or, if the disciplines are not identical, in what do they consist?

Vs. 3 suggests drought and famine ("make her like a wilderness . . . parched ground . . ."), and these also provide a reasonable

[5] Cf., Deut. 6:20–25; 26:1–11; Josh. 24:1–27.

explanation of vss. 9–10, 12 ("take back my grain . . . , wine . . . , wool and . . . flax . . . , expose her bare loins . . . , lay waste her vines . . ."). When we reach vs. 14, however, we have to do with deportation from the land ("I am abducting her . . . to the wilderness . . ."). If these passages represent a chronological sequence, that is, a discipline of drought followed later by a harsher one of exile, then vss. 6–7 may be out of place. The image of a blocked path suggests deportation rather than drought or the like. We have already observed, in the textual notes, that some commentators are disposed to move vss. 6–7 from their present position to one following vs. 13. This change would have the added advantage of placing the wife's confession of her desire to return to her husband (vs. 7b) immediately before the description of his effort to regain her obedient love (vss. 14 ff.).

The deprivations described in vss. 8–12 are best explained as the result of invasion, despoliation, and exile. Israel's loss of the fruits of the soil (vs. 9) and the reversion of the land to a wilderness (vs. 12) are as easily related to drought or pestilence as to invasion and deportation, but the cessation of the cult (vs. 11) would certainly not have occurred because of a merely natural calamity. On the contrary, famine or pestilence would have produced a quickening of ritual activity. However, the deportation of the Israelite people would have put an end to the contemporary cult. Vss. 9–13, are best interpreted, therefore, as the afflictions accompanying the military destruction of the kingdom and the exile of its people.[6] The images employed in vs. 3 are also explainable in this way. The language of vss. 3 and 6 is highly figurative. It is a mistake to try to ascertain precisely what the poet had in mind when he used these images. The poem is, after all, an allegory.

All things considered, it is best to retain the canonical order of the verses and not attempt to find an exact chronological sequence among the various threats. We should also not insist upon a precise

[6] If it is primarily the revelling and gaiety of the cult that are to cease (vs. 11), then this would happen after a natural disaster. Nötscher comments that because of the drought Israel will have nothing to offer in sacrifice. If it is the cult itself that is to stop, as I believe, then this explanation does not suffice. Commentators have never been able to agree entirely on the particular ritual occasions mentioned here. In all probability the poet was not merely concerned with the enumeration of particular celebrations that would be stopped but, by citing typical, important celebrations, meant to indicate that the practice of the cult itself would cease.

definition of the "lovers" in vss. 5, 7, and 12. One thinks immediately of the local Palestinian Baals, and rightly so (cf., vss. 16–17). But Israel's prostitution was a complex affair that included also selling herself to foreign powers and to their tutelary deities. The poem calls to mind various political and cultic aberrations and various natural and social consequences. These are sufficiently recognizable for the general intention of the poet to be grasped, without the hearer's knowing their exact dimensions.

If the Masoretic verse order is preserved, there is an excellent irony in the confession of the frustrated "prostitute" in vs. 7. Finding her lovers unable to maintain her in comfort, she protests a sudden willingness to return to her former husband, who is of course Yahweh, the speaker. What she does not know, however, is that it is not her lovers who have ceased providing for her, but precisely her former husband, who has been responsible all along, first for supplying her and then for denying her (vss. 8 ff.). Her lovers have been fantasies all the while. If vss. 6–7 are separated from 8–9 this irony is lost.

One might argue that admittedly the move entails the loss of a good text but that it entails also the gain of a better one, namely the description of the wife's eventual awakening and repentance (vs. 7). But, what kind of repentance is this? Her motive, candidly asserted, though only to herself, is that she was "better off then than now." Actually she intends to seek the same goals by the same means with what she thinks is another partner. She cannot change her husbands, however, although she does not know it. Since she has not changed her means or goals, she has not changed at all. The juxtaposition of vss. 7 and 14 does not yield the sequence, repentance — forgiveness, in any case, because the first action of vs. 14 is a forceful abduction into the wilderness and not one that issues from repentance and willing obedience. These come later, *in* the wilderness.

Near the beginning of the poem there is a strange comment about the children of the faithless wife. "And her children I'll not pity, for whorish children are they . . ." (vs. 4 f.) is an almost parenthetical remark, in which the mother's punishment is arbitrarily imposed upon her seemingly innocent children. The explanation of this harsh judgment seems to lie in the fact that the speaker here is more the wounded husband than the compassionate judge. A husband would certainly not be required to give his name or a share in his estate to the illegitimate children of his adulterous wife. So much seems clear at least on the surface of the allegory. But we must also ask how such a comment from the prophet illuminated the actual situation in Israel.

First of all, we must remind ourselves not to demand absolute correspondence between the allegory and Israel's history. We may find then an excellent analogy between the two. The woman's children could not escape the evil consequences of their mother's behavior. These would fall as heavily upon them as upon her. Similarly, the rising generation of Israelites would inevitably suffer the consequences of policies instituted generations before them. The analogy breaks down only if we ask about the similarity of guilt. The children in the allegory themselves are not responsible for their mother's crimes, whereas the Israelites of the rising generation could be probably expected to perpetuate the crimes of their fathers. Nevertheless, this dissimilarity does not vitiate the analogy in its essential point, namely the pronouncement of coming disaster. The dissimilarity would probably not have seemed as great to the ancient hearer as it does to the modern reader, incidentally. He would not have individualized guilt to the extent we do, and probably would have considered the children as tainted as the mother. And even a modern man who rationally judges such a child to be innocent, may be irrationally disposed toward it as if it were guilty. However, the issue of guilt or innocence is not what is really at stake in Hos. 2:4.

As we turn our attention to the promise of reconciliation and covenantal renewal in 2:14–23, the first thing we must say is that Hosea's vision of the future is not a program for social reconstruction or a calendar of particular future events. He says nothing here about the forms of public worship or government and nothing concrete about the constituency of the new community. Here, as elsewhere in his predictions of the new era, Hosea leaves the mystery of future happenings unprobed. Every future is the product of interaction between the transcendent, free will of God and the finite, free wills of countless men, and Hosea's visions are based on a complete respect for these freedoms.

What is certain about the new era is that Yahweh's determination to create a people faithful to himself will be fulfilled. Israel will understand her relationship to Yahweh (vss. 20, 23) and to the order of nature (vss. 21 f.), as she does not now (vss. 8, 12, 13); and she will demonstrate her knowledge in works of justice and compassion (vss. 19–20). Blessed once more by the fruits of the land (vs. 22) and by a harmonious relationship with nature (vs. 18), the people's ignominious names will be cast aside. It is not merely that Israel will be acknowledged once more by God, for even in judgment he had never failed to do that. It is rather that she will know him as the one by whom she is supremely known.

In the new epoch, Israel's preoccupation will be the sovereignty of God's righteous love, as the source and norm of human action. To this final concern all others will be subordinated. The centrality of the language of betrothal and of personal dialogue, of speaking and answering, in vss. 18–23, makes this clear. One is also struck by the prominence in these two strophes of the divine "I." It is God who speaks the words of forgiveness and covenant-making. He speaks and Israel answers. He, he, he; though always as "I", in the language of dialogue, where Israel is always "you." Contrast the self-interest of Israel in the earlier strophes: "Let *me* hurry after *my* lovers, who give me *my* bread and *my* water, *my* wool and *my* flax, *my* oil and *my* drink" (vs. 5). And again, "Let *me* go back to *my* former husband; for *I* was better off then than now" (vs. 7). And this: "These are *my* wages"; said she, "*my* lovers gave them to *me*" (vs. 12). On the occasion of the new covenant, Israel speaks one single word, *'Elohay,* "My *God*" (vs. 23).

There is no asceticism in prophetic religion and none in Hosea's vision of the future fulfilment of Israel's relationship to God. The fruits of nature are to be enjoyed by man, and God withholds none of them from his people (2:21–22; 14:5–8). The deprivation described in 2:9–13 ("I will take back my grain in its time . . .") is specific and not general. It is to be imposed on Israel through military conquest and deportation from the land, as the particular consequences of the policies and actions of her present time in history. From the standpoint of God, it is a temporary disciplinary measure. The first wish of God the Creator was to "give her the grain, new wine, and oil . . ." (2:8), and his ultimate wish as the Lord of nature was to give these again.

In Hosea's view, the moral problem of the possession of the land, with its potentiality for agriculture and commerce, was not whether to have or not to have. It was a matter of attitude, namely, whether a man regarded the land as his own possession, disposable according to his autonomous will, or whether he counted it as a gift that should be looked after according to the wider interests of the men for whom he was responsible as a fellow child of God. It was a choice between acquisitiveness and gratitude, as well as between the corresponding modes of behavior toward the neighbor.

What distinguishes Israel's relationship to nature in the new era, from that of the old, is that she will understand it as derivative and not primary. Her bonds of faith to God and of righteousness, love and compassion to man (2:19–20), will take precedence over her appropriation of nature. Therefore, warfare will be eliminated from the covenantal people. By acting on the basis of gratitude to God and loyalty to man, men will be incapable of resorting to the techniques of self-aggrandizement (2:18).

It needs to be said, in this connection, that it is a great mistake to deny the Hosean origin of 2:14–23 and of chapter 14, as has often been done in the past, on the ground that the interest in nature shown in these passages is uncharacteristic of the prophet. It is alleged in this connection that he was interested only in ethical issues. It need only be observed that Hosea is everywhere concerned with nature as an ethical problem and that there can be no prophetic ethic without an ethic of nature.

We have observed that coercion will have no place in the new covenantal relationship and, therefore, it will be possible to abolish arms and warfare (vs. 18). It is impossible to say whether Hosea believed there would be actually an age when physical force or its threat would not be employed either in the order of nature or in the order of society. There is a considerable measure of transcendent, or perhaps we should say eschatological, idealism in this climactic vision of chapter 2, and one hesitates to press the imagery too far, especially in an allegorical poem. Yet, what is most important here does not depend upon how we treat this issue. The central affirmation is that coercion will have no place in the new covenant between God and man. Israel's obedience will be free, willing, and spontaneous. Only so can the true covenant be established or maintained. Anything else would fall short of the covenant of Person and person, of "Husband" and "wife," of *ṣedeq, mishpaṭ, ḥesed, raḥᵃmim, ᵉmunah,* and *daʿath Yahweh* (righteousness, justice, love, compassion, faithfulness, and the knowledge of Yahweh; vss. 19–20).

We have been making constant use of the terms "covenant" and "covenantal people" in our discussion of Hosea's oracles, and will continue to do so throughout this book. It is time, therefore, to justify this procedure and explain what we mean by these terms. Hosea did not often use the word "covenant" in his oracles. It appears as a reference to Israel's relationship with God only in 6:7 and 8:1. In addition, however, he uses terms that presuppose this covenant. The most important of these terms are *torah* (instruction, direction, or law), *ḥesed* (loyalty, devotion, or steadfast love [*RSV*]), *ṣᵉdaqah* (righteousness or justice), *misphaṭ* (justice, judgment, or right), and *da'ath 'Elohim* (knowledge of God).[7]

By "covenant" I mean the relationship of mutual obligation between Yahweh and Israel, expressed in the twofold promise that he would be their God and they would be his people. This "contract" was universal in the scope of its application, that is, there was no aspect of the people's behavior and experience that could be excluded from God's concern and Israel's obligation. It was also permanent; it extended indefinitely through time. This covenant was therefore analogous to a human marriage or to a relationship between parent and child, and Hosea's choice of the marital and parental metaphors in describing God's relationship to Israel was a particularly appropriate one. God's covenant with Israel was more like a parental relationship perhaps, because God was clearly the superior and prior being, and Israel the wholly dependent one. An ancient Hebrew wife, however, was cast in a similarly dependent role toward her husband and did not enjoy the equality in marriage that some modern wives do. Both metaphors were therefore appropriate to the God – man relationship as it was understood in Israel.

The relationship was established on the love of God for Israel, which was concretely expressed in his deliverance of Israel from the anonymity, paganism, and suffering of their Egyptian captivity and in his empowering them to become a community of mutual obligation, as defined by the ethical principles of Mosaic Yahwism. Israel's primary motives for obedience were grateful love and a proper fear of the one being who was truly holy. From this fear and this love

---

[7] The references are as follows: *torah*, 6:1; 8:1, 12; 13:2, 4; *ḥesed*, 2:19; 4:1; 6:4, 6; 10:12; 12:6; *ṣᵉdaqah*, 2:19; 10:12; *mishpaṭ*, 2:19; 5:1, 11; 10:4; 12:6; and *da'ath 'Elohim* (or the equivalent), 2:8, 20; 4:1, 6; 5:3, 4; 6:3, 6; 8:2; 11:3; 13:4, 5. See the discussion of 4:1 ff. and 6:1 ff.

flowed the basic ritual and the ethical attitudes of Israel. These in turn gave rise to the specific regulations for worship and human relations collected in the codes of law in the Old Testament. The fruits of obedience were the maintenance of a just society and the full appropriation of the gifts of creation, within the limitations God himself had imposed upon the children of men. The ultimate fruit of faith was faith itself, the knowledge of one's true place in the world and trust in his creator.

Israel was the community of those who shared this understanding of their existence and who were determined to create the social conditions within which they and other men could give maximum expression to it. The determination had to be perennial, because the flow of human events in history was so fast that new problems were constantly being encountered. Israel could never create permanent conditions of justice, because justice had to be achieved anew with each change in the complex structures of society. In that sense, the "true Israel" is never achieved. On the other hand, Israel could entirely cease to be, if she yielded her fear of Yahweh and her obedience to the ethical corollaries of her faith, in favor of some idolatry. Hosea believed that the empirical Israel of his day had ceased, in this very way, to be the people of God.

Hosea's many references to the time when Yahweh brought Israel up out of Egypt show that he believed the Israel of God had been brought into existence at that time (2:15; 9:10; 11:1–2; 12:9, 13; 13:4–5). He never refers to the concrete events of the exodus–wilderness tradition, such as the deliverance at the Red Sea or the people's survival of the obstacles on their "journey" to Canaan. He speaks only of God's meeting them in the wilderness, of saving them to be his people, and the like. Thus, according to Hosea, the event of the exodus was God's creation of a people of faith and covenantal obedience. This community survived the hazards of its early history, but its faith was as much the means of survival as the result of it. It is a mistake to suppose that Israel learned to believe in God by interpreting certain outward happenings, like the escape from the Egyptian chariots at the Red Sea, as acts of God.

The decisive events of Israel's history were as much the products of faith as its occasions. The community of faith created the events of its life by seeking the natural and political conditions within which the people could obey God and worship him. In the process of creating these events—the exodus, the passage through the wilderness, the settlement in Palestine, the mastery of the Philistine threat, and the establishment of the monarchy—Israel gained new insights into the nature of God and her own existence. Thus the new events were revelatory. They also involved a successful appropriation of the external circumstances thrust upon Israel from without. In that sense, the great events of her history were responses to objective occasions and not merely creations of her own will. Things happened to her, certainly. Some of these happenings were natural, others political. Her faith in the Lord of both nature and history demanded that she see his hand in all these happenings. She was able to see his hand in them, however, because of her prior faith in him as Lord. These happenings did not create her faith; they provided the context within which the faith could be lived, tested, deepened, and corrected.

Israel's faith in God was not merely the private speculation of a "religious man," like Moses, for instance. It was more objective than that. Yet its objectivity lay in the fact that it was shared by a community of men, who found it the soundest possible foundation for objective existence as a society in space and time. Its objectivity did not consist in its being produced or confirmed by happenings in the natural order. Israel's faith was able to survive all kinds of embarrassments to her interpretation of the natural order, precisely because it had another foundation.

I have said that Israel created the revelatory events of her history. I do not mean thereby that her faith was nothing more than an act of will. It was a gift of God. He acted to give her faith, as he acted upon her to provide the occasions for her obedience. This belief in the prior grace of God is fundamental to Israel's perspective. If we ask, however, what the chief *medium* was that God used in bringing about revelatory and redemptive events, we must answer that it was the people's will to shape the future in the service of God. Faith presupposes faith. There is no way to break through this circle of faith to find some external and "objective" cause.

The faithful community's comprehension of its relationship to God changed in the course of time, under the stimulus of prophets and others with theological imagination. The relationship itself was more than their words could articulate. It was the total ground and context of the community's being, acted out in ritual and in daily life. It was expressed in creeds and laws, in the writing of history and in changing social institutions. It was a way of being, under God. This is what the covenant was.

The great song of renewal (2:18–23), which climaxes the allegory of Israel's history, celebrates the faith of the new covenantal community, but leaves the mystery of the future inviolate. The editorial poem that comprises 1:10–2:1 is altogether different. It is concerned with the question of the constituency of the new community, its form, and its importance among the peoples. The veil of the future is pushed aside, and we are shown a reunion of the descendants of the kingdoms of Israel and Judah, grown to enormous numbers and ruled once more by a monarch. The poem descends, in short, to the level of the "old wife," who cared so much about this sort of thing. The poem does not entirely violate the spirit of Hosea's promise to Israel, but every genuine echo of 2:18–23 connotes redundancy over that more eloquent song, and every note that does not reflect the other is a stranger to the repertory of Hosea.

On the surface, this brief poem seems to be merely a reversal of the names of Hosea's children and, therefore, a reasonable word to expect from Hosea.[8] We already have his expression of that hope, however, in 2:21–23. Any imitator could have constructed the second one. It differs from Hosea's own visions of the future, however. These visions do not depict a reversal of the effects of the nation's calamity by a *return* to the conditions and institutions of the past. On the contrary, they imply the creation of new conditions. The single exception is the return to the land, and even this note is played softly. The return to the land is the symbol of Yahweh's provision of the natural requirements of life in community. The particular land of Palestine has no special status or sanctity in Hosea's promises for the future (incidentally it has none in 1:10–

---

[8] Mauchline defends the Hosean authorship of 1:10–2:1 on this ground. Wolff supposes that this oracle was given to those who suffered in the invasion of 733 B.C. It is impossible, however, to believe that Hosea could have made them such a promise, which presupposes the extension of existing institutions into the future, at the same time that he was denouncing those institutions in "Ephraim." The events of 733 B.C. changed nothing. Why should Hosea suddenly have become soft-hearted about the kingship? Wolff compares 1:10–2:1 with Isa. 8:23 ff. and thus, to my mind, helps refuting his own defense of the Hosean origin of the former; for Isa. 8:23 ff. is utterly alien to the spirit of Hosea.

2:1 either).[9] Hosea's silence about the kingship in 2:18–23; 11:10–11; and 14:1–8, however, stands in sharp contrast to the royal viewpoint of 1:11.

It is especially significant that the reversals of the three names in 2:22–23 are not all alike. There is a word play on Jezreel ("God Plants") in the promise to plant the people, i.e., God's bride, in the land. Not-Pitied is now to be pitied, and this, too, in this context, can only mean that God will have compassion upon the people. In neither case is there any reference to the house of Jehu or to the "House of Israel," which were the original objects of these prophetic signs. Only in the case of the third name is an effort made to preserve the original meaning of the sign and to pronounce a direct reversal. Not-My-People becomes explicitly My-People. The inner relationship between God and the people is thus reversed in the new era, but the outer circumstances of the new community are not mentioned, not even in the change of the first two names.

I consider Hos. 1:10–2:1 an editorial addition to Hosea. Among other things, the passage contains an alien note of Judean national messianism. It is a bland form of royalism, to be sure, and not a serious intrusion into Hosea's oracles.[10] It is an intrusion, nevertheless. On the other hand, there are two ideas contained in this poem that are worthy of any prophet. They are the convictions that the people of God are to think of themselves as sons of a transcendent Father (1:10b) and that these sons can be his true sons only when they are one covenantal people (1:11a). It is difficult to imagine a better summary of the Law and the Prophets.

[9] See the discussion of 9:3 (p. 164) and 9:15 (pp. 167–168). The statement in 1:11 that "they will go up from the land" seems to me to allude to a great pilgrimage to the national sanctuary. No particular "holy hill," either Mt. Zion (Jerusalem) or Mt. Ephraim (Shechem, Bethel), is named. This vagueness is consistent with the spirit of the other predictions of restoration in Hosea, as against the Zionism of post-exilic Judean writers. If this interpretation is correct, the common effort to make the line denote a return from exile (usually by emending to "the lands") is unnecessary. Vs. 2:11 has predicted the cessation of the national pilgrimage-festivals; thus, the reversal of that punishment in the new era (1:11) is an appropriate one, whether the statement is Hosea's or that of an editor.

[10] See the comments on the Judean edition of Hosea in Additional Note C.

3 THE SIGN OF THE RANSOMED BRIDE: HOSEA 3

1   *Then Yahweh said to me again:*
     "Go, love a woman,
          lover of a paramour and an adulteress,
     As Yahweh loves the sons of Israel,
          while they turn to other gods,
          and love raisin cakes."

2   So I ransomed her for myself for fifteen pieces of silver
     and a homer and a lethek of barley.

     And I said to her:
     "You will wait for me for many days
          —without prostituting yourself
          or belonging to any man—
          and I, too, (will wait) for you.
4   For the sons of Israel will wait for many days,
          without king and without prince,
          without sacrifice or sacred pillar,
          without ephod or teraphim.
5   Afterward the sons of Israel will return
          and seek Yahweh their God
          [and David their king.]
     They will come in fear to Yahweh and his goodness
          in the latter days."

NOTES ON THE TEXT

Verse 1. "Said again" is adopted by Rowley (*BJRL* 39 [1956/57], 206), Gordis (*HUCA* 25 [1954], 29), *Chicago,* Robinson, and Pfeiffer (*Introduction,* p. 570). Were the adverb עוֹד meant to modify "go," it would follow the imperative (see *BDB,* p. 729a). There are a few cases in the OT where עוֹד precedes an imperative (cf., Zech. 1:17. Zech. 11:15 is sometimes cited in this connection, but it is identical with Hos. 3:1, and the adverb there, too, may actually modify the preceding "said" and not the following "take"). "Go again" is therefore possible (so, the English versions and many commentators), but "love again" (W. R. Smith, *The Prophets of Israel*, 1897, p. 412; Brown; and F. Buck, *Die Liebe Gottes beim Propheten Osee*, 1953, pp. 12–13) is not.

MT has "loved (אֲהֻבַת) by a paramour," but the parallel, "turn . . . love," is complemented better by an active participle (thus, *LXX, Moffatt,* Sellin, Robinson, Weiser, Nötscher, and others). The difference in vocalization is slight (אֹהֶבֶת). Gordis (*loc. cit.*) observes that the passive form may have an active meaning (comparing Ps. 103:14; 1 Sam. 21:9; Song of Sol. 3:8).

רֵעַ ("paramount"; cf., *Moffatt, Chicago, RSV, Harper,* and others, and Jer. 3:1) has sometimes been translated "husband" here (Smith: "loved of her husband, though an adulteress") and Jer. 3:20 cited in support of the translation (cf., *BDB* and Smith). The word is "paramour" or "lover" in Jer. 3:20 also, however, (cf., e.g., *Chicago* and *Moffatt,* against *KJV, ASV, RSV;* see, further H. L. Ginsberg in *Y. Kaufmann Jubilee Volume,* Jerusalem, 1960, p. 51). The *LXX* understood the word to be רַע ("evil") and this interpretation has been accepted by Sellin and Scott (*Message,* p. 127). A. D. Tushingham has interpreted the term to mean friend or proxy ("best man") of the god in a sacred marriage, i.e., the priest who mates with a sacred prostitute, who in turn represents the goddess (*JNES* 12 [1953], 150–59). רֵעַ is parallel to "other gods," but the term is too ambiguous to be assigned such a technical meaning, without a great deal more evidence than Tushingham has produced. His interpretation is certainly not impossible, of course.

The raisin cakes were employed in the cult (Isa. 16:7; 2 Sam. 6:19; Song of Sol. 2:5; 1 Chron. 16:3; and compare the cakes for the queen of heaven in Jer. 7:18; 44:19). The usage presumably originated in the cults of fertility.

Verse 2. I have interpreted the וָאֶכְּרֶהָ of the MT, which has given the translators no end of trouble, as a scribal error for וָאֶפְדֶּהָ ("and I ransomed her"). The question of Yahweh's ransoming (פדה) Israel is raised at other crucial points in Hosea (7:13 and 13:14). Whether or not this emendation of the verb in 3:2 is correct, the line apparently describes a ransom payment of some sort. *LXX* translates "hired." Nyberg (p. 23) regards this meaning as legitimate for II כרה, which many consider to be the root of the Masoretic verb (*BH*, Robinson, Wolff, Weiser, Wellhausen). Others take it to be נכר, which has a Ugaritic cognate, *nkr*. Yet, the advocates of this theory disagree over the meaning of the Ugaritic word. Gordon, who has changed his mind several times, takes it to mean "purchase in remarriage" (*Ugaritic Manual*, p. 296), but he supports his theory by referring to Hos. 3:2! "Purchase in marriage" is advocated by Gray (*The Krt Text*, 1955, p. 37) and Gordis (*loc. cit.*), and "recognize legally as one's wife," by Tushingham (*op. cit.*, pp. 153 f.). The word may have been as highly technical as these interpretations indicate, but the number of occurrences is still far too small to prove it. If the verb in 3:2 means "hire," it may indicate securing the services of a prostitute (cf., Isa. 57:8, where כרה should probably be read for כרת; cf.; *Köhler*, p. 454).

Lethek appears nowhere else in the OT, though *1tḥ* appears in the Ugaritic texts as a unit of dry measure. Generally it has been assumed to be a half-homer.

Verse 3. The first phrase (תשבי לי) should be translated "wait for me" (thus, the Vulgate, Syrohexaplar, and Symmachus; cf., Ziegler, *Septuaginta* XIII, *in loc.*). ישב ל never means "dwell with" in the OT. Gordis's contention that the phrase means "dwell in a husband's house," i.e., marry, is completely unconvincing (*loc. cit.*). The common occurrence of ישב (ב)בית (literally, "sit in the house [of]"), in the OT, hardly justifies translating תשבי לי "dwell in my house." To "dwell with" is expressed by the prepositions ב, את, and עם. ישב with ל occurs in Jer. 3:2, Judg. 16:9; Gen. 21:16, 22:5; Exod. 24:14; 2 Kings 10:30, 15:12; and Job 15:20 (cf., Ps. 132:12). שבו־לכם פה in Gen. 22:5 is literally "sit yourselves down here" (i.e., wait here). תשב לה, in Gen. 21:16 is "sat herself down," or "sat by herself" (*JPS*). In 2 Kings 10:30 and 15:12 בני רבעים ישבו לך על־כסא ישראל means "your sons of the fourth (generation) shall sit on the throne of Israel" (*RSV*), or literally, "sons of the fourth (generation) shall sit for you upon the throne of Israel." ישבו לכסא־לך (Ps. 132:12, "shall sit upon your throne") is similar. ישב ל is used only in Job 15:28 in the sense of "dwell in," and the text there may be incorrect, since a singular pronoun (למו) is used with the noun and verb in plural. Even if the text were correct, the usage is unlike that in Hos. 3:3, for the pronoun in Job 15:28 refers not to a person, but to houses, which are explicitly mentioned. That usage is much closer to the common "sit upon" (ישב ל, e.g., Ps. 9:5).

Exod. 24:14 and Jer. 3:2 confirm the translation "wait for me" (literally, "sit for me"). The first is שבו־לנו בזה עד אשר־נשוב אליכם ("wait for us here until we return to you"), and the second is על־דרכים ישבת להם ("by the roads you wait for them," i.e., Israel waits for her lovers). Judg. 16:9 (וישב לה) also uses the verb in the sense of "lying in wait," but, since the same statement in 16:12 omits the לה, and since the feminine pronoun is used in 16:9 for Samson, the לה should perhaps be left out. תשבי לי ... אני אליך in Hos. 3:2 is so close to Jer. 3:2 that one wonders whether the former originally had a verb of coming or returning in the last clause, such as the latter has. Compare the parallel, Hos. 3:5, "afterwards they shall return" (ישבו). This line is not precisely parallel, because in 3:2 the action or disposition is that of Hosea toward the woman (the symbol of Israel), whereas in 3:5 it is that of Israel toward God. It is better, therefore, to take the initial verb ("wait") as governing the last clause as well as the first. The intervening clauses, introduced without a conjunction, are then to be understood as modifiers of the initial verb. The manner of the woman's waiting is defined by her not fornicating or having intercourse with a man (these may be synonymous, or the latter may include legitimate intercourse, i.e., with Hosea). The four stichs of this couplet are chiastic (ABBA). The two adverbial clauses in the middle are synonymous parallels and so are the first and the last clause. On the adverbial use of finite verbs in Hebrew, see G.K. 120g.

תשבי לי in Hos. 3:3 is translated "sit (still) for me" by LXX, Jerusalem, Harper, Brown, Sellin, Robinson, and Weiser, and "abide for me" by KJV and ASV. JPS renders it "sit solitary for me." This is essentially what the line means, but not precisely what it says. These translations properly preserve the suggestion of unengaged waiting for Hosea. "Dwell as mine" (Chicago and RSV) does not, and is therefore less satisfactory.

וגם־אני אליך ("and I, too, for you") refers back chiastically to the first clause and is governed by the initial verb. Hosea's action resembles that of the woman in that he waits for her. It is absurd to link it to the prohibition of fornication, and it is tautological to link it to the preceding clause, because her not belonging to any man (i.e., sexually) subsumes also her not belonging to Hosea. Furthermore, the clause is not parallel to the preceding one because it lacks the negative (לֹא). It has often been surmised that a phrase (לֹא אָלֵךְ or לֹא אָבוֹא) has dropped out (recently, *Chicago, Moffatt,* Robinson, Weiser and Wolff). However, the lines as they are, are a well-balanced, chiastic couplet, 3+2, 3+2 (A+B, B+A), and the addition of the allegedly missing phrase would make the last line a grotesque 3+4. There is no versional support for the addition. Ziegler lists a number of ancient witnesses, however, which transpose the clauses so that the last in MT comes immediately after the first! (*Septuaginta* XIII, *in loc.*). These translators understood the parallelism, whether or not their *Vorlage* was arranged in this way. The chiasmus in this verse is complemented by another in vs. 5 (see the note, below). Thus, the same stylistic device is found both at the beginning and at the end of this final segment of the prophet's great sign-narrative.

Verse 4. יֵשֵׁב in vs. 4 means what it does in vs. 3, i.e., "wait." "Abide," with the connotation of waiting or enduring, is also acceptable (so *KJV, Chicago,* and others). *Moffatt's* "remain" is good, too (cf., Wolff).

For "ephod and teraphim," the *LXX* has "priesthood and signs," but this is merely interpretive and does not presuppose a variant text.

Verse 5. "And David their king" and "in the latter days" have been regarded by many scholars as marks of a later (perhaps exilic) hand. The passage has been handled by these men in various ways, however. The principal alternatives are: (1) to delete the allusion to David as an editorial expansion (thus, *BH,* Wellhausen, Nötscher, and many others; this is easily the favorite expedient); (2) to delete that phrase, together with 5b (Sellin; Weiser deletes "and David their king" and "in the latter days"); (3) to delete the whole of vs. 5 (Harper); and (4) to treat the entire fifth verse as integral to the chapter, but date the whole in the post-exilic era (Batten, *JBL* 48 [1929], 271 f.; May, *op. cit.,* p. 286; and the following, cited by Pfeiffer, *Introduction,* p. 576: W. R. Smith, Volz, Marti, Haupt, Hölscher, and R. E. Wolfe). On the other hand, a few recent critics have allowed vs. 5 to stand as Hosea's: M. Buber, *The Prophetic Faith,* 1949, p. 123; Gordis, *op. cit.,* p. 31; Buck, *op. cit.,* p. 17;

Knight (apparently); and G. A. Smith (who questions only the name "David"). I consider the phrase "and David their king" a crude intrusion, incompatible with the context. Verse 5 is a homogeneous chiastic couplet (3+3, 3+2; A+B, B+A). The insertion destroys the poetic line. Hosea often employs tristichs, especially at strategic points in his poems, but this stich introduces an anticlimactic digression that cannot be justified by appealing to the appearance of tristichs in other places. In the genuine tristichs of Hos. 1–3, the third stich is always parallel synonymously to one or both of the other stichs (1:2b, 9; 2:2a, 3b, 5b, 7a, 9a, 10, 12a, 13a, 14a, 18a, 18b, 19, 23). In 3:5, the third stich is an editorial afterthought. See Additional Note C: References to Judah in the Book of Hosea.

The literary form of this narrative is strikingly similar to that of chapter 1: the divine command and its explanation occupy a single line each. The four-word introduction is almost identical with the one in 1:2. The prose connective between the two spoken words is merely long enough to hold the parts together. The second speech is prefaced in the standard way, this time with two words; and it contains the usual, simple command and an explanation of standard design. The differences from the form of chapter 1 are dictated by the contents of the last action, which, being complex in performance, requires a longer explanation than usual. Again, the first person is required because of the dialogue with the woman. Hosea addresses her face to face, just as Yahweh does his new "wife" in 2:19–20.

The placement of chapter 3 after chapter 2, rather than after chapter 1 is probably due to its similarity to the last part of chapter 2. We can do no more than guess whether chapters 1 and 3 once formed a continuous narrative. The shift in persons from third to first has led many scholars to conclude that they were written at different times. The opinion once advocated that the first-person address in chapter 3 gives it a better claim to authenticity than chapter 1 is not tenable, however.[1] I believe that we still lack sufficient knowledge of the composition and transmission of the prophetic literature

---

[1] The significance of first- and third-person narratives has been most vigorously studied in connection with the Book of Jeremiah. The formal difference between the biographical and autobiographical materials has not proved to be a useful criterion of authenticity. A thorough discussion is presented in W. Rudolph, *Jeremia* (*Handbuch zum Alten Testament,* 2nd ed., Tübingen, 1958), pp. xiii–xx. See, also, S. Mowinckel, *Prophecy and Tradition* (Oslo, 1946), and W. Holladay, *JBL* 79 (1960), 351–67.

to draw any definite conclusions from the mode of reference to the prophetic speaker/actor.[2]

THIS DRAMATIC PARABLE of the ransomed bride is an epitome of the Book of Hosea. All the salient themes of his oracles are presented in the symbolic actions described and the brief accompanying words. Israel's corporate life (the woman's former marriage) has been internally destroyed by idolatry (her love for a paramour). This corruption has resulted in the loss of corporate identity and of the benefits of Palestinian settlement (the bride's dismissal and enslavement). However, the punishment thus suffered is not only a divine penalty for Israel's sin, but it is also the occasion for a change of heart. God will ransom the people from slavery, as an earnest of his intention of restoring them as his true people (Hosea's purchase of the destitute woman), although they will be required to endure a period of deprivation to test their penitence and faithfulness (her trial "for many days"). Only after this time of discipline will the social and sacral instruments of Israel's life be recreated (the woman's acceptance by her waiting husband).

Once again, the pattern of events derived from sacred history forms the basis for interpreting the future. The people's immediate destiny is the return to "slavery," as in Egypt, and the loss of the land. From that exile, however, they will be delivered in a new exodus (symbolized by the prophet's purchase) and disciplined in a new wilderness. From there, they will be led again into the land of promise and empowered to fashion a new life, founded on the recognition of God's sovereignty. The past redemption will be recapitulated in the future, although the ultimate outcome of God's action on Israel's behalf is, naturally, indeterminate. Because of the people's freedom, the future remains open.

Recent criticism of the Book of Hosea has been preoccupied with the identity of this adulteress, rather than with the meaning of the text as it is. The interpretation presented here is not dependent upon

---

[2] Lindblom's discussion (*Prophecy in Ancient Israel,* pp. 222–23, 235–36) generally shows proper caution in this regard. His conclusion (p. 255), that Hos. 1 and Hos. 3 are doublets, the first written by a disciple and the second by Hosea, contradicts, however, the reserve he himself has otherwise shown, and certainly fails to take sufficient account of the great difference in substance between the two narratives. See below, pp. 54 f.

any particular conclusion concerning the woman's identity. Nevertheless, this problem is not irrelevant to the meaning of the sign and must be therefore discussed. Only if the story is pure allegory, that is, if it has no basis in action in Hosea's life, then only is the identity of the woman wholly irrelevant. In that case, the meaning of the story lies simply in the explanatory words that accompany the action.[3] If the narrative records an actual experience of Hosea, however, as most contemporary scholars believe that it does, there are three possible interpretations to be considered.

The first theory is that chapter 3 is a duplicate account of Hosea's marriage to Gomer, referred to also in 1:2 f.[4] If this theory is correct, however, one of the writers misconstrued the symbolic character of the action. Chapter 1 indicates that the woman immediately conceived a child, whereas in chapter 3 the woman is immediately isolated from men, including Hosea. This obstacle to the theory cannot be eliminated by juggling the time sequences. One such effort is the supposition that chapter 3 describes a trial relationship that came into being between the receipt of the command (1:2) and the actual marriage (1:3). Another is the supposition that there was actually a longer period between the marriage and the birth of the first child than is implied in 1:3. Each of these theses has a certain plausibility, but each fails to reconcile the two narratives. In both reconstructions, the consummation of the marriage to the woman of chapter 3, after the period of trial, issues in the birth of the child Jezreel and, subsequently, in that of the other children. These children become symbols of divine punishment and of the impending era of deprivation. Thus, according to these theories, the eventual fulfilment of the marriage, after the period of isolation, relates directly to Hosea's pronouncements of disaster. But, in chapter 3 the pronouncement of punishment is symbolized by the period of isolation, and it is strongly

---

[3] Chapter 3 had been interpreted as a parable of Israel in exile, written long after Hosea's time, by Paul Volz (cf., Harper's summary on p. 217 of his commentary), H. G. May (op. cit.), L. W. Batten (op. cit.), W. F. Stinespring (Crozer Quarterly 27 [1950], 200–07), G. Hölscher (Die Propheten, Leipzig, 1914, pp. 426–28), R. E. Wolfe (ZAW N. F. 12 [1935], 92–93), and Y. Kaufmann (op. cit., pp. 370 f.). Recent scholars who have interpreted the whole of chapters 1–3 allegorically are listed in Rowley, "The Marriage of Hosea," BJRL 39 (1956/57), 214.

[4] See, Robinson, O. Eissfeldt, Einleitung in das Alte Testament (3rd ed., Tübingen, 1964), pp. 522 f., and Lindblom, op. cit., p. 225). Buber eliminates the problem of duplication surgically, moving 3:2 after 1:3a (op. cit., p. 111). The problem is only partly solved in this way, however.

implied that the eventual consummation of the marriage will symbolize the era of covenantal renewal for Israel. In chapter 1, the consummation of the marriage symbolizes judgment and destruction; in chapter 3, the consummation of the marriage symbolizes reconciliation and restoration. Therefore, these narratives have nothing to do with each other. They describe two different occasions that have utterly different meanings.

A second embarrassment to this theory is that the woman of 3:1 ff. is described as an adulteress. If the marriage in chapter 3 is the same as that in chapter 1, that is, Hosea's original marriage to Gomer, then her adultery had to be against another husband. In that event, Hosea's marriage to her (3:2 f.) would not be as good a symbol of Yahweh's persisting love for his old, faithless wife, Israel (3:1). I say, this is an embarrassment, because the consensus is to regard the two women as one; it is certainly not a disproof, because the consensus could be wrong.

A second alternative is to take the action of chapter 3 as Hosea's second marriage to Gomer. This is the prevailing view. If it is correct, the event was a perfect symbol of covenantal renewal, that is, the reconciliation of an estranged wife with her husband. The term "adulteress" is easily accounted for by this theory, although it requires the assumption that Gomer was unfaithful to Hosea prior to his purchase of her. There is very little evidence to support this assumption but none that really stands in its way. My personal preference is for this theory.

The third alternative is embarrassed, as is the first, by the word "adulteress," but it does not suffer from the other deficiency of the first theory. This alternative is that chapter 3 reports an experience with a woman other than Gomer.[5] Had the woman been the adulterous wife of another man and become a derelict, Hosea's action on her behalf would not have symbolized directly the restoration of a previous covenant. However, the action would still have been a startling representation of God's intention to redeem the degenerate people of Israel, especially if the woman were a sacred prostitute, as many suppose.[6] It has been argued that unless the partners of the action in chapter 3 were Gomer and Hosea, the bride's return could

[5] Cf., Tushingham, *loc. cit.,* and Pfeiffer, *op. cit.,* pp. 568–69. The latter gives the names of recent advocates of this theory.

[6] E.g., Tushingham, *op. cit.,* T. H. Robinson, and H. W. Robinson, *Two Hebrew Prophets* (London, 1948), p. 14 (also published as *The Cross of Hosea,* Philadelphia, 1949).

not have symbolized Israel's return to her first "husband." [7] However, if Gomer had not been available for this role, because she had not been unfaithful to Hosea (after all, we do not know that she was), then another woman would have had to suffice. Her previous history, leading up to her present plight, would not have been the symbol of Israel's history, to be sure, but the present plight itself and her subsequent submission to Hosea's discipline would have symbolized Israel's present condition and her coming chastisement and restoration. The action would have been doubly significant if the woman were Gomer, but it would have been highly significant even if she were not.[8]

Hosea's action represented the deliverance of Israel from bondage to a baalized form of worship (3:1). It is not unreasonable, therefore, to assume that the woman ransomed was a prostitute, perhaps a temple-prostitute. She herself would thus have been a victim of the grossest aberration in the popular religion of the day and a perfect symbol of adulterous Israel. The text will certainly bear such an interpretation, even though it does not demand it.

Hosea was commanded to love this woman as God loved apostate Israel. This command is the heart of chapter 3. Its meaning is not altogether obvious, however. One of the most appealing current explanations of it is that of Martin Buber. "That a particular person should be bound to love another particular person in utter concreteness, is there such a thing as this? The word can only be spoken to one who already loves." Otherwise, the love could not be commanded.[9] This is an attractive defense of the identification of the woman with Gomer. The Lord grants permission to Hosea to *continue* loving Gomer, even though she has committed a crime against him. In spite of this eloquent defense of the theory, however, it must be observed that the command is not directed to the sentiment of love, but to love-as-action, and this *can* be commanded in utter concreteness.

[7] Rowley, *op. cit.*, p. 207.

[8] Hosea's purchase of the woman undoubtedly gave him a legal right to her, so that, in the event she was originally another man's wife, Hosea was not himself committing adultery by taking her as his wife.

[9] *The Prophetic Faith*, p. 113; cf., Mauchline and Knight. Tushingham rejects Buber's interpretation of 3:1 on the ground that "love" is purely erotic here (*op. cit.*, p. 151). He translates אהב, "crave, desire." This is the standard word for erotic love in Hebrew and at the very least it has erotic overtones here.

Genuine acts of love are motivated by the sentiment of love, but how is the latter to be defined? Is there a unique sentiment of love, a passion of a peculiar quality that makes it possible to speak of acts of love as of those that issue from this source? Perhaps there is; but is not love defined primarily by what it does? At least, this seems to be the case here. Hosea was commanded to love a derelict woman as a sign of God's resolve to deliver Israel from her moral predicament. The effort to help the one in distress marked the act as an act of love, whether the woman was already Hosea's wife or someone else. Hosea did not merely save the woman from her dereliction, however. He brought her to himself to love as a woman, as his wife. He even purchased the right to her as a woman. He did not exercise this right immediately but enforced a period of continence upon her. They waited many days before consummating the marriage. The obvious implication of the story, however, is that he intended to consummate it eventually. He waited first of all to see whether she would accept her discipline and be ready to be his wife without returning to her adultery. The narrative does not tell whether she passed the test and, accepting him as her husband, was accepted as his wife.

The first stages of this marital drama symbolized God's love for Israel and the necessity of her chastisement. These were certainties to Hosea, and his certainty was embodied in his action and his words. He was not sure of Israel's response. He hoped it would come. As a prophet he was the spokesman of God and harbinger of his acts, but not the spokesman of Israel. His hope for Israel's proper response was well symbolized by his waiting for the woman's fulfillment of his desire. The actual consummation of the marriage, however, would have been the sign of Israel's actual fulfillment of God's desire, and that sign he could not yet enact. He may have married the woman—we do not know—but if he did, it was not a prophetic sign, to be made a part of his public message.

The evident source of Hosea's knowledge of God's love was his interpretation of Israel's history. God had come to Israel in the exodus–wilderness era as a loving parent (11:1, cf., 9:10; 12:13; 13:4). A new relationship was established, one which Israel had not known before. This divine act of love had no precedent. It was not merely the expression of a mutually acknowleged relationship but was itself the occasion and power by which that relationship was created. In fact, the love persisted in spite of the meager response it evoked (11:2–4; 9:10; 12:14). Far from loving God in return, Israel learned to love the magical rites of the agricultural cult (3:1; cf., 4:19; 9:1, 10; 10:11) and other illegitimate devices of self-aggrandizement (12:8). Nevertheless, God's love continued. He would now enact new measures of discipline and healing (14:4). The cure involved radical surgery but its aim was health and not death. The same love God had shown to Israel in the past was now proclaimed in the remarkable prophetic action undertaken by Hosea (3:1 ff.).

Hosea's knowledge of love, and especially its conditions and capacities, was undoubtedly fostered by what he experienced as a father and husband. The general truth of this assumption is inherently probable. We cannnot reasonably go further than this, however, and speculate about particular experiences and insights he might have had, because the Book of Hosea tells us nothing about such family experiences or husbandly insights. The bittersweet story so often told about Hosea's agony over Gomer's infidelity, his mounting indignation and her eventual expulsion, and his helplessness before a deathless love that led him to take her back against reason and law, is a pure fabrication. The sooner it disappears from the textbooks of Old Testament study the better.

Hosea's actions toward the woman of chapter 3 were first of all symbols of God's love for Israel. Hosea speaks decisively of God's former acts of love and presents the coming action as a repetition of the old. We must therefore understand his action chiefly in relation to his interpretation of Israel's history rather than his own. He mentions his own story only in so far as it is the direct expression of his understanding of the history of the people of God. It is quite impossible to probe into his untold biography for sources of his teaching and action, and, fortunately, it is not necessary. His oracles provide sufficient clues to the source of his understanding.

The familiar argument that the radical shift in Hosea's attitude toward Israel's future, from despair to hope, may be accounted for only on the assumption that Hosea experienced a radical change in his own sentiments toward Gomer, is a counsel of interpretive despair.[10] Such a defense of the authenticity of the oracles of hope is not likely to succeed. Fortunately, the case rests on firmer foundations. The promises of renewal in Hosea do not mitigate the threats

[10] See Mauchline, for instance.

of doom but presuppose them. Hosea's attitude toward Jehu's dynasty did not change, nor did his attitude toward the extant Israelite state, or the baalized cult and its priesthood, or toward the international policies of his time. He never promised restoration of what he had condemned. He promised a new beginning, based on God's changeless and persistent love. He did not change his mind about it, any more than he did about God's determination to bring an end to the old dispensation. His hatred of the old order and his love of the people are consistent throughout—concurrently. There is no change of heart toward Israel or her future and no need to account for such a change.

Hosea's purchase of the guilty woman (3:2) fits well into the pattern of his proclamations, though certain aspects of the transaction are unexplained. Regardless of the identity of the woman or the precise nature of her offense, the purchase itself is a splendid symbol of the new exodus of Israel. Hosea secures the marriage rights to the woman and simultaneously effects her release from an obligation that in his mind is illicit and degrading. He does not exercise his right immediately but tests first the woman's chastity for an extended period of time. He waits hopefully for her to prove herself and accept him faithfully as her husband. She waits patiently to see whether she will be accepted as an honorable wife.

Thus, Israel's release from her illicit and degrading bondage to alien powers and practices may lead to the re-creation of a covenantal community if she proves, in her time of trial "in the wilderness," that she can accept Yahweh faithfully as her "husband" and Lord. This is the meaning of the episode taken as a whole. No explicit indication is given in the narrative that the purchase itself was meant to have special significance. It has generally been assumed that the purchase was mentioned simply because it took place. Since the particular woman Hosea secured had to be paid for, he paid. She may have been a slave or a prostitute.[11] It is unlikely that the pay-

---

[11] Wellhausen, Harper, Mauchline, Sellin, Robinson, Smith, Rowley, (*op. cit.*, p. 225), and others think she was a slave. Harper called the purchase inexplicable, though he too attempted to guess at the reasons for the stated amount, the circumstances which might have led to her predicament, and the nature of the servitude itself. The theory that she was a cult prostitute, whose release was obtained in this manner, has an increasing number of advocates (e.g., Tushingham, *op. cit.*, pp. 150 ff.; Nötscher; and May, *op. cit.*, p. 287).

ment was the bride-price for a free woman or a bribe to the woman's lover.[12] The writer apparently did not think it important enough to explain.

The suggestion of the text that Hosea married Gomer (chap. 1) and bought the adulteress (chap. 3) as symbolic expressions of God's purposes toward Israel may strike the modern reader as a callous exploitation of a human being for extraneous ends. There is perhaps a certain justification to this reaction, for one cannot preclude the possibility that Hosea's actions were entirely motivated by prophetic rather than personal concerns. Surely, this conclusion is more likely than the opposite one, namely that his initial motivation was entirely personal and that later only he came to regard his action as having symbolic meaning. I reject both the mechanical and the sentimental views of his behavior, however, and regard Hosea's marriage to Gomer and his purchase of the adulteress who, I believe, is identical with Gomer, both as genuinely personal acts aimed at securing a real and self-authenticating marriage and as prophetic acts symbolizing God's relationship to Israel.

The modern reader must bear in mind that a "self-authenticating" marriage in ancient Israel, as in most cultures, was not entered into because of romantic love between the marriage partners. Few, if any, marriages presupposed the existence of a bond of affection between the man and the woman. Marriages were based upon other considerations, and the two partners might be perfect strangers to each other before the marriage. The modern insistence that a marriage be based primarily upon the couple's prior regard for each other as unique individuals is, therefore, an entirely inappropriate basis for judging any marriage in ancient Israel, including that of Hosea. It is not fair to say that Hosea was merely exploiting Gomer for professional reasons, as if the alternative were a compelling love for her as a person. According to ancient concepts of marriage, there was nothing wrong with a man's choosing a particular woman for his wife because she met certain objective qualifications. In Hosea's case, these would have been suited to his prophetic intentions. His choice of a particular woman for such a reason would not at all preclude his

---

[12] If she was actually an adulteress, she was no longer a "marriageable" woman who could command the customary bride-price (*mohar*). Her lover would have been in no position to demand payment for her release, since he would have been guilty of a capital crime!

wanting the marriage to become a relationship of mutual love and personal responsibility. As a matter of fact, Hosea's marriage to Gomer had to have this relationship as its ultimate aim and hope (chap. 3), to fulfill his prophetic intention as a symbol of God's covenant with Israel.

The love Hosea shows toward the adulteress in chapter 3 is not without erotic affection. The word used here is precisely the usual Hebrew word for that. But the trouble with the woman in this narrative, and with Israel generally, is that, in Hosea's experience, they are moved only by erotic affections. Hosea demands of the woman that she show fidelity as well. This is what must distinguish the new marriage from the old, as it must distinguish Israel's new covenant from the old one. The new will also be marked by love in the affectional sense of the term, as is made clear by the whole tenor of Hosea's proclamation of God's love toward Israel (2:14–20; 11:1–11).

Hosea's redemption of the debauched woman in chapter 3 has important ethical implications that follow from the foregoing considerations. We have rejected the notion that this act was intended *only* as a symbol of God and Israel. To be a good symbol of that relationship, which was nothing if not one of love, devotion, righteousness, and knowledge, it had to be a relationship characterized by these qualities. It could not be a mock drama. It had to be a genuine effort to achieve a good marriage with the woman. The discipline imposed upon her had to be taken seriously, as an aid to her rehabilitation as a responsible person in the community. This is true regardless of what precise personal sentiments toward the woman we may wish to attribute to Hosea. Here then we have a concrete illustration, involving an actual human being, of the meaning of the prophetic ethic of *ḥesed* and *ṣedaqah,* loyalty and righteousness.

Was the purchase of the woman understood as a symbol of the second exodus from slavery? The allegorists of an earlier age often interpreted the action in this way.[13] Such an inference from the action in its present context in Hos. 1–3 is not unreasonable. Chapter

[13] See, e.g., C. F. Keil, *The Twelve Minor Prophets* Vol. I (*Biblical Commentary on the Old Testament,* by C. F. Keil and F. Delitzsch, Grand Rapids, 1949; reprint), *in loc.* Among recent commentators, Knight is the only one, to my knowledge, who mentions the exodus in connection with chapter 3, though he does not interpret the purchase itself as a symbol of a new exodus.

2 describes the new wilderness era and the second entry into the land of promise and, elsewhere in the book, Hosea speaks of the coming exile as a "return to Egypt" (8:13; 9:3; cf., 11:11). Therefore, it is quite natural for the reader to attach this significance to the purchase of the woman, whether or not it was originally intended.

Hosea did not know what would be the outcome of Israel's coming period of trial, but he seemed confident that the divine pedagogy would finally succeed in eliciting a faithful response from the people. Once again, as in chapter 2, he makes no attempt to predict the institutional character of the new community. It has one essential feature, renewed faith in Yahweh as sovereign and benevolent God, faith defined as turning back, seeking, and fearing the Lord. The fearfulness of Yahweh would have been amply demonstrated in the intervening experiences, yet not because he was an intrinsically demonic power. He willed Israel's good. He was the final source of this good, as he was also the only one they needed to fear. So, the people would approach him in confidence and in awe. Their seeking would be a persistent single-mindedness, turning again and again to the Lord of their existence, who, though present, was forever eluding their comprehension and control, and demanding that they seek him again and again.

Faith in Yahweh is exalted as the supreme quality of man's life. The creation of men's faith is presented in both chapter 2 and chapter 3 as the last goal of God's own work in Israel. Faith in God is the one thing needful. It is not the penultimate act or disposition of man, which serves the attainment of some other, ulterior good. It is itself man's ultimate good. Vss. 3:5 and 2:14–23 are eschatological in this sense; they affirm the finality of faith. Whether they are eschatological in a chronological sense is a matter of opinion. It is possible to interpret them as a description of a future time when a community of men will attain the condition of faith as a permanent endowment, a level of understanding and obedience that will distinguish them from the unfaithful, disobedient men of the present age. If this inference is correct, then Hosea was saying in effect that the kingship of God would be established in the final phase of the story of Israel, that it would be a manifest kingship, unlike his hidden kingship in the present time.

Alternatively, it is possible to interpret the time of faith, as Hosea presents it, as a recurring possibility for Israel, one that awaits her continually in the wilderness of her disobedience and faithlessness. This is not to suggest that Hosea simply described the possibilty of perennial renewal of man's faith. He spoke chiefly of corporate renewal. He spoke to Israel, inheritor of a covenantal tradition, and not directly to every man. His allegory of renewal (chap. 2) and his parable of the ransomed bride (chap. 3) presented models of God's judging and redeeming activity that illuminated the particular future he and his contemporaries were facing. They also served as models of God's creative activity in other crises of Israel's existence.

The historical relativity of Hos. 1–3 is highest in those segments that deal with the past, that is, with the story of the Israelite commonwealth in Canaan, and lowest in segments that deal with the consequences of this story. The reason is not merely that Hosea did not know the end of the story and was therefore vague in his treatment of it. He could have said a good deal more than he did about the specific outcome of the events transpiring before him, as other Hebrew prophets did. The more probable reason is that such an analysis would not have been so relevant to his hearers as the one he actually made. His vocation was not to analyze current events and their implications for politics and society, but to proclaim the ways of God with Israel. These ways are perennial, even though the circumstances under which men find them and respond to them are always new. Hosea addressed men in terms of their covenant with God, and not first of all as citizens of a particular political order, either of the present or of the future. What he said has immediate relevance to men of the covenant in every new wilderness of their corporate existence.

The hope for a re-establishment of David's line is an alien feature in Hosea's promise (3:5). It is one of the marks of the Judean revision of the book.[14] This revised text presents the absurd image of the Davidic dynast, alongside Yahweh, as the object of eschatological faith! The people's final turning and seeking (5a), which are identical

14 See the textual note to 3:5. Even if, after all, the reference to David were a genuine part of the original oracle (something that probably will never be known), it would have to be interpreted as the symbol of a united people under God and not as a fragment of Judean propaganda. Until such time as its originality is proved, however, I shall read chapter 3 without this phrase. As a matter of fact, I should do so even if it were proved, for the chapter has greater literary and theological integrity without it, regardless who it was who wrote it.

with fearing (5b), can have only one object. It is conceivable that Hosea should have spoken of the gathered Israelites of the future appointing a single ruler over a unified social order (1:11), but it is inconceivable that he should have placed their allegiance to the Judean royal house on a level with their ultimate faith in God.

This redactional reference to the Davidic dynasty shows the good intention of the editor and, at the same time, his misunderstanding of vss. 3–5. As a Judean, he believed in the sole legitimacy of the Davidic dynasty, its sanctity, and eternity (2 Sam. 7; Ps. 89). He probably believed also in the sole legitimacy of the Jerusalem cultus (Deut. 12). He regarded therefore the northern Israelite kingship and its cultus as schismatic, apostate, and heretical (1 Kings 12:25 ff.; 13:33 ff.; etc.). Armed with these prejudices, he took the oracle in Hos. 3:4–5 as a contrast between the illegitimate kingship and cultus of the old Israelite state and the legitimate kingship and cultus in which the Israelites of the future would take part. Hosea's promise contained what the editor thought was a reference to the restored cultus, but since it lacked an allusion to the future kingship he supplied the missing piece.

From Hosea's viewpoint, the illegitimacy of the old Israelite kingship had nothing to do with its non-Davidic character. Such a notion never appears in his oracles against the northern kings. The illegitimacy of the Israelite royal establishment lay in the fact that the selection of kings and the conduct of political affairs were not expressions of faith in Yahweh or subject to the norms of action implicit in the Yahwistic covenant. Precisely the same illegitimacy characterized the Israelite cultus. That is why both were to cease "for many days." Moreover, vs. 5 does not predict the restoration of the monarchy and the cult. It predicts the renewal of faith. The temporary cessation of state and cult was a necessary condition, but not a sufficient cause, of this renewal.

The woman's situation before Hosea (chap. 3) is similar to that of Israel before God. Hosea loves her as Yahweh loves Israel, but she does not yet love him. She must be deprived of marital relations for a time in order to learn to love him, that is, to accept her relationship with him faithfully. She is deprived of all sexual relations, even of those formally legitimate, as the necessary condition, but not the sufficient cause, of becoming inwardly faithful. Similarly, Israel is deprived of government and cultus, even though they are outwardly proper, in order to become inwardly faithful. The narrative does not describe either the future establishment (re-establishment, if she is, indeed, Gomer) of outward marital relations between the woman and Hosea or the future re-establishment of the external forms of Israel's political and cultic life; it is implied that both of these will take place if Israel and the woman come to maintain their respective relationships to God and Hosea faithfully. Only the reference to the Davidic dynasty disturbs the elegant symmetry of this sign-narrative and its corresponding theological proclamation.

Hosea was certainly no propagandist for the Judean royal line. None of his denunciations of the northern kingdom was based on the claims associated with the tradition about Yahweh's election of David. These included hegemony over the tribes of Israel (Gen. 49:8), as well as sovereignty over neighboring nations (Num. 24:17–19; Gen. 49:10–11), and even the mastery of western Asia, from the Nile to the Euphrates (Ps. 89:26–28 [Eng. 25–27]; cf., Pss. 2 and 110). Furthermore, this title was everlasting (Ps. 89:19–37; 2 Sam. 7:12–16). It is difficult to believe that Hosea would not have been as severe in his criticism of these Judean pretensions as he was of the political schemes of Israel, had he prophesied in the south. For Hosea, the instruments of national power were intended to be the servants of the covenant, that is, means by which to achieve justice and promote the knowledge of God. When the servant became master, the prophet denounced him. Surely, he would not have endorsed the Judean claim of the absolute validity of the Davidic line.

There is no need to suppose on the other hand that the new dispensation, for which Hosea hoped, was to be a universal church, whose membership would transcend national, geographical, and social distinctions. Such an institution is not mentioned in his oracles any more than it is in the other pre-exilic writings of the Old Testament. Nor is it likely that he conceived of a future community simply as consisting of those who had faith in Yahweh, without any external ecclesiastical structure. At the very least, he would have assumed the necessity of common means of worship and the transmission of sacred traditions, and we may reasonably interpret his statements about the renewal of Israel's relationship to Yahweh as including such means.

Hosea based his hope for the future of the people of God not upon the survival of the Judean state but upon a renewal of faith and a concomitant re-establishment of the community, after the national disaster. Had Hosea been chiefly concerned with the problem of Israel's political independence, he might have considered the southern kingdom a better hope than the northern, by the time his ministry was over. After the debacle of 735–32 B.C., Israel was reduced to half her former size, was once again tributary to Assyria, and was in constant danger of Assyrian annexation. However, Judah's situation was little better politically. She did not enjoy genuine self-determination from that time until the end of the Assyrian Empire, and then only briefly, under Josiah. Hosea's hope would have been a forlorn one if it had rested on Judah's political prospects.

According to the analysis of Micah and Isaiah, Judah's religious condition was no better than that of Israel. We do not know what Hosea's opinion of the southern situation was, but probably it would have been as critical as Micah's and Isaiah's. Surely, he would not have thought Judah more faithful to Yahweh than Israel, and thus more worthy of preservation. The only remaining reason for placing his hope upon Judah, then, would have been a blind belief in the Davidic messianic dogma. However, that dogma was promulgated in Judah after the separation of the two kingdoms and was never accepted by the Israelites of the north, to our knowledge. It is extremely unlikely therefore that Hosea accepted it.

Hosea spoke to the men of Israel about their life together as people of God. He spoke essentially about faith and faithlessness and the effects of these upon their common life. Their faithlessness was about to lead to the violent dissolution of the structures and supports of their corporate existence. But Hosea proclaimed the faithful love of God, who would turn their just disaster into the occasion for a renewal of their faith and, thereby, into a renewal of their common life. The eternal possibility of the renewal of faith was a practical necessity for Israel in the middle of the eighth century B.C. The same necessity and possibility exist for the people of God in every century and in every land. This is the meaning of Hosea's preaching.

It was not the prophet's task to design the structures of common life in the new era. Since the growth of social institutions is not wholly subject to rational control or prediction, we should not expect the prophets to have engaged in speculation about such things. Occasionally, we have the impulse to upbraid them for condemning existing institutions, without proposing alternatives. Yet, they were not called to formulate social legislation or execute programs of political control. They were called to declare the eternal love and justice of God and thus to maintain the people of the covenant in the knowledge of God and of their mutual loyalties. In performing this task, Hosea spoke of the ultimate needs and responsibilities of the men of his day, even while he spoke concretely of the events and conditions of their lives. The eternal gospel of God is especially clear in chapters 2 and 3. It has meaning not only for the ancient sons of Israel but for all the children of Adam.

HOSEA'S MARRIAGE

A vast amount of energy has been spent in the modern debate over the character of Gomer and the history of her marriage to Hosea, but the results of the expenditure are rather meager. There is simply not enough information provided in the book to enable the reader to reconstruct the story of the marriage. We do not know whether Gomer's "whorishness" (1:2) was actual fornication, or infidelity to Yahwism, or both. The literal interpretation is dominant among contemporary scholars, but the figurative interpretation is also vigorously defended by many. We do not know whether Gomer's harlotry had actually manifested itself before Hosea married her or whether it took the form of overt behavior only afterward. The conviction that she was already known to be a prostitute, either sacred or secular, before Hosea married her, is most prominent among recent writers on the subject, but the theory that she had only an inclination to prostitution, until after her marriage, is still very popular. We do not know whether the adulterous woman of chapter 3 was Gomer or a second woman. The theory that she was Gomer is ascendant today, but the alternative has its advocates, nevertheless. In the event that this woman was Gomer, we do not know whether the purchase described in chapter 3 came before or after the marriage mentioned in chapter 1. The theory that chapter 3 concerns Hosea's second marriage to her is the current favorite, but a case may still be made for the alternative view.[15]

Because the story of Hosea's marriages is largely unknown to us,

[15] All these theories are described and evaluated in H. H. Rowley, "The Marriage of Hosea," *BJRL* 39 (1956/57), 200–33. A full bibliography of recent discussion is also provided there.

we cannot use it as a foundation for interpreting his message; rather, we must rely entirely upon the actual declarations of the book. Nevertheless, important theological conclusions have actually been drawn from hypothetical reconstructions of the story, and it is necessary therefore to comment upon them. Two kinds of use are made of the marital story. One is to clarify the content of his message and the other is to deduce the motives of his preaching. Both uses are invalid.

The most important example of the first type is the effort to show that the reality of Hosea's love for his faithless wife confirms the authenticity of his oracles of hope.[16] It presupposes that chapter 2 describes Gomer's infidelity to Hosea and his rejection of her and that chapter 3 relates his subsequent display of redemptive love toward her. These suppositions may be correct, but they are too uncertain to support the conclusion that Hosea's behavior toward Gomer guarantees the Hosean authorship of the promises to Israel. There is no guarantee of authorship. However, it does not matter. Even if we knew that Hosea wrote both the threats and the promises in the book, but if we found the two to be theologically and logically incompatible, we would have to discredit one or the other, in spite of their origin. Conversely, if we found the two to be fully compatible logically and theologically, it would not be important who wrote them, as long as both together provided a cogent interpretation of the crisis of faith and culture in Israel in the eighth century B.C.

The second use to which the marital story of Hosea is put is encountered far more often than the first. It enjoys such wide currency, in fact, that it may be called almost a dogma of twentieth-century Old Testament criticism. It is the supposition that the origin of Hosea's belief in the wrath and love of God for Israel was his experience of husbandly wrath and love for his faithless wife Gomer. This supposition, like the one described above, requires also the prior assumption that Gomer was unfaithful to Hosea after their marriage, and that she was the woman of chapter 3, whom Hosea lovingly sought to redeem.

The two assumptions are reasonable enough, but there is almost no evidence to support them. Hence, the inference drawn from them is extremely precarious. When it is set beside the explicit statement of the text that Hosea did what he did with these women, primarily as

[16] See, e.g., Cornill, *op. cit.*, pp. 48–52, and Brown (pp. 34–37).

an expression of a prior theological conviction, it must be rejected as fallacious. In other words, the text (1:2) says that Hosea first came to the conclusion that God was "married" to a "harlot," and so himself married a harlot in order to symbolize this, and that subsequently (3:1) he came to the conclusion that God loved his "adulterous wife" and wanted to redeem her and, in order to symbolize that, Hosea acted to redeem an adulteress by means of loving discipline. The text could be wrong. It should not be set aside, however, unless there is important objective evidence to support the alternative. In fact, the evidence is extremely weak.

There is nothing decisive in chapter 3 to suggest that the woman was Gomer. Again, nothing in chapter 2 indicates that the "wife" represents an actual woman. The chapter is pure allegory from its first word to its last. The supposition that its story of Israel and Yahweh reflects also the story of Gomer and Hosea is mere fancy.

A common argument concerning Gomer's initial character as a bride has been made on the assumption that chapter 2 is telling the stories of Israel and Gomer, concurrently. Since Israel was originally faithful to God, according to 2:15 (so this theory goes), Gomer must have been also initially faithful to Hosea and could not have been a prostitute whom he deliberately married. Several objections can be made to this argument. One is that Gomer's possible prostitution prior to her marriage to Hosea has no direct bearing on the question of her fidelity to him afterward. A second is that chapter 2 seems to have nothing whatever to do with Gomer.

If we must seek a parallel between Gomer and Israel, however, it seems to me that it lies in the presentation of both as prostitutes from the beginning and not in their innocence. Entirely too much weight has been placed on Hos. 2:15. Among other things, it has been used to contrast Hosea's interpretation of Israel's early history with that of Ezekiel. Hosea is often said to represent the wilderness era as one of fidelity, whereas Ezekiel represents it as a time of apostasy (Ezek. 16, 20). The fact is that Hosea likewise, regarded the wilderness era in Israel's history as a time of apostasy. Every other reference to it in the Book of Hosea makes this point (11:2; 9:10, 15; 13:6). Israel was faithful to Yahweh to the extent that she came out of Egypt, made a religious covenant with him, the God of Moses, and entered the land under the direction of Moses' successors. That much, however, would have to be said also of Ezekiel's view of

Israel's past. On the other hand the apostate attitude, which Ezekiel attributed to earliest Israel, is precisely the same attitude which Hosea saw manifested in the earliest times.

According to Josh. 24 (and to modern historians of the Hebrew religion) the fathers of Israel worshipped other gods than Yahweh before the exodus from Egypt. We may use Hosea's term and say that Israel was a prostitute at that time. What this ancient tradition affirms is confirmed by the picture of Jacob that Hosea draws in chapter 12 (although he does not use sexual metaphors there). For what it is worth, therefore, I suggest that the argument for parallels in Hosea's presentations of Israel and Gomer points toward Gomer's being a prostitute of some sort when he married her, rather than toward her innocency. The prophet's representation of Israel's history is more important for its own sake, of course, than any possible implication it might have for the character of Gomer.

Chapter 1 reports that Jezreel was borne by Gomer to Hosea (1:3) but does not say explicitly that he was the father of the second and third child. It has often been inferred from this omission, and from the names of the second and third child, that Gomer conceived them illegitimately. The inference is problematic but not impossible. If it were true that Gomer had had children by adultery after her marriage to Hosea, however, he would not have been at all surprised, since, according to the text, he had deliberately married a prostitute. It is impossible to construct a romance of broken faith, wounded affection, wrathful indignation, and love-in-spite-of-everything, out of these materials. The bittersweet story of Hosea's deathless love for a wayward wife and of his discovery of a parable of God and Israel in his own experience is the fabrication of sentimental critics.[17]

---

[17] George Adam Smith popularized the notion that Hosea learned about God's wrath from Gomer's sin (*op. cit.,* pp. 234, 244–45, 250–51) but he held that Hosea's compassion for the woman of chapter 3 (whom Smith considered to be identical with Gomer) was not the source of his belief in God's love for Israel, but the *result* of it (pp. 250–51). A host of others after Smith has deduced Hosea's knowledge both of God's wrath and of God's love from his personal responses to Gomer. The most influential version of this theory, in English, has probably been that of H. W. Robinson (see, *Two Hebrew Prophets*). Occasional voices have been raised against the fixation of the dogma, e.g., those of L. W. Batten (*JBL* 48 [1929], 257–73), H. G. May (*JBL* 55 [1936], 285–91), and W. Stinespring (*Crozer Quarterly* 27 [1950], 200–07). They have had little effect upon the majority opinion, however, perhaps because their rejection of the love story was accompanied by an unnecessary rejection of the oracles of hope from among the authentic utterances of Hosea.

I do not wish to deny that Hosea's family life confirmed and enriched his understanding of the covenant. Very likely he discovered in the intimate associations of marriage and fatherhood something of the interior meaning of God's covenant with Israel. That much is implied in his adoption of the metaphors of marriage and parenthood in his preaching. Certainly, these metaphors were close at hand in the cultic symbolism of baalized Yahwism. Yet it is hard to account for his choice of them merely on the ground of their appropriateness in a polemic against the syncretized cult. There was a great danger that this use of the metaphors would be misunderstood. In addition, his preaching was no mere polemic. These metaphors were also central to his constructive proclamation, as chapter 3 demonstrates. We are forced to posit a source of understanding in which the creative possibilities of marriage and fatherhood were apprehended. One reasonable hypothesis is that his own family experience provided such a source; yet, because of the speculative character of this opinion, it is critically more responsible to say that the fragmentary evidence implies that the prophet's knowledge of the demands and powers of God's love was *deepened* in his experience within his family, than it is to say that he first *discovered* these powers and demands in familial love and then boldly projected an analogous sentiment upon God. His appropriation of Yahwistic tradition and his reflection on the story of Israel, according to the positive evidence of the book, were the primary sources of his understanding of God. Chapter 11, for example, makes this clear. However, we must finally admit that we do not know how Hosea was led to his convictions. How is any man?

If we *must* have a story of Hosea's marriage to Gomer, however uncertain, I prefer the one defended by Rowley.[18] It is that Gomer was a prostitute, of either the sacred or the common variety, when Hosea married her, that the three children named in chapter 1 were theirs, that Gomer committed adultery against Hosea, and that he brought her back to make a responsible wife of her by means of love and discipline (chap. 3). Whether he was successful we cannot even guess. Hosea fulfilled his *ḥesed;* the rest was up to Gomer.

---

[18] *Op. cit.* However, I find his treatment of chapter 2 to be unconvincing as an argument for Gomer's actual infidelity to Hosea. I find no positive evidence in the text for this infidelity except the *possibility* that Gomer was the adulteress of chapter 3. I believe chapter 2 does not help us at all.

PART TWO

THE FACES
OF INFIDELITY

CHAPTER

4 LIKE PRIEST, LIKE PEOPLE: HOSEA 4

I. *The Prosecutor's Summons*

1   Hear the word of Yahweh, O Israelites,
        Yahweh's indictment of the inhabitants of the land.
    There is no faithfulness, nor devotion,
        nor knowledge of God in the land.

2   Cursing, perjury, and murder,
        robbery, and adultery, are everywhere!
        And bloodshed follows bloodshed!

3   Therefore the land withers,
        and all its inhabitants languish,
    With the beasts of the field and birds of the air;
        and even the fish of the sea are dwindling away.

II. *The Priest's Malfeasance*

4   Yet, let no man accuse;
        let no man convict;
            for against you, (too), is my indictment, O priest.

5   You stumble by day,
        and the prophet stumbles [with you] by night;
        so I am destroying your people.

6   My people are destroyed for lack of knowledge.
        Since you have rejected knowledge,
        I will reject you as my priest.
    And since you have forgotten the teaching of your God,
        I, too, will forget your descendants.

7   The more they multiplied, the more they sinned against me.
        I will change their honor to disgrace.

8   They feed upon my people's sinning,
        and they long for their offenses;

9   and so it is, like people, like priest.

I will punish them for their ways,
    and repay them for their deeds.
10   They will eat but not be satisfied,
    promote prostitution but not increase;
For they have forsaken the Lord,
    to maintain prostitution.

III. *The People's Malady*

11   Wine and new wine take away the senses:
12   my people ask oracles of a tree,
        and a stick gives them revelations.
Because a whorish spirit misleads them,
    they go whoring away from their God.

13   Upon the hilltops they sacrifice;
    upon the heights they burn offerings,
Beneath the oaks, poplars, and terebinths
    because their shade is pleasant.

Thus your daughters become prostitutes,
    and your daughters-in-law commit adultery.
14   But I will not punish your daughters for their prostitution
    nor your daughters-in-law for committing adultery;
Because the men themselves consort with whores
    and offer themselves to sacred prostitutes.
    Thus a people without insight comes to ruin.

IV. *The Prophet's Warning*

15   Though you prostitute yourself, O Israel,
    let Judah incur no guilt.
Keep away from Gilgal;
    do not go up to "Beth-evil";
        and do not swear, "As Yahweh lives."
16   Like a stubborn heifer Israel rebels.
    Can the Lord now tend them like lambs in a pasture?

17   Ephraim is joined to idols.
    Let him alone!
18   A band of drunkards, utterly debauched,
    they relish the shame of her protectors.
19   A wind has wrapped her in its wings,
    and they will be ashamed of their altars.

NOTES ON THE TEXT

Verse 1. The word translated "devotion" is the familiar *ḥesed,* which denotes both steadfast loyalty and creative affection toward fellow participants in a community of obligation. "Mercy" (*KJV*), "steadfast love," and "kindness" (*RSV*), as well as "loyalty" and "devotion," convey various nuances of this richly suggestive word. Both the sentiments and the behavior implied in these terms are ingredients of true *ḥesed,* though even *ḥesed,* if it is man's, can be hollow and ephemeral (cf., 6:4, where an impulse toward devotion, unmatched by sustained loyalty, is meant). *Hesed* is linked elsewhere in Hosea with "the knowledge of God" (2:21 f.; 6:6), "justice" (*mishpaṭ,* 2:21 f. [Eng. 2:19]; 12:7 [Eng. 12:6]), "righteousness" (*ṣedeq,* 2:21; 10:12), and "faithfulness" (*'emeth, 'ᵉmunah,* 2:21 f.).

Verse 2. The relationship between this verse and the Ten Commandments is discussed in Additional Note B.

The five infinitives are best understood as subjects of the finite verb פרצו (literally, "break forth"). The latter does not, then, enumerate a sixth crime (contrary to *ASV, Chicago, RSV,* and others). Cf., *LXX,* Robinson, and Budde (*JBL* 45 [1926], 282).

Verse 3. I regard this verse as part of the indictment (with *JPS, RSV, Chicago,* Harper, Sellin, Weiser, and Mauchline) and not part of the sentence, and have used therefore the present tense and not the future (the Hebrew will bear either).

The standard translation of the first verb, "mourns," produces a marvelous irony: the people mourned the amoral calamities of nature, especially the death of the vegetation god, in their baalized cult; but, here nature is "mourning" because of the moral calamity that has befallen the people. I should like to be able to retain this translation. G. R. Driver (cited by Wolff) and Köhler (*Lexicon, Supplement,* p. 210) are apparently right, however, in deriving this verb from אבל II, "to wither or dry up," rather than אבל I, "to mourn." Where אבל is predicated of the soil or its plants it is usually associated with יבש ("be dry," Jer. 12:4; 23:10; Amos 1:2; Joel 1:10) or אמל ("wither," Isa. 24:4, 7; 33:9; Joel 1:10). Exceptions are Jer. 4:28 and 12:11. אמל is the parallel verb in Hos. 4:3a, also. It never clearly means "mourn," except perhaps in Isa. 19:8. Elsewhere it means the withering of vitality and the cessation of fertility and productivity. The implication of 4:3 may well be that the land is mourning, but what it says is that it is withering.

Verse 4. MT: "Thy people are like those who contend with the priest" (וְעַמְּךָ כִּמְרִיבֵי כֹהֵן). Although *KJV, ASV,* and *JPS* preserve this reading, virtually all modern commentators have thought it made nonsense and have proposed textual changes. The reconstruction that has claimed the widest (now almost universal) support is "for with you is my contention, O priest" (וְעִמְּךָ מְרִיבִי כֹהֵן), which necessitates the change of two vowels and the excision of a single consonant (the second כ having crept in, presumably, by dittography). Since the prophet accuses the priests later on (4:8) of living handsomely off their "contentions" with the people, i.e., the traffic in sin-offerings, the priest is the implied subject of the injunction "Let no man contend . . ." (4:1b). The proposed textual change in the last clause, then, provides an elegant complement to what precedes, and a fitting transition to the following indictment of the priests. I should like to propose one refinement in this reconstruction. Instead of deleting the second כ, read it as an error for ג and divide the words thus: וְעִמְּךָ גַם רִיבִי כֹהֵן ("for with you, too, is my contention, O priest"). This proposal has the following advantages: (1) It is more probable that a ג was misread כ than that an initial כ arose from a final ך by repetition; (2) the noun רִיב occurs in the Hebrew Bible about sixty times, including Hos. 4:1a; and 12:3 [Eng. 12:2]), whereas the Hiph. participle מֵרִיב occurs elsewhere only once (1 Sam. 2:10, the only other Hiph. form of any kind); (3) the meaning thus obtained corresponds more fully than the alternatives to the whole burden of the oracle, namely, that both people and priest are objects of divine punishment (4:9, "like people, like priest"). The prophet proposes nowhere to contend *only* with the priests, but *also* with them. They are, then, incapable of assaying the people's crimes or punishments, because they stand with them in the dock.

Verse 5. MT: ". . . and I will destroy your mother" (so *KJV, ASV, RSV,* and *JPS*). Various alternatives to this perplexing object have been suggested: "people," "urim [and thummim]," "fortune," and "you," recently. The first, which has been adopted here, requires only a slight change (עַמְּךָ for אִמְּךָ) and makes excellent sense. *Chicago, Jerusalem,* Weiser, and Nötscher adopt this emendation, and Mauchline and Junker (*BZ* 4 [1960], 165 ff.) agree that "mother" means "people" here (cf., 2:4, 7 [Eng. 2:2, 5]). "Mother" means Israel, of course, in Hos. 2:2, 5, and also in Isa. 50:1; but in these passages the use of the marriage metaphor for God's relationship to Israel makes clear sense of the term. In vs. 4:5 the priests are addressed, and it is not at all clear who the "mother" is. In 2 Sam. 20:19, the city of Abel is called "a mother in Israel." Could Hosea have been referring to the sanctuary-city in which the priests of chapter 4 lived? Robinson, Wolff, and Lohfink (*Biblica* 42 [1961], 303 ff.), argue that Hosea was addressing a particular priest; but, if this were the case, which seems unlikely, no reason was given why the man's mother should be destroyed. Junker's rebuttal to this position is a good one (*BZ* 4 [1960], 168 f.), but his contention that "mother" means the priesthood is not very convincing. The association with vs. 6a supports the conclusion that "mother" means the people. I have translated the perfect consecutive verbs of vs. 5 into the English present tense, rather than the future, which is used by the English versions. Weiser ("have destroyed"), Wolff ("is destroyed"), Mauchline and Nötscher ("you are destroying"), and the Jerusalem Bible ("have destroyed"), translate the line similarly. "Am (are) destroying" is better than "have destroyed," however, since we would expect simple perfects (as in vs. 6) or imperfect consecutives if the latter were intended. These lines comprise a part of the indictment (invective) and not of the punishment (threat).

Verse 9. The perfect consecutive verb (וְהָיָה) in the first clause has been treated here as have those in vs. 5, and for the same reasons (thus, also, *JPS,* G. A. Smith, and Brown; cf., *Chicago*). This clause belongs with vs. 8 as the closing line of the invective against the priests. Note that the first, third, and sixth lines end with the decisive word "priest."

Verse 10. "Prostitution" is now almost universally transferred from vs. 12, where it is superfluous, to vs. 11, where it completes an otherwise unfinished sentence ("For the Lord they have forsaken to keep . . ."). See, e.g., *RSV, Chicago, Jerusalem,* Weiser, Mauchline, Wolff, Nötscher. T. H. Robinson transposes the text: כִּי לִשְׁמֹר אֶת־יְהוָה עָזָבוּ ("for the observance of the Lord they have abandoned"). שָׁמַר is often used of observing the *commandments* of the Lord and the like, but there is no parallel in the OT to the usage proposed by Robinson (see, also, *KJV, ASV, JPS, Moffatt*). The passages cited by Junker (*op. cit.*) are actually not parallel (Prov. 27:18; 1 Chron. 12:29; Gen. 26:5; etc.). They speak of guarding one's master, maintaining one's service to a king, and the like.

פרץ (literally "break forth") has been variously translated "be fruitful," "get children," "multiply," "prosper," etc., all on the basis of the context. Children would be appropriate if the reference were to secular prostitution (*Jerusalem,* Cheyne), but, if it were to cultic prostitution or to a more general religious "prostitution," then the withheld increase would be material blessings of all sorts.

Verse 15. A large majority of the commentators delete vs. 15 as a Judean gloss that has crept into the text. Only Harper, Nötscher, Knight, Brown, and Scott (*op. cit.,* pp. 43 f.), retain the MT. Surely this is not so obviously a Judean gloss as the majority vote suggests. As a warning against incurring the particular corruptions associated with the Israelite cult, it is neither pro- nor anti-Judean, as are the really suspect Judean allusions in Hosea (favorable: 1:7; 3:5 ["and David their king"]; unfavorable: 5:5; 6:11; 8:14; 10:11; 11:12 [?]; 12:2). Furthermore, who is the addressee in vss. 15 and 17, if not Judah? Certainly it is not Israel. The point is precisely that Israel/ Ephraim is to be left by his neighbors and God, to suffer the consequences of his acts (cf., vs. 10). This is not a command to repent of the cultic evils of the past. Nowhere in this poem does Hosea imply the hope or even the possibility of repentance.

Several scholars have supposed that vs. 15 originally referred paronomastically to Beersheba as well as to Gilgal and Bethel (Bethevil) (cf., Amos 5:5): ". . . swear not at Beer-sheba ("Well-of-swearing")." Cf., *Chicago, Moffatt,* Wellhausen, G. A. Smith, Harper, Robinson, and Nötscher. In the absence of textual or versional support, this emendation is arbitrary.

The name *Beth-aven* ("House of evil") occurs here and in 5:8 and 10:5, and the similar name *Aven* ("Evil"), in 10:8. Although Beth-aven is distinguished from Bethel in Josh. 7:2 and 1 Sam. 13:5, these terms seem to be used by Hosea as sarcastic designations of *Bethel* (which means "House of God"). In order to preserve the allusion to Bethel and also indicate the sarcasm, I have translated the first term "Beth-evil."

Verse 17. The last two verses of the chapter are textually difficult ("corrupt," perhaps, though this term may be a rationalization of our ignorance) and have occasioned a host of reconstructions, some of which have also affected vs. 17. The second half of this line contains a single term, according to the Masoretic pointing (הנח־לו), and Procksch (*BH,* followed by *Jerusalem,* Weiser, Nötscher, and Mauchline) has proposed "completing" the line by including in it the first two words of vs. 18 (emended): "Leave him alone in the company of drunkards." We may disregard the Masoretic hyphenation in vs. 17, however, and properly stress each of the last two words, whose meaning is "Leave him to himself!" ("Let him alone!" in the English versions is, of course, more vivid). As an exclamatory command, the line is as complete as it need be. *Chicago*'s "A maker of images is Ephraim; he has set up for himself a fat bull!" involves a more extensive textual emendation in vs. 18 than the principal alternative, although it yields a good parallelism.

Verse 18. MT is סר סבאם, which probably means "their liquor is gone," and which is intelligible when taken with the following line, "(so) they grossly promote fornication." Nevertheless, most scholars are dissatisfied with this version, which does involve uncertainties. A change to סר סבאים, "a company of drunkards," is adopted by a great many scholars and is presupposed by *RSV, Moffatt, Knox,* and *Jerusalem,* among recent versions. The principal alternative is one proposed by Sellin and accepted by *Chicago,* i.e., "a fat bull," which must be joined to vs. 17. The changes in the consonantal text are hardly more extensive than those in the first proposal (שר for סר and מאבס for סבאם, yielding שֹׁר מְאָבָס). This is very attractive. Nevertheless, the ancient versions support MT in referring to an alcoholic debauch; so, the first alternative is the better one.

The last word is literally "her shields" (מגנה). The noun is a common metaphor for rulers, as protectors (Pss. 84:10; 89:19), and the feminine singular pronoun is no serious problem in a passage that symbolizes Israel as a heifer (vs. 16). G. R. Driver's suggestion (*JTS* 34 [1933], 383 f.), which is supported by *Köhler* and Wolff, that the word is II מגן ("insolent"), is plausible ("they loved the shame of the shameless"). Less likely is the reading מגאנה ("her pride") or מגאני ("my glory," in "they love shame rather than my glory," i.e., Yahweh), although the first of these enjoys the support of the *LXX.*

Verse 19. The shift in numbers among the pronouns is identical in vs. 16, the last line of the previous strophe, and here, the last line of the present strophe (she . . . they). It is impossible to keep the pronouns consistent since Ephraim, the heifer, and the people are all involved (he, she, they), and there is really no need to, although many have tried.

The parallel construction of the two final strophes confirms the rendition that has been adopted here: (a) Israel, prostitute yourself (15a)// Ephraim, joined to idols (17); (b) let Judah incur no guilt

(15a)// debauchery (perhaps cultic) (18); (d) stubborn heifer (16a)// a wind has wrapped *her* in its wings (19a); (e) *they* cannot be tended (16b)// *they* will be ashamed . . . (19b). The formal similarity is impressive and establishes the fundamental rationality of the last five verses, against those who have found them fragmentary and hopelessly corrupt.

IN ANCIENT ISRAEL, legal indictments and pleas of defense were presented orally before the judges and witnesses, although they might be also in writing (Job 31:35; Dan. 7:10). Prophetic accusations were often cast in the technical form of such indictments and employed the standard terminology of judicial procedure.[1] In fact, we are inclined to imagine the Hebrew prophets proclaiming their oracles "in the gate," very much in the fashion of a public prosecutor speaking for God. Some of their "briefs" may originally have been in writing; the extant ones, at least, were ultimately recorded. Hosea used this form with great force in chapters 2, 4, 5, and 12. The effectiveness of the device in these oracles is due in large part to the use of the full muster of dramatis personae of the law court. Judge, prosecutor, defendant, and witnesses are all present in the persons of God, the prophet, the people, Israel (personified variously as Jacob or the bride of God), and the priests and rulers. The roles in the great court drama shift from time to time and frequently overlap, for the scene is only an analogy, after all, to the actual situation that Hosea wished to describe.

His indictment of the Israelite priests in vss. 4:4–10 has special significance, because the priests constituted one of the chief judicial corporations of the nation. It was their prerogative to administer ritual law on the basis of historical precedent, as well as to employ the sacred oracle (the lot and "urim and thummim," which may have been identical) for decisions in unprecedented cases. Their jurisdiction was primarily sanctuary-practice and ritual purity, but the necessity of resorting to the sacred oracle in cases that could not be settled

---

[1] See, B. Gemser, *op. cit.*, p. 123. Examples of such prophetic usage are Isa. 3:13–17; 41:1 ff., 21 ff.; and Mic. 1:2 ff. I am speaking here of juridical forms in a strict sense and not of prophetic "judgments" in the broad sense of that term. That this term has become a synonym for "threat" shows the influence of the prophetic adoption of juridical forms and phraseology into their oracles.

by other means extended their influence considerably. As mediators between men and God and arbiters of men's status before the law, they enjoyed a lucrative and privileged position in Israelite society (4:7–8). Yet, to Hosea, they were unfit to judge others and fully liable to judgment themselves (4:4). The heart of his accusation was that they had perverted the knowledge of God, theirs and that of the people, and therefore had brought about the ruin of the community. We must examine the major terms of this charge.

It is easy to make general and superficial observations about the knowledge of God as a central concept of Hosea, but difficult to expound its meaning concretely in the poems where it is found. That the term denotes what we call faith or "true religion" is well known, as is the fact that Hosea considered it the source of morality. Virtually all handbooks on the prophets compare Amos and Hosea on this point. It is commonplace to observe that, whereas Amos taught that ritual propriety without social justice was an abomination in the sight of God, Hosea taught, more profoundly, that just behavior springs from a just heart, the heart that knows God through faith. However true this formula may be as a characterization of Amos and Hosea, and it is partly true, all interpretive formulas need to be scrutinized. What kind of knowledge is the knowledge of God, according to Hosea?

First of all, it is knowledge of the nation's historic experiences of deliverance from Egyptian slavery (13:4) and starvation in the wilderness (13:5), by the hand of Yahweh, the God of the covenant. The memory of these experiences, which were central events in the salvation-history, was transmitted by the congregation of Israel, especially in the rituals of its annual pilgrimage festivals. This memory and its implications were salient features of the *torah* (teaching), for which the priests were responsible (4:6). But Israel forgot this when she settled in Canaan and began to enjoy the fruits of the land (2:8). This failure to acknowledge that Yahweh, their God from the land of Egypt, was also the source of blessing in Canaan, was tantamount to a denial of the real presence of God in the prior experiences in Egypt and the wilderness (11:3); for it was only in being able to acknowledge Yahweh's sovereign presence in Canaan, as a power continuous with the one they had known in the past, that the events of the past could be actually acknowledged as revelatory. The ultimate purpose of God's demonstrations of saving power in Egypt and in the wilderness was the creation of a worshipping and morally responsive community in his name. This continuing acknowledgment of Yahweh as Lord was the absolute condition of knowing that the prior events were Yahweh's purposive acts, and not merely happy accidents. The power and glory of God can be known as power and glory without a retrospective commitment to the source of power, but they cannot be known as the power and glory of *God* without it. This aspect of the biblical understanding of God is brilliantly symbolized in the story in Exod. 33:17–23, where Moses is able to see God's glory only after God has passed by.

It seems to me that when Hosea says in 11:3, "they did not know that I healed them," he means not so much that the people of Moses' generation did not acknowledge Yahweh as their Physician in the wilderness, but rather that their descendants, some of whom were Hosea's contemporaries, by denying the continuing Lordship of Yahweh their Benefactor, were effectively denying the revelatory character of the events of sacred memory. They formally acknowledged that memory (8:2; 13:4). But what sort of God is a God who can be confined to sacred memories? Obviously not the Lord whom Hosea knew, but merely an anonymous, divine athlete who entered the cosmic arena one season long ago, to contest with some others the momentary destinies of a group of Hebrew slaves and miscellaneous Egyptians and, having won a fleeting championship, soon disappeared from view.

When Hosea's compatriots hurried to the altar in hours of peril to reaffirm their knowledge of God (8:2; 6:3), they were merely resorting to whatever devices might serve to avert their peril. But, in doing this, they did not acknowledge Yahweh, for they had not the slightest idea who he was (5:4). They sought someone else, that nameless champion of a previous season, who, they hoped, might once again win the day and use his momentary supremacy in their behalf. But even this people without knowledge of Yahweh, who sought the deification of themselves in seeking their anonymous champion, could be made to know that the knowledge they had was not the knowledge of Yahweh. When their quest met its absolute denial in the impending death of the nation, they would know that they had not known him (5:9; 9:7).

It is possible that Hosea meant by this assertion that the disaster would bring a new acknowledgment that the power shaping Israel's life, that is, the one who had brought about their destruction, was Yahweh, their covenantal Lord. He does not actually say this, however, and, in the light of his statement in 2:20, that Israel would know Yahweh after the *new* "exodus" and new covenant, it seems likely that he did not expect this positive recognition at the time of the national catastrophe. At the very least, however, Israel would know then how vacuous was the knowledge upon which their recent cultic behavior had been based.

In the light of Hosea's usage, one may distinguish between true knowledge of God, accompanied by obedience to one's covenant with him, and mere knowledge of the covenantal traditions communicated by the priests to the worshipping congregation.[2] And yet, one who saw in the sacral traditions a God who did not demand exclusive and total obedience could not be said to know these traditions, that is to say, he would not be affirming that these traditions communicated genuine *knowledge* of God. He would actually be denying the truth of what they claimed about God's nature and his demands. He would not have received the knowledge that the traditions carried and, therefore, it could be said that he did not even know the traditions. So, in one sense, knowledge may be spoken of as something distinct from a moral assimilation marked by obedience to the One who is known; and, in another sense, it may be understood as something that involves the acceptance of the known as valid, true, significant, and binding. It is in this second sense that the term is used in Hos. 4. The lack of the knowledge of Yahweh,[3]

[2] That the knowledge of God in Hosea means this last kind of knowledge has been advocated by H. W. Wolff (*Hosea*, to 4:1–3; and *Ev. Theol.* 12 [1952/3], 533 ff.) and G. von Rad (*Theologie des Alten Testaments II*, Munich, 1961, pp. 151 f.). This opinion has been criticized as superficial by G. Fohrer (*TZ* 11 [1955], 169), for whom knowledge of God involves an intimate and enduring relationship. Wolff's insistence that cognitive knowledge about God (*"Wissen um Gott"*) is the primary sense of the term has been further challenged by E. Baumann ("'Wissen um Gott' bei Hosea als Urform der Theologie?" *Ev. Theol.* 15 [1955], 416–25), who prefers to define it as a personal relationship. In replying, Wolff acknowledges the centrality of man's personal relationship to God in the thought of Hosea, but reaffirms his conviction that *da'ath 'Elohim* is essentially cognitive. ("Erkenntnis Gottes im AT," *ibid.*, 426–31).

[3] "Knowledge of God (*'Elohim*)" seems to be synonymous with "knowledge of Yahweh." Sellin, Wellhausen, and Harper, among others, have described the first as a general, human, moral knowledge, and the latter as a specific knowledge of the Yahwistic teachings of Israel. I agree with Brown, however, that this distinction is invalid for the usage in the Book of Hosea (see Sellin

in this sense, was both faithlessness to his covenant and forgetfulness of the covenantal traditions. However, in the other sense of the term, which Hosea also uses, it is possible to speak of being faithless to one's knowledge and still, in a measure, of having it. (6:3; 8:2).

When we come to the question of the relationship between the knowledge of God and morality, we must distinguish these two connotations of the word "knowledge." Knowledge that involves obedience is not the source of morality; it is itself morality. Here the relationship between the two is a matter of definition. The situation is different, however, in the case of knowledge understood as rational assimilation of information about God. Here knowledge means belief, rather than trust or obedience. It is not entirely clear what relationship Hosea believed there existed between this kind of knowledge and obedience. Under some circumstances, the relationship might be negative, that is, belief unaccompanied by obedience. This dissociation of the two characterized the Yahwistic congregation of Hosea's time, according to his denunciation. Yet, under other circumstances, the relationship might be positive, as, for instance, in the new Israel of the future (2:12–21). Why should one relationship prevail in the first case and the other in the second?

At first glance one may be tempted to say that in times of prosperity men are disposed to believe without obeying, whereas in times of adversity they are more inclined to obey as well as to believe. In Hosea's oracles, however, it is not the coming time of adversity that is to witness the union of belief and obedience, but the subsequent time of blessedness (2:12–21; 13:16–14:7). Adversity may be the occasion for a renewed obedience; it is certainly not its cause. There is one aspect of Israel's coming adversity, however, which Hosea considers especially useful for creating the occasion for obedience to the Lord. It is the forced removal of the means of access to Yahweh's Canaanite rivals (2:4–11; 3:2–5). This deprivation will constitute a special remedy, then, for Israel's moral disease. Like many medicines, however, this one merely clears the way for the organism to regain its health. Another aid, even more effective, will be the love of God, manifested in communal well-being (2:13–21; 13:16–14:7; 11:11).

All of these are spurs to obedience; none can guarantee it. God

---

and Brown on 4:1). The only *'elohim* that Hosea had in mind, when he spoke of knowing *'Elohim* (4:1; 6:6; 8:2; 13:4), was *Yahweh* (2:22; 6:3; cf., 2:10; 11:3), and there is therefore no ground for saying that *knowing 'Elohim* was different from *knowing* Yahweh.

had loved Israel before and she had become faithless. On the other hand, the future would also disclose new rivals for Israel's affection. Obedience is a free act of the human will, and the "explanation" of the relationship between belief and obedience, in any particular case, is hidden in the mystery of that freedom. There is no other source of obedience of the will than the will itself. Hosea expresses the hope, indeed the confidence, that God will finally succeed in eliciting that obedience; but it will be a free response, as free as the bridal love of a maiden or the homing flight of a bird (2:13 ff.; 11:11).

It is impossible, then, to trace fully the course of man's mental and volitional activity from belief to obedience. It is not difficult, however, to trace the course of social interaction from the corruption of men's wills to the dissolution of a genuine community, or, better, its drift in a circle from the one to the other, over and over again. Hosea assures us mightily of his conviction that a collection of crooked hearts will produce a crooked society, and that crooked institutions both perpetuate the crime and produce new criminals. This is the burden of the introductory poem in chapter 4 (vss. 1–3), as well as that of other statements that follow (4:12, 16, 17–19).

This insight into the dynamics of immorality may be used to illuminate further the relationship between knowledge and morality that we have been discussing. Although it is true that no necessary link can be discovered between knowledge and obedience, as has just been said, nevertheless, there is a pragmatic connection between the two that might be called disciplinary. It involves a circular interaction between the two, analogous to the interaction between social institutions and individual behavior, each shaping the other.

The knowledge of God, as Hosea uses the term, is founded upon acquaintance with the sacred traditions of the worshipping community. These traditions include memories of the redemptive events of the community's history, viewed as acts of Yahweh, and instructions concerning his moral demands upon its members. This knowledge may be acquired in its rudiments by means of catechetical training in the cult (religious education). All the while a person is learning the meaning of the tradition intellectually, he is participating in the life of the community. According to his role, he carries various privileges and obligations that are defined, at least in general terms, by the covenantal *torah*. His willingness to commit himself to others in the community as their servant, in the highest sense, constitutes *ḥesed* (devotion, loyalty). This attitude is partly characterized by mercy (as the older English versions translated the word) and compassion, because the men to whom one is devoted are both fallible and finite. The catechumen's knowledge of God is fragmentary and tentative, and so is his *ḥesed*. But his persistence in *ḥesed* is the means by which his knowledge of God deepens. This is so because the relationship between himself and God is analogous to the relationship between himself and his neighbor. Commitment to each means commitment to both and increasingly yields understanding of both. Knowledge deepens, therefore, as commitment persists.

However, loyalty to others in a community does not inevitably foster knowledge of God. The ideals, institutions, and modes of behavior sanctioned by the society may be idolatrous. *Hesed* shown toward such a society may be an obstacle to the knowledge of God. In prophetic teaching, knowledge of God's revelation is a necessary source of true knowledge of God, and knowledge of his revelation is given first of all in the exodus—wilderness traditions of redemption and covenant-making. Commitment to a community of persons who celebrate this revelation in corporate worship and who seek to create institutions and personal relationships that honor the God who is thus revealed, and the creatures made in his image, does in turn deepen a man's understanding of the very revelation upon which his commitment is based. This is the circle of *ḥesed* and knowledge.

There are several other facets of Hosea's ethical teaching in chapter 4 that might be overlooked and that we may comment on here. First of all, he describes the destruction of communal life, not merely as coming in the future, through the deliberate intervention of God, but as already well under way. "My people *are* destroyed!" This is not a "prophetic perfect" tense, whereby an actual future is described as if it had already come to pass, because of the certainty that God would do what he promised. It is a real perfect. The covenantal community has already destroyed itself. The evidence for this is on every hand, as Hosea graphically illustrates!

This process of communal decay is not merely an automatic one, even though it is to a considerable extent self-propelling. To Hosea it is, nevertheless, an immediate expression of the will of God. "I am destroying your people" (4:5). At the stage of the process to which Hosea testifies, the action of God is not an intervention but a withdrawal. God is the Healer, Preserver, Defender, of his people, indeed of his whole creation. Righteousness is his work, at least in the sense that the community discovers the sources of righteousness, namely, ethical motivation, guidance, and forgiveness (power, wisdom, and renewal), in a relationship with God that is sustained by acts of worship. When God "withdraws" from that relationship, and Israel encounters some other power (most likely her *alter ego*), she no longer draws upon these resources (cf., Hos. 5:6, 15), whether she knows it or not. God leaves them alone and they come to ruin. This is the wrath of God. His grace is withheld, the power to repent is lost, and even the awareness of sinfulness disappears. This condition is the last phase of moral dying, over which even God might be tempted to despair.

So Israel is the self-destroyed people, whom God leaves to their own vicious devices as the punishment for their prior, habitual faithlessness. Hosea spells out a number of features of this ruin, over and above the corruption of human relations and the outbreak of violence. They are shame (4:7), insatiable and pleasureless desire (4:10), and hopelessness (4:6, 10). If 4:10a refers specifically to childlessness, as it may, then this implies the reversal of the old patriarchal promise that the line of Abraham would flourish and fill the land. In these brief but telling lines we have the first explicit insistence by a teacher of Israel that sin is punished in its moral and psychological consequences. In asserting this, Hosea describes a cosmic order that is neither independent of God and automatic, nor merely dependent on God and voluntaristic, but both self-regulating and divinely ruled.

Finally, we must take notice of what these poems suggest concerning the relationships among several segments of Israelite society. Hosea seems to consider the priests and the laity equally culpable for the national decay. The laity supports a mechanical cultus to foster its own interests, and the priests oblige it for a considerable price. "And so it is, like people, like priest" (4:9). It is impossible to sort out the measures of blame. Each is sufficiently guilty.

While he seems to divide the guilt evenly across the clergy–laity line, Hosea apportions unequal shares to the men and the women. In 4:13–14 the corruption of the women is laid squarely at the feet of the men. These lines imply not only the rejection of the usual double standard of sexual morality, but a reversal of it. Instead of condemning the aberrations of the women and tolerating those of the men, Hosea holds the men directly accountable for the guilt of both. Perhaps this should not be taken to mean that he exonerated the women; yet, this appears to be the case. They were the victims of a patriarchal social structure in which they had few rights or opportunities. Women could easily be divorced by their husbands, and the divorcee had few means of support. Barring remarriage or a return to the protection of her father's house, she had little more than slavery and prostitution to choose from. The biblical injunction to provide for the widows and orphans, which was an ineffective welfare measure at best, did not cover her situation. If the fate of women was to be ruled by their husbands (Gen. 3:16), then the men, according to Hosea, were to bear fully the consequences of this relationship, including the guilt for supporting cultic institutions that debauched the women and corroded family life.

We have been considering some of the ethical implications of chapter 4. No less important is Hosea's picture of the Israelite institutions of worship. He accuses the priests of turning the rituals into mechanisms for effecting easy atonement (4:7–8) and of peddling oracles by divination (4:11 f.). In the process, the ancient and honorable office of covenant-mediator, which carried the responsibility for preserving the Yahwistic traditions and for instructing the people in covenantal obedience, was debased (4:6). Professional prophets were included among the sanctuary-personnel (4:5). Their duties were probably divinatory.[4] The temptation for professional prophets to deliver agreeable oracles for a proper fee was perennial in ancient as in modern times (cf., Mic. 3:5–8, 11; Jer. 28:9; 29:8 f.). There is every reason to believe that the Israelite prophets succumbed as their Judean counterparts did, though there is no way to be sure that Hos. 4:5 alludes to such traffic in oracles.

It is impossible to divine what specific "harlotrous" practices Hosea meant in 4:13–14. The unusual use of the term "daughters-in-law" has led Leonhard Rost to the conclusion that Hosea was condemning the custom whereby a father-in-law had sexual intercourse in the sanctuary with his daughter-in-law-to-be, prior to her marriage to

---

[4] Several commentators have deemed the reference to the prophet in 4:5 a gloss: Wolff, Budde (*JBL* 45 [1926], 284 f.), Sellin (who reconstructs the whole line: "I compare your day to night"). The verse does seem to be too long, but it is better to delete, if anything, the unnecessary "with you" (עִמָּךְ). This word could easily have crept in by assimilation to neighboring clauses (the last clause of vs. 4 contains וְעִמָּךְ, and the last clause of vs. 5, אִמֶּךָ). In most recent treatments of the passage the reference to the prophet is retained: Robinson, Nötscher, G. R. Driver (*JTS* 39 [1938], 155), N. Lohfink (*Biblica* 42 [1961], 303 ff.), and Weiser. Weiser makes the interesting observation that "by day" may mean the priestly oracle (divination by mechanical means) and "by night," the prophet's oracular dream.

his son, in order to provide a sacral guarantee of the fertility of the union.[5] This interpretation is an improbable one, although not impossible. The imagination of man in the domain of sex is highly inventive, and the popular cults of ancient times sanctioned wide varieties of sexual practice in a ritual context. Many possibilities lie behind Hosea's cryptic allusion. Since vs. 14b refers specifically to sacred prostitutes, that office is probably meant in 13b–14 as well.

The principal Yahwistic cult-centers of the northern kingdom were implicated in the practices that Hosea condemns here (4:15). Since there is no evidence that formal Yahwism was abandoned in these places during Hosea's time, we must conclude that the behavior he describes was common there, in Yahweh's name, as well as at the rural high-places (4:13), where out-and-out Baalism was most likely to have survived from pre-Israelite times, or to have been revived after an initial Yahwistic displacement. Hosea's charge, then, is directed primarily at baalized Yahwism.

The great irony of Israel's life was the curious contradiction between what she aimed at in her religious practice and what she actually obtained. She had accommodated her cultus, in both obvious and subtle ways, to the ubiquitous nature-cult of the ancient world. It existed in countless varieties, but one of its cardinal and universal features was that it employed semimagical rites to insure the fertility of the earth. These rites presupposed a mythological idealism that linked the processes of nature to the cult drama by means of purely formal similarities (patterns) of action. Man's bond to nature was ostensibly strengthened through sympathetic mourning rites for the dying and rising god and through sexual rites imitative of the indispensable mating of god and goddess.

Hosea describes the actual relationship between man and nature in utterly different terms. The association is intimate, to be sure, but quite the reverse of what the people imagined. The people were not stricken because of the non-moral death of the powers of nature, but nature was stricken, or was soon to be, because of the moral death of the people (4:1–3). This was the tragic irony of Israel's existence.[6]

---

[5] *Festschrift für A. Bertholet* (1950), pp. 451 ff., cited by Weiser (*in loc.*). Rost refers to *Herodotus* I, 199, for evidence of this custom. Weiser rejects Rost's conclusion.

[6] Compare Hos. 4:1 ff. with the cursing of the ground on account of man's disobedience in Gen. 3:17–18, and the cursing of all creation on account of man in Gen. 6:7.

CHAPTER

5

AN ABANDONED
LEADERSHIP:
HOSEA 5:1–7

I. *Summons*

1   Hear this, O priests;
        Take heed, O House of Israel;
        Hearken, O house of the king;
            for the judgment concerns you:
        You have been a trap at Mizpah,
        A net spread out upon Tabor,
2   And a pit dug deep in Shittim;
            therefore, I am chastening you all.

II. *Indictment*

3   I know Ephraim,
            and Israel is not hidden from me.
        Even now Ephraim promotes harlotry;
            Israel is defiled.
4   Their deeds do not allow them
            to turn back to their God,
        Because a whorish spirit controls them
            and Yahweh they do not know.
5   The pride of Israel will testify against him,
            and Ephraim will stagger in his guilt.

III. *Sentence*

6   With their flocks and herds they will go
            to seek Yahweh.
        But they will not find him.
        He has abandoned them.
7   They have proved treacherous toward Yahweh;
            for they have borne alien sons.
        Now the new moon
            will devour them with their shares.

NOTES ON THE TEXT

Verse 1. If "House of Israel," in the Book of Hosea, meant the whole people, this call to them might be out of place in a summons to the officials to appear for trial, and there would be a possible justification for the textual changes that have been proposed ("prophets of Israel," or "princes," or "judges"). However, this is not what the term means in Hosea, as I have tried to show in the discussion of 1:4 and in the Additional Note A. The context demands a reference to governmental leaders, as those who emend the text conclude, but the present phrase is synonymous with the monarchial state and should be therefore retained. Weiser and Wolff are surely correct in saying that Hosea had in mind the officials who were responsible for the administration of justice (*mishphaṭ*, vs. 1). Yet there is no basis for limiting the scope of the phrase "House of Israel" specifically to the local elders (Wolff) or free citizens (Weiser) who were responsible for the maintenance of law. The phrase is more general, meaning simply the governmental officials who were accountable to the king. This much at least is established by the parallel, "house of the king." It is of course possible that the three phrases here denote three distinct official groups, but, if this is the case, we are not told who constituted the third. It is as reasonable to think of the army as of the judiciary, and it is best to interpret the phrase as comprehending all royal departments, including the official priesthood. The expedient of deleting the second line entirely (Welch, cited by Brown; and Budde, *JPOS* 14 [1934], 2 f., following Oettli and Meinhold) is unwarranted on grounds of content and is prohibited by the form (see the note on the literary form, below).

The commentators' disposition to see the judiciary in the term "House of Israel" has been conditioned by לכם המשפט (vs. 1b), which has been taken by many to mean "the responsibility for justice is (supposed to be) yours," rather than "the proclamation of guilt and punishment is directed against you" (thus, for instance, Robinson, Knight, and Wolff). Read in this way, or as a deliberately ambiguous statement carrying both meanings, the line is an ironic thrust at the alleged champions of order and justice, who actually stand condemned at the bar of divine justice. This interpretation is certainly

attractive. It is supported by similar constructions in Deut. 1:17,
"for justice is God's" (כי המשפט לאלהים הוא; note the article, as in
Hos. 5:1), and especially Mic. 3:1, "Hear now, O leaders of Jacob
and rulers of the house of Israel. Is it not for you (לכם) to know
justice (המשפט)?"

Verse 2. The elegant threefold parallelism in 1b–2a, which is
formally identical with that in 1a, is secured by means of the slightest
change in the Hebrew text (ושחתה שטים or ושחת השטים‎ for בשטים‎).
Such a change is now almost universally accepted. The verb is active
in the MT ("they have made deep"), and the corresponding pronoun
in vs. 2b is third plural ("to them all"). The original may have been
a Qal pass. pt. (עמוקה), however, corresponding to פרושה in the preceding line. The change to the more common Hiph. would have
been an easy one for a scribe to make. It would have necessitated
changing the pronoun in 2b from second person (לכם or לכלכם) to
third (לכלם). Budde's proposal to read הָעֲמָקָה gives the result we
prefer, but involves the addition of ה to the consonantal text. Compare Moffatt's translation. Alternatively, G. R. Driver defends the
MT (with the exception of a single word-division, reading ושחט
השטים). On the basis of cognate languages, he argues for a root שחט,
"to corrupt," distinct from the homograph which means "to slay,"
and translates, "They deepened the corruption [i.e., fornication] of
Shittim" (*JTS* 34 [1933], 40). This interpretation has the merit of
preserving the MT, though it sacrifices the threefold parallelism of
the line. The change of שחת to שחט, on the other hand, would have
been easy for a scribe to make, especially if he were copying from
oral dictation of the text.

Verse 3. The verb in MT is 2 m. s. pft. Hiph., הזנית. This form
could easily have arisen from a third feminine singular spelled de-
fectively (הזנת), which would have been consistent with the parallel
(3bb) and the remainder of the strophe (4–5). The feminine gender
is correct here, since the subject is the country (cf., 5:9, where
"Ephraim" is again the subject of a feminine verb; and *G.K.* 122
h–i). The adverb "now" (עתה) should not be emended to "you" (אתה),
as is often done (cf., עתה again in vs. 7).

Verse 5. Two deletions have been made here. A second "Israel" in
the second line of MT is redundant and destroys the meter. Its removal entails the change of the plural verb and pronominal suffix
in this line to the singular. This deletion is almost universally adopted

by the commentators. The second excision is the Masoretic line "Judah also has stumbled with them." This line is an obvious afterthought and probably comes from a Judean editor. Its origin is further betrayed by the presence of the perfect tense of the verb (כשל) alongside the preceding imperfect (יכשלו) and perfect consecutive (ועצה). It is treated as a gloss by Sellin, Robinson, Weiser, Wolff, Mauchline, and others.

Verse 7. The point of 7a is not the begetting but the alienness; so, it does not matter whether we follow MT in treating ילדו as a verb or repoint it (ילדו) and translate "his children are alien sons" (Budde, *loc. cit;* cf., Wellhausen's "for they are bastards from birth"). The first alternative undoubtedly contains a jibe at the fertility aspects of the baalized cult, by which, of course, they have alienated themselves from Yahweh. In this context, the play on the new moon is especially telling, that is, the irony that the cultus will produce calamity rather than the sought-after prosperity, perhaps by the time of the next new moon.

Numerous alternatives have been suggested for "new moon" (חדש). The principal ones are "plowman" (חרש, as being consumed with his fields; so Duhm, followed by Budde, and *Chicago*), "destruction" or "a destroyer" (משחית; *BH, Moffatt, Jerusalem,* Sellin, Robinson, Weiser), and "locust" or some form of crop disease (חסיל or חרש/חרס; Wolff, and Scott, *op. cit.,* p. 132). The ironic statement of MT is hardly improved upon by these speculative changes, and is to be retained with *ASV, RSV,* G. A. Smith, Harper, Brown, Mauchline, and others.

The Literary Form of 5:1–7. In the face of the bewildering variety of strophic analyses that have been made of chapter 5, we cannot expect to achieve a final solution of the problem of its internal structure. A tentative justification for our arrangement is nevertheless possible.

That a major break comes after vs. 7 is acknowledged by most of the recent critics, although several have insisted that the associations with 5:8 ff. are as close as those among the components of 1–7. My principal reasons for treating 1–7 separately from 8 ff. are that it has formal and substantial integrity and that its chief concern is not that of 5:8 ff., namely, Israel's international policy during the period marked by the Syro–Ephraimitic war.

Internally the poem falls into three parts. Elliger's study of the formal integrity of 1–2 seems conclusive to me (*op. cit.*). In 1a, three parallel lines are set off by a fourth standing apart. All four are in two-stress meter. The pattern is repeated in 1b–2, with three-stress lines. The emphatic "you" punctuates the final lines of the two parts, and the emphatic "I" in 2b is an important link with what follows ("me" in 3a, "God/Yahweh/Him/He" in 4a, 4b, 6a, 6b, and 7a).

Weiser alone among recent translators divides the rest of the poem as I have: 3–5, 6–7. My reasons for taking 3–5 as a unit are as follows: (1) The alternation "Ephraim/Israel" dominates the first and the last line of this strophe, both of which, together with 4b, have a 3+3 meter. (2) The dominant tense of this strophe is present, whereas that of the first (1–2) is past and that of the third (6–7) is future. But the fifth verse, which is in the future tense, belongs precisely to the second strophe and not to the third, just as the last line of verse 2, which is present, belongs to the first strophe and not to the second. These are bridges between strophes, both in form and in content. (3) The meter supports this division: the last strophe is symmetrical (3+2, 2+2, 2+3, 2+2) and has no 3+3 lines to match those in verse 5. (4) The resulting structure defines an eloquent court drama, the chief moments of which have been marked by the headings added to the translation.

Covenantal knowledge is necessarily reciprocal. Each party knows the terms of the covenant and, even more importantly, knows the other and knows that he is known by him. For Hosea, Israel had lost this knowledge. God was hidden from them (5:6). Accustomed to the established places and forms of worship, they knew where his presence could be found and they sought him there. But they had forgotten whom they sought, and he did not, indeed could not, disclose himself to them. Yet, his knowledge of them was not lost. It may have been distorted, because it was knowledge of those who were not aware that they were known. Yet they were not hidden from him. Though they were blindly led toward alien objectives, their way and their total condition were fully revealed to God. Therefore, his judgment was inescapable, however secure Israel may have felt in her self-delusion.

A modern believer in the God of the Bible, who has been thoroughly taught the omnipresence of God, may be offended by Hosea's declaration of the absence of God. Yet Hosea's declaration is unequivocal. God has abandoned them. They will not find him. Insincerity, incidentally, has nothing to do with it. There is no suggestion that he thought Israel's search for the source of power to be insincere. Quite the contrary. If anything, they were so intent upon their quest, impelled by the "whorish spirit" that possessed them, that they had no vantage point from which to observe themselves in action. Their deeds and mind were one; therefore, critical (or even hypocritical) reflection upon their behavior was impossible. They were sincere enough and wholehearted in their religious quest. Yet, God had abandoned them.

The clear implication of Hosea's shocking doctrine of the absence of God is that "more religion" was not the solution to Israel's moral predicament. His denial of God's presence in Israel's midst placed him squarely against the notion that all religious paths lead to God, and the idea that wholeheartedness is the chief criterion of valid worship. "They will go to seek Yahweh. But they will not find him." This is not to say that Hosea's teaching of God's absence represents a denial of God's omnipresence. God was still present. As judging Lord he was all too close at hand. Never for a moment was Israel hidden from him. As a power subject to Israel's disposal, however, he was absent. He was effectively absent as far as their search was concerned.

Because Israel's spirit and deeds were one, there was no possibility of self-criticism, no chink in the armor of religious pride through which redemptive humility might strike. What was required was a "new spirit," that is, a new cultural and moral orientation. This renewal is analogous to an individual's change of heart (repentance), but it is even more complex an event and even less subject to deliberate control. No man can transform his will by taking thought, and no men, though they be prophets of God, can transform the spirit of their age by conscious design. This is true even of men who see the need of renewal and earnestly desire it. In Hosea's opinion, his compatriots did neither. Under these circumstances it was futile to preach repentance, and Hosea's oracles are notably silent in this respect.

Nevertheless, though a cultural transformation by deliberate action was out of the question, was it impossible to hope for a renewal by means of those dynamic processes of history that transcend human calculation and that control, and yet involve, creative human endeavor in politics, religion, and law? Perhaps it was, theoretically, and no doubt many of the leaders of the nation believed that their policies were the most creative ones available to them. However, Hosea gives no indication that he had any confidence in the capacity of such processes and policies to avert a national disaster. He was persuaded that Israel would fall in her pride (5:4–5).[1] In the present oracle, this is Hosea's final word. Elsewhere, however, he makes it clear that the end of the Israelite kingdom was precisely that historical event that would create the occasion for renewal, which the society was unable to bring about from within. It would force upon the people that self-criticism that was impossible as long as their present system was "working," however minimally. Such critical awareness was the first condition of renewal. It was not the only condition, of course, for the means and opportunity for social construction were also required. Hosea could only believe that God would provide these. He could not surmise what they might be or how they would be employed.

Nothing is said in chapter 5 about Hosea's ultimate hope, and we must not let our knowledge of that hope obscure our recognition of the finality of the end that he predicted for the extant Israelite civilization. Oracles like 5:1–7 must not be softened by an appeal to the oracles of reconstruction. For most of Hosea's countrymen, the collapse of the Israelite state meant the end of the institutions that gave structure to their lives and defined the aims and values of their common endeavor. It meant the actual end of their cultural world. It was the close of an era. Furthermore, great numbers of Israelites would perish. Property losses would be enormous. All the major cities of the land would be obliterated. Thousands would be deported. From the people's viewpoint, there was no hope for them as Israelites. Even those who, like Hosea, defined Israel primarily in terms of faith and not in those of culture, could hardly have appraised the

---

[1] "Israel's pride" has been taken to mean Yahweh (Cheyne), or the affluence of Jeroboam II (Weiser and Nötscher), or trust in ritual (Harper), as well as arrogance and self-congratulation. Pride is parallelled by guilt in vs. 5, however, so that the last alternative is the best. The second and the third definition are not entirely excluded thereby, since each was a factor in creating the guilt. The first interpretation is improbable in this context.

disaster itself as anything but the end. Socially, politically, economically, and cultically, it was to be a total calamity.[2]

In this oracle, Hosea decries the role of the political and cultic leaders in bringing about Israel's demise. The accusation leveled at the priests in chapter 4 is here broadened to include the whole leadership within the monarchical establishment. No specific charge is made. They are accused implicitly of corrupting the offices that served to maintain *mishpaṭ* (justice, or order) into stations of abuse. The order of service has been reversed. The resources of the community have been put at the disposal of the hereditary tyrant and his subordinates. They have become, in effect, predators upon the people (5:1–2). The preying is universal in the kingdom, from Mizpah (south?) to Tabor (north) to Shittim (east), because the kingdom itself is built upon it. The policies of the monarchy have been such that the present modes of action are irreversible. "Their deeds do not allow them to turn back (5:4)." One might argue that this is not always true of state policies, but Hosea was sure that the current alternation between subservience to and rebellion against Assyria, combined with internal political instability and religious syncretism, was a web of her own spinning in which Israel was inextricably caught.

This total wrongness of the system as such is denoted also in the statement that the shepherds of Israel (5:6) have "borne alien sons," that is to say, they have finally produced a whole generation of leaders who are not sons of the true Israel. They belong to another family. Their "spirit" is not that of the ancient covenanters with Yahweh. It is a "whorish spirit," belonging to absolute despotism, which the monarchs of Israel had copied from other nations, along with the idolatry of the state and nature.[3]

This analysis of the relationship between deed and spirit suggests an analogous situation in the psychology of individual behavior,

[2] Most commentators infer that the destruction referred to here was to come by means of an Assyrian invasion, though several accept the *LXX*'s witness to a pestilence of some sort (see the textual note to vs. 7). I accept the majority judgment.

[3] "Alien sons" has occasionally been interpreted as the illegitimate children born as a result of sexual rituals, including those performed in conjunction with the new moon festival. It has also been suggested that these children were sacrificed in the baalized cult and that Hosea's threat (vs. 7) was that these crimes would be fittingly punished by the loss of legitimate children. See Wolff's discussion, where the various theories are presented.

namely the interaction of deed, habit, and desire. The analogy should not be misconstrued as a direct comparison, however. Corporate institutions do not behave merely as individual human beings do. The conjecture by some scholars that this poem (note, especially, vs. 4) was influenced by Gomer's infidelity to Hosea,[4] aside from its problematical assumption that she was unfaithful to him, could lead to the confusion of individual and social levels of psychological analysis in the interpretation of Hosea. His metaphors can be easily distorted if regarded as allegories.

Because the political system is falsely oriented, the ritual offerings made by the state cannot be the tokens of a larger service to Yahweh. They are tokens instead of the spoils exacted from the community (5:1–2). This is suggested by the word *ḥelqehem*, "their shares." The context must determine what the shares consist of. The term is used for shares of booty in Gen. 14:24; Num. 31:36; 1 Sam. 30:24; and Isa. 17:14; and in the present poem it is reasonable to take them as spoils of the hunt at Mizpah, Tabor, and Shittim. The last word of the oracle, then, is that the spoilers will be spoiled (5:7). If this is a correct interpretation of the line, then Isa. 17:14 is a striking parallel:

> At evening time, behold, terror!
> Before morning, they are no more!
> This is the portion (*ḥeleq*) of those who despoil us,
> and the lot of those who plunder us.

Israel's plunderers are her own priests and courtiers (5:1–2), but their reward will be as sudden and effective as that of the nations in the oracle from Isaiah.

In citing Mizpah, Tabor, and Shittim, Hosea may have had specific events in mind, official actions so well known publicly that his audience would have recognized the allusions at once. If he did, we do not know what these were. It is possible that he named these places as symbols of the territories lost to Assyria in the aftermath of the Syro–Ephraimitic invasion of Judah (735–32 B.C.).[5] In that case, the first site must be Mizpah of Gilead (cf., Gen. 31:49; Judg. 10:17). Yet Mizpah of Benjamin is a better choice. It was in the

---

[4] Cf., Lindblom, *Hosea literarisch untersucht*, pp. 74 f.

[5] Alt stated this opinion in a footnote to his article on Hos. 5:8 ff., but without full discussion (see *Kleine Schriften* II, p. 187, note 1). Sellin, Robinson, and Budde have taken similar positions.

immediate vicinity of the heartland of Ephraim, which was the probable scene of Hosea's ministry, and it may have been a principal
boundary fortress between Israel and Judah (1 Kings 15:16–22).
If it can be identified with modern Tell en-Nasbeh, as many scholars
believe, it was an important place for the administration of justice.[6]
Since justice (*mishpaṭ*) is the key word of the introductory strophe
(Hos. 5:1), such an allusion would be entirely appropriate. The three
places might then denote the limits of Israelite jurisdiction, from Mizpah in the south to Tabor in the north and Shittim in the east.[7]
Cultic associations are not excluded by this interpretation, since the
cult was related in many ways to the administration of law.[8]

Regardless of the minor uncertainties in the meaning of the poem,
there is no question about its major thesis. Israel's leaders are no
longer the servants of God and God's people, nor the defenders of
their welfare and freedom. They have brought the community, as
they wished to bring the power of God, into the service of alien goals
of their own choosing. They have enslaved the people and, though
they do not know it, they have also enslaved themselves.

[6] See James Muilenburg's discussion in *IDB*, K–Q, p. 407. The Mizpah
of 5:1 is placed in Benjamin by Grollenberg (*Atlas of the Bible*, London
and Edinburgh, 1957) and May (*Oxford Bible Atlas*, London, 1962), though
not by Wright and Filson (*Westminster Historical Atlas to the Bible*, Philadelphia, 1945).

[7] Knight also interprets Mizpah and Tabor as "south and north."

[8] Many commentators regard the crimes referred to in Hos. 5:1–2 as
cultic; cf., Harper, Robinson, Nötscher, and Wolff. Weiser questions the
cultic view, however, and prefers interpreting these verses entirely in relationship to the administration of covenantal law.

CHAPTER

6

THE INTERNATIONAL CRISIS OF 735 B.C.: HOSEA 5:8-15

I

8   Blow the shophar in Gibeah,
     the trumpet in Ramah!
   Cry an alarm in "Beth-evil";
     I will terrify Benjamin!

9   Ephraim will be a desolation
     in the day of rebuke.
   Among the tribes of Israel
     I make known what is sure.

10 Judah's officials have become
     like those who move boundaries.
   Upon them I will pour out
     my wrath like water.

11 Ephraim is oppressed;
     justice is suppressed;
   For he has determined
     to pursue vanity.

II

12 So I am like a disease to Ephraim,
     and rottenness to the house of Judah.

13 Yet when Ephraim sees his sickness,
     and Judah his wound,
   Then Ephraim goes to Assyria;
     and he (Judah) sends to the great king.
   But *he* is unable to cure you;
     he cannot heal your wound!

14 Because I am like a lion to Ephraim,
     like a young lion to the house of Judah.
   I, I will tear and go away;
     I will carry off and there is none to rescue.

15   I will go back to my place,
        until they are confounded.
      And then they will seek my presence;
        in dire straits they will seek me.

NOTES ON THE TEXT

Verse 8. Beth-aven ("House of evil," here rendered "Beth-evil") is Hosea's regular taunt-name of Bethel ("House of God"), the chief (and now baalized) sanctuary-city of the northern kingdom (4:15; 5:8; 10:5. Cf., "high places of Aven," 10:8.)

A slight change in the MT is required to give the fourth verb, "I will terrify (אחריד) Benjamin!," in place of "behind you (אחריך), Benjamin." The *LXX* already regarded the word as some form of the verb חרד, and modern commentators are nearly agreed that some form of that verb should be substituted for the Masoretic preposition.

Verse 9. The word translated "rebuke" (from יכח) has a judicial connotation. It has been appropriately translated "decision" (Brown), "punishment" (*Moffatt, Chicago,* Harper), and "chastisement" (*Jerusalem* and most German commentators).

Verse 10. It had become the standard critical procedure to change "Judah" to "Israel" in this verse (and in 5:12, 13, 14; 6:4) before Alt's interpretation of this oracle against the background of the Syro–Ephraimitic invasion of Judah (735 B.C.) was widely adopted (see, *Kleine Schriften* II, pp. 163–87. The article was published originally in 1919). Robinson is the only dissenter among the post-Alt commentators (Budde, *op. cit.,* p. 18, also substituted "Israel" in 5:12, 13, 14 and 6:4, but not in 5:10).

Were it not for vs. 10b, there would be no reason to hesitate before accepting Alt's interpretation. The attack announced in vss. 8–9 is to come from the south of Ephraim, moving northward from Gibeah to Ramah to Bethel, and the reference to Judah's landgrabbing in vs. 10a is therefore perfectly natural. However, the condemnation of Judah's officers in vs. 10b is a digression in the movement of the monologue. Except for this remark, one's attention would be riveted upon Ephraim's approaching crisis and its justness. The substance of the condemnation of Judah may well be Hosean, but the pace of this highly dramatic warning is badly disturbed by the digression in

vs. 10b. This problem ceases to exist, of course, if the piece is frag-
mented into independent oracles (8–9, 10, 11), following Alt. The
unity of tone and rhythm imply the integrity of vss. 8–11, however.

Verse 11. The passive participles of the MT ("oppressed,"
"crushed") are demanded, against the *LXX*'s actives (which many
scholars have accepted) by the circumstance that it is Ephraim who
is attacked here.

"Vanity" is now standard for the last word. The Hebrew צו may
be the equivalent of the more common און (according to most
critics), or it may be a vulgar taunt, with the same meaning (Wolff).
It appears in the taunt against Isaiah in Isa. 28:10, 13. See, also
Köhler, *Lexicon,* p. 796. The word might even be a corruption of
סוא (= Sib'u, king of Egypt; cf., 2 Kings 17:4).

Verse 12. "Disease," or "pus," instead of the English versions'
"moth" (for עש, from עשש), with Köhler *(Lexicon),* Wolff, and Knight,
following G. R. Driver (in Rowley, ed., *Studies in OT Prophecy,*
1950, pp. 66 f.).

Verse 13. Since the parallel Ephraim/Judah is maintained in vss.
12, 13a, and 14a, it seems likely that it is also intended in 13b. The
simple insertion of "Judah" *(Jerusalem,* Brown) disturbs the meter;
so, the more common device to secure the desired end is to substitute
it for the second (expendable) verb (ישלח) (Alt, Nötscher, Sellin, Wellhausen, and others). Of course, ישלח could have arisen more easily
from ישראל than from יהודה; so, the suggestion has been frequently
made to substitute "Israel," but only by those who are willing to
emend "Judah" to "Israel" elsewhere in the chapter (Nowack,
Cheyne, Harper, Budde, and others). It seems safe to say, however,
that, barring the discovery of new evidence, this expedient is now
critically impossible for the bulk of OT scholars.

A major difficulty arises, moreover, when "Judah" is added to this
line, for it implies then a simultaneous quest for Assyrian aid by
Ephraim and Judah. We know of no such circumstance, though the
historical records are admittedly fragmentary. An alternative is to
assume a foreshortening of perspective on the part of the poet and
look for respective appeals of different times. The last course is to
interpret the pronoun as referring not to Judah but to Israel.

"Great king" (מלכי רב or מלך רב in place of the מלך ירב of MT) is
now universally adopted (contrast the "King Jareb" of *KJV)* as an
Assyrian designation of the king (*šarru rabu*). Cf., "the great king,

the king of Assyria," 2 Kings 18:19, 28; although the Hebrew adjective is a different one there (הגדול). G. R. Driver considers וָרָב to be an Aramaism (from רבב or רבה) and reads "great king," without any change in the text (*JTS* 36 [1935], 295).

Verse 15. "Confounded" (ישמו) is based on the *LXX* ἀφανισθῶσι, brought to naught). It is adopted by *BH,* Wellhausen, Nowack, Marti, Harper, Budde, Alt, Sellin, Oettli, Mauchline, and Wolff. The א in the יאשמו of MT could be a copyist's error, influenced by the preceding word (אשר; indeed, ten of the preceding thirteen words contain an א in the first syllable!) and the parallel verb (אשובה). If אשם is retained, it should be translated "paid the penalty," as in 10:2; cf., T. H. Gaster in *IDB,* R–Z, p. 152.

This verse has been assigned by some to the oracle that precedes, by others to the one that follows; there are no final grounds for settling the debate. In my opinion, the argument from form supports the former alternative. Vss. 5:12–15 form an elegant and coherent strophe of eight lines, matching the eight-line construction of 5:8–11. Verse 15 consists of distichs, such as 12–14 (and 8–11), whereas the following material is dominated by tristichs (6:1, 2, 3b). Comparison of meters is impossible, unfortunately, because the meter of vss. 12–14 is uncertain. The argument from content is futile. One may argue that the editor placed 5:15–6:3 after 5:12–14 because of catchword similarities between verses 14 and 15, but one may equally well argue that he placed 6:1–3 after 5:12–15 because of catchword associations between 5:15 and 6:1. *LXX* adds "saying" after 5:15 and thus links it to 6:1 (thus, *RSV, Moffatt,* Brown, and Harper). The arrangement I have adopted is also employed by Nötscher, Wolff, Weiser, and Schmidt (*Sellin – Festschrift,* 1927, pp. 111–26). The Jerusalem Bible separates 5:15 from both 5:14 and 6:1!

T HEOLOGICAL EXPOSITION is inseparable from historical exegesis; so, the historical setting of a prophetic oracle must be always carefully examined. Some oracles are fairly general in their application, relating to a habitual mode of action or to the dynamics of a social institution. The oracle at hand was formerly interpreted in this fashion, for the most part. There are oracles, however, that deal directly with particular historical events and the roles of the principal actors in them. Most recent commentators on Hosea have been persuaded by Albrecht Alt's study of Hos. 5:8–6:6 that at least the larger part of this material belongs to the latter type. Only rarely do exegetical studies have such widespread and lasting influence as this one by Alt.[1] Our discussion of 5:8 ff. may well begin by stating his conclusions.

Alt considered 5:8–6:6 as consisting of five originally independent oracles that commented on various phases of the international crisis of 735–32 B.C. (5:8–9; 5:10; 5:11; 5:12–14; 5:15–6:6). The first (5:8–9) was published shortly after the first phase. The kingdoms of Israel and Damascus had mounted an invasion of Judah (2 Kings 15:37; 16:5; Isa. 7:1–9), apparently in an effort to force the unwilling king Ahaz of Judah into a revolutionary alliance against Assyria, to whom they were tributary.[2] The invasion was initially successful, and Jerusalem itself was finally put under siege (2 Kings 16:5; Isa. 7:1). We may reasonably conclude, therefore, that the Judean fortresses along the Israelite border to the north were taken by the invaders. These, according to Alt, included Gibeah and Ramah (Hos. 5:8), in the traditional territory of the northern tribe of Benjamin. This buffer-zone between Israel and Judah had been controlled by Judah for about one hundred and fifty years, after Asa of Judah had taken it from Baasha of Israel (1 Kings 15:16–22). Ironically, Asa's success in that venture had been gained through an alliance with Damascus! Ramah was just north of Gibeah and, together with Mizpah and Geba (1 Kings 15:22), it formed the line of Judean outposts, until the last years of that kingdom (2 Kings 23:8).[3] They were temporarily regained, then, by Israel in 735 B.C.

In his oracle, Hosea presupposes the Israelite control of Gibeah and Ramah, which stood on a direct line betwen Judean Jerusalem and Israelite Bethel ("Beth-evil," 5:8). He anticipates Judah's retaliation against Israel in an assault moving northward from Jerusalem to Gibeah, to Ramah, and finally to the great Ephraimite city of Bethel. Thus the whole of Benjaminite territory would be "terrified" (5:8). This retaliation could only take place, of course, after Assyria had forced the superior forces of the allies to withdraw from

---

[1] "Hosea 5:8–6:6 . . . ," *Kleine Schriften* II (Munich, 1953), pp. 163–87.
[2] See, e.g., Martin Noth, *The History of Israel* (2nd ed., London and New York, 1960) pp., 257–61.
[3] See, Noth, *ibid.*, p. 235.

Judah, on the petition of the Judean king Ahaz (2 Kings 16:7–9). In this campaign, Tiglath-Pileser III of Assyria incorporated the territories of Damascus and the northern (Galilee) and eastern (Gilead) portions of Israel into the administrative domain of his empire (2 Kings 16:9; 15:29).

According to Alt, Hosea's second oracle in this series (5:10) is a condemnation of Judah for carrying her retaliation beyond the recovery of her border fortresses to an acquisition of Ephraimite territory. The third oracle (5:11) refers to a "crushed Ephraim," that is, the rump state to which the Israelite kingdom had been reduced by Assyria's annexation of Galilee and Gilead in 733 B.C. All that is left is the central hill country of Ephraim. This disaster has befallen Israel, because she has "pursued [her] foe" (5:11),[4] that is, her traditional enemy, Damascus, with whom she had fought for over a hundred years (cf., 1 Kings 22, for example).

Verses 5:12–14 condemn the political schemes of Israel and Judah during this era, specifically their pro-Assyrian policies. This is not an allusion to a collective action by the two powers (we know of none at this time) but to separate actions (possibly Menahem's tribute in 738 B.C. and that of Ahaz in 735 B.C.; cf., 2 Kings 15:19–20 and 16:8). Thus, Hosea decried both the pro-Assyrian and the anti-Assyrian activities that produced intra-Israelite conflict and religious syncretism and increased, moreover, the people's subjection to Assyria. Finally, according to Alt, 5:15–6:6 depicts Israel's turning to the future, after the debacle of 735 B.C. They seek a new national program; but, because they have now been completely disillusioned by recent events, they seek a non-political one.

Alt's major thesis, that this chapter is a commentary on the Judeo–Israelite conflict of 735 B.C., and on the policies of the two kingdoms vis-à-vis Assyria during this critical period, has been all but universally accepted. Nearly every commentator has found fault with details of his interpretation, but nearly all have been persuaded of its general validity. The most questionable feature of his analysis, from a literary standpoint, is his division of 5:8–14 into four independent oracles that supposedly were published over a period of several years. I agree with Lindblom that the poem is too well integrated, in its form and substance, to be chopped up as Alt

---

[4] Alt accepts Duhm's emendation of צָר to צִי ("enemy") here.

has done.[5] That the various comments in the oracle relate to different aspects of the international situation in 738–32 B.C. is certainly no indication that each line was composed at the time of the particular event to which it refers. Furthermore, I am sufficiently impressed by Budde's comment about Hosea's use of the term "Ephraim" as a designation of the Israelite kingdom, to demur to Alt's treatment of this term in vs. 11. Budde rejected Alt's hypothesis concerning the basis of this usage, chiefly because it is found in all of Hosea's oracles, including those that seem to have been written before 735 B.C.[6] These and similar criticisms of Alt's work do not affect the fundamental worth of his exposition, however, nor the theological significance of the oracle itself.

An altogether different kind of objection to Alt's theory has been raised, however, which is far more fundamental: G. A. Danell has denied that 5:8–6:6 deals with the historical events of 738–32 B.C. and has declared this material to be the deposit of a ritual drama that Israelites and Judeans enacted jointly at a principal northern sanctuary in the course of a major festival.[7] Georg Fohrer has similarly rejected the theory of Alt, on the ground that 5:8–6:6 is not concerned with politics. The issue, he says, is not "politics or faith," but "cultus or faith." [8] If these two men were correct, we would have an entirely different ethical situation to expound from the one we have actually assumed in the following discussion. I consider their conclusions erroneous, however.

Danell merely states his thesis in the most casual manner and offers no objective evidence for his cult–dramatic interpretation of 5:8–15. On the face of it, it is improbable. Cult dramas generally deal with perennial problems and are fashioned in such a way as to admit of a very wide application. Hos. 5:8–15 treats a particular situation. Its terms are not stereotyped but specific. At the most, it might be conceded that this could be the liturgy of a ritual drama

[5] *Op. cit.*, pp. 76–80.

[6] *JPOS* 14 (1934), 8 f. Budde accepted Alt's attribution of 5:8–10 to the Syro–Ephraimitic crisis but considered the remainder of 5:1–6:6 to date from before 735 B.C. See, also, the comments at the end of Additional Note A, and Lindblom's comment on the meaning of "Ephraim" here (*A Study of the Immanuel Section in Isaiah*, p. 28).

[7] *Op. cit.*, p. 138.

[8] *TZ* 11 (1955), 165. He claims the support of Hans Schmidt in this position, but Schmidt's opinion relates to 6:1–6 and not to 5:8–15, which Schmidt deemed independent of the other. See, "Hosea 6, 1–6," *Sellin Festschrift* (Leipzig, 1927), 111–26.

that was celebrated on only one occasion, in order to deal cultically
with a problem presented by a particular historical crisis. But, in that
case the ultimate background of the text would be the actual historical
crisis and not the ritual celebration of it. Nothing in 5:8–15 itself,
however, implies that the events described were the subject of such
a drama. It is also incredible that Israelites and Judeans would have
conducted a joint celebration of this sort—a mock war—during a
period when the two nations were actually hostile toward each other.

Hos. 6:1–6 does indeed mention a ritual act, and it is possible to
connect it with the events described in 5:8–15. But the ritual action
covers only 6:1 ff. Vss. 5:8–15 are presented to us, not as a scene
from the sanctuary, but as a scene from the world of political affairs;
they must not be cut to fit the mold of 6:1–6. In yet another way,
Fohrer has made the same mistake as Danell. He has let the issue
of 6:1–6 obscure the issue of 5:8–15. These poems may be related,
but they are not the same. The best course to follow in expounding
the oracles in these chapters, therefore, is to take them individually,
before trying to relate them to each other. In this way, an over-
simplification will be hopefully avoided.

The only direct accusation made by Hosea in the first part of this
oracle (5:8–11) is that Judah has embarked upon a program of
territorial aggrandizement, apparently at Israel's expense (5:10). The
chiastic form of the second strophe (10–11) places Ephraim under a
parallel charge, and this inference is confirmed by Alt's interpretation of vss. 8–9. Judah's present territorial seizure (10a) will be
punished (10b), just as Ephraim's past program (11b) is now being
punished (11a). Ephraim's punishment, that is, his oppression, follows
from Judah's retaliation; but, since this act is in itself criminal, even
though it brings a punishment to Israel that she deserves, the prophet
can say that justice is suppressed by it (11a). God is equally opposed
to the policies of both nations, although he can use the evil action
of the second as a just punishment of the first. This divine justice,
working through the realities of political and military engagement, is
proclaimed by God's prophet to all the tribes of Israel (9b). Only
through his oracles are the dynamics of history recognized as judgments of God, and not merely as the interactions of nations. Clearly,
this justice transcends the special interests of both Judah and Israel.
Hosea speaks for God and for the ancient covenantal ethic and not
for one party against the other.

Budde refused to see any condemnation of Israel in vss. 8–10, but insisted (against Alt) that Hosea was a loyal Ephraimite who merely described his country's devastation as a fact. It was not a just war that Judah waged, and so Hosea condemned that kingdom, not his own.[9] In order to sustain this estimate of Hosea's sentiment, Budde carved vss. 8–10 out of their present setting, and dubbed them an independent oracle. He justified this procedure by noting that the punishment in vss. 8–10 lies in the future, whereas that in vss. 11 ff. is already past. Though Budde's conclusion is wrong, to my mind, it is worth discussing, because it serves to sharpen important issues in the explication of this poem.

Even if the independence of vss. 8–10 from 11 ff. were conceded, it would still be necessary to recognize in them a note of stricture against Israel. Hosea describes Ephraim's desolation as coming in the "day of rebuke" (tôkeḥah, vs. 9). The term is judicial and may be properly translated as "punishment" (thus, Moffatt, Chicago, Jerusalem, Harper, and most German commentators). I have followed the authorized English versions in translating it "rebuke," in order to preserve the connotation of judicial decision (Brown actually renders it "decision"), as well as that of chastizement, however imperfectly that word may serve this dual purpose. The note of punishment is unmistakably there, in any case.

The temporal shifts in 5:8–15 are indeed significant, but not as Budde believed. There is no need to separate the future tenses from the past tenses. Taken together, they form a reasonable sequence of divine judgments. Ephraim's recompense for attacking Judah is now being administered (vs. 11a), though that of Judah is still to come (10b). However, Ephraim's experience at Judah's hand does not constitute the whole of God's punitive action against him. His final desolation is still in the future (9a, 14–15). It is one that Judah will not administer alone, but one in which he will share (12, 13, 14). In short, Hosea deals in 8–15 with a complex situation that has developed through several phases and is yet to be resolved in the last event. God is already a "disease," afflicting the two nations (12, 14a). Part of his deadly work is done. The decisive part remains (9a, 10b, 14b–15). Hosea's metaphors and his tenses are fully appropriate to the historical events that he surveyed and the consequences he expected.

From the perspective of later times, Israel's shifting foreign policies

[9] Op. cit., p. 18.

of the 730's and 720's B.C. seem madness. Much of the vacillation, between bold plans for national self-determination and frightened surrender to Assyria's tyranny, was inevitable. Israel was too small to succeed in a consistent program of self-determination, located strategically as she was athwart the Palestinian corridor between Africa and Eurasia. Many of her political decisions were dictated by the desperate needs of the passing moment. Also, rapidly changing dynasties meant rapidly changing policies. Could anyone have prevented the resulting chaos? It seems strange that the Old Testament prophets took no account of these extenuating circumstances. Instead, they were uncompromising and intolerant in their appraisal of the conduct of national affairs. Yet their oracles deal only indirectly with the motives and decisions of individual men, and it is on that level of moral criticism that one is most inclined to make allowances for the natural limitations of men and for their partial successes. The immediate targets of the prophets' criticism were the covenant–community and the monarchial state. Although these corporate entities were frequently personified in the prophetic writings, they did not act as an individual would, nor did they merit the kind of sympathetic appraisal that most men would bestow on an individual. The evils that men do are magnified and complicated in the massive and intricate workings of large communities, and these communities generate evils of their own that are not simply attributable to the deliberations and deeds of individuals. The prophets concerned themselves with such corporate evils. They were not called, for the most part, to be the judges of particular men.

In any case, Hosea's judgment of Israel in 738–32 B.C. was uncompromising. The policies of those years were hurrying her toward the final loss of her covenantal identity and, beside this monumental fact, no other considerations were important. In expressing his judgment in the present oracle, Hosea chose two brilliant metaphors of God's chastisement, the wasting disease and the ravaging lion. Here is anthropomorphism running to theriomorphism and beyond. If God cannot be identified with any of the objects or processes of nature, there is, on the other hand, nothing in nature that cannot be used as a simile of divine activity. "Disease" suggests that the working out of God's punishment of Israel and Judah was internal to their social affairs. Here again is Hosea's insight that the evil deed is punished in its natural consequences and even in itself. Concretely, we may say that the Judeo–Ephraimite conflict of 735 B.C. cost more through the loss of potential covenantal values between the sister states than could be justified by any gain in the pursuit of their separate causes.

It is probably not an illicit allegorization of the second part of this oracle (5:12–15) to regard the shift in similes from the disease to the lion as denoting a new act in the tragic drama of Israel and Judah. The point of vs. 13 is that the two nations have tried to bolster their strength, in relation to each other and generally in their Palestinian sphere of involvement, by means of military aid from Assyria. What they have failed to comprehend is that this expedient can only lead to an entanglement more lethal than the pestilence of the Judeo–Ephraimite conflict. In the end they will be torn to pieces, beyond repair. Hosea does not say explicitly here that this end will come through Assyrian invasion, but he says so in other oracles, and it is surely implied here. Even the choice of the lion as the metaphorical destroyer may have been significant in this connection, for the lion was a favorite symbol of royal power in the ancient world. Thus, the "great king" to whom Ephraim sends (vs. 13) will be in the end a devouring lion (vs. 14).[10]

Yahweh is Lord, and the destruction that Israel brings upon herself in the war with Judah and the entanglement with Assyria is finally God's judgment. His righteous decision to chastize lies behind the whole sequence of events, and there is no escaping the execution of his decree. Therefore, Israel's successive remedial measures are bound to fail. Israel is in Yahweh's hand, throughout the drama, and that hand is intent upon justice. These theological statements may be translated into terms appropriate to the history of culture. From this other perspective, one may say Hosea was persuaded that the aims of Israelite civilization in his time were inimical to the principles of covenantal existence, and that the last consequence of their pursuit

---

[10] This is not to say that Ephraim sought Assyrian aid in 735–34, B.C., for it was Judah who did that. Hos. 5:12–15 is not a precise reflection of the course of events in the Judeo–Ephraimite war but a commentary on the whole policy of international alliance as practiced by the kings of the time. One will find more than a single historical error in this oracle if he reads it as a simple chronicle of the events of 735–32 B.C. Not only is Ephraim mentioned (vs. 13b) as the petitioner of Assyrian aid, but Judah is assigned the same fate in the struggle as Ephraim (vss. 14–15). Neither nation fell immediately after the crisis of 735 B.C., although Israel did not survive for very long. In principle, however, Hosea was correct. His oracle is not an historical timetable, after all.

was the death of "Israel," the people of God. No further political measures, of the sort adopted by the contemporary state, could avert this disaster, for these measures themselves were subversive of covenantal loyalty and justice. One might take also Hosea's analysis as an astute reading of politico–military probabilities, but there is no evidence in his oracles that he consciously engaged in such a calculation. Nevertheless, his theology was so thoroughly grounded in the realities of human life that his analysis was fairly accurate on that level, too.

When Yahweh had finished his deadly work, he would "go back to his place" to wait for Israel's honest return to him (5:15). This statement should be interpreted anthropologically and not mythologically. As far as Israel's life is concerned, Yahweh has departed. He is not cultically or psychologically available. He has not literally withdrawn to a super-terrestrial heaven, though the line has occasionally been interpreted in this way.[11] He has "gone away" in the same sense in which he has "abandoned them" according to the previous oracle (5:6). He has finished his work of judgment and is effectively absent from any significant relationship to Israel. He waits for Israel to appropriate the meaning of his "confounding" (5:15) and seek a new, creative relationship with him. This repentance is not something that comes on this side of national disaster or one that may avert the final calamity. It is on the other side of disaster. Israel must first be totally confounded in the political game she is playing. Nothing short of this will produce the proper insight and change of purpose. Until Israel "dies," the nation will not be able to comprehend the true nature of her disease (vs. 13). So, the repentance that finally comes to the survivors of the nation's death is not one that will serve to heal the nation as a whole and let it live. It is one that will effect an entirely new life with Yahweh, on different terms. This is the consistent message of the oracles of Hosea.

[11] The following "places" have been suggested: heaven (Weiser, Cheyne, Harper, and others), the desert sanctuary of covenantal memory (Sellin in *Mose und seine Bedeutung für die isr.–jüd. Religionsgeschichte,* Berlin, 1922, p. 26), and the "lion's" den (cf., 5:14 f.; M. J. Buss, *A Form–Critical Study in the Book of Hosea,* unpublished dissertation, Yale University, New Haven, 1958, p. 84). Buss's judgment seems correct to me; that is to say, the surface meaning of "place" is the metaphorical lion's den. Having said this, we must go on to ask what is the theological intention of this statement.

CHAPTER

7   A COMMUNAL CONFESSION
AND PROPHETIC RESPONSE:
HOSEA 6:1-6

I. *Confession*

1   Come, let us return to Yahweh;
for he has torn and he will heal us;
he has smitten and he will bind us up.

2   He will revive us after two days;
on the third day he will lift us up.

2/3   Let us live in his presence that we may know;
Let us press on to know Yahweh.

His going forth is as sure as the dawn;
and he will come like rain to us,
like the spring rain that waters the earth.

II. *Response*

4   What will I do with you, O Ephraim?
What will I do with you, O Judah?
Your devotion is like a morning cloud,
or like dew that goes early away.

5   Therefore I have hewn by the prophets;
I have slain them by the words of my mouth;
and my judgment goes forth as the light.

6   Because I crave sure love and not sacrifice,
the knowledge of God, rather than burnt offerings.

NOTES ON THE TEXT

Verse 2. Like the verbs in 1a (נשובה, "let us return") and 3a (נרדפה, "let us press on"), the verb in 2b (נחיה, "let us live") is best taken as a cohortative. The last two words of vs. 2 should be joined to the following line: (literally) "Let us live in his presence and let us know."[1] The resulting parallelism is an elegant one, the idea being that by living in the (cultic) presence of Yahweh the diseased pilgrims will soon come to know his healing power, the attributes of which are subsequently recounted (3b). The Masoretic verse-division produces reasonable sentences, but a very bad poetic form. If it is retained, vs. 3a has the 1 + 3 rhythm ("Let us know,/let us press on to know Yahweh"), or at best an awkward 2 + 2 ("Let us know, let us press on/to know Yahweh"). Furthermore, the pattern of the strophe (vss. 1–3) is tristich, tristich, distich, tristich, that is to say, one that is unparalleled in Hosea. However, if the poem is divided as in the accompanying translation, the line in question becomes a fine 3 + 3 ("Let us live in his presence that we may know;/let us press on to know Yahweh"), and the strophic pattern becomes tristich, distich, distich, tristich. This balanced (chiastic) form is also found in 2:2–3; 2:21–23; and 9:1–3 (cf., the similar forms in 4:6–9a; 2:8–10; and 13:15–16).

Verse 3. Verse 3a is frequently emended to secure a synonymous parallelism: "Let us know, let us press on to know Yahweh.//When (as soon as) we seek him, we shall find him" (כשחרנו כן נמצאנו) for the כשחר נכון מוצאו of MT). The change consists merely in the addition of two letters, the transposition of two others, and a slight modification of the word-division. The *LXX*'s "we shall find," for the last word, may be an interpretation of MT and need not imply a variant Hebrew text (i.e., the translator understood the verb to be מצא, rather than יצא, and supplied the missing נ of the first plural). The altered text has been adopted by many authorities. The MT should be retained, however (with *Moffatt, RSV, Jerusalem,* Nötscher, and others). The last three clauses form a climactic tristich whose subject is Yahweh (cf., the tristichs in vss. 1–2 and 5), and the simile in 3ab accords perfectly with those in 3b and 5.

Verse 4. Judah is appropriately mentioned (in the third person) in 5:8–15 as a participant in the crisis of 735–32 B.C. Can Judah be the co-speaker with Ephraim in 6:1–3? If 6:4–6 is a response to 6:1–3, as virtually all commentators believe, then the answer must be yes, if the address to Judah in vs. 4b (MT) is correct. Elsewhere

[1] I owe the suggestion for the translation of 2b–3a, and the resulting restructuring of the strophe, to Donald Riggs, a student in my seminar at Perkins School of Theology.

in Hosea, nothing is said about Judah's *cult* practices, though one might argue that 4:15 implies that Judeans were engaging, or were tempted to engage, in cult practices like those of Ephraim, perhaps at some of the same sanctuaries. The name "Judah" in 6:4, however, may have replaced an original "Israel" by assimilation to the paired Ephraim//Judah in 5:9 f., 12, 13, 14 (cf., *Jerusalem,* Harper, and Robinson, among others).

Verse 5. Several scholars have sought by means of textual emendation to secure an allusion to the Sinaitic–Mosaic tradition and even to the Decalogue: "I have hewn in stone (באבנים, i.e., the tablets of the Decalogue)," or "hewn by a prophet" (i.e., Moses, in place of the plural of MT), and "I have taught them (הורתים or הודעתים) by the words of my mouth." See, *BH;* Nötscher; Peters, *Osee,* p. 21; Schmidt, *op. cit.,* p. 120; Sellin; and Spiegel, *HTR* 27 (1934), 105–44. The change is entirely arbitrary and has been properly rejected by most recent commentators. It might be possible, on the other hand, to translate the Hebrew, "I have hewn the prophets . . . ; I have slain them" (*LXX;* cf., Zolli's discussion in *ZAW* 57 [1939], 288, where the 1929 edition of Sellin's commentary is cited along with Nyberg's work), except that the meaning of the passage is thereby obscured unnecessarily.

Verse 6. Verse 6b should perhaps be translated ". . . *more than* burnt offerings." The parallel (6a) is "not" (לא), but 6b may still be comparative, not privative, as Budde asserts (cf., *KJV, ASV,* Brown, Mauchline, and Robinson, for instance, as opposed to *RSV, Chicago, Moffatt,* Harper, Wolff, and others).

The Literary form of 6:1–6. In addition to the comment made above on vss. 2–3, attention should be called to the powerful effect created by the constantly repeated pronouns, "He . . . us," in 6:1–3. The worshippers' attention is entirely concentrated upon the immediate relationship between God and themselves. This purpose is reflected in the repetitions, and is served by them, in turn, when the worshippers chant this song.

The absence of tristichs in 5:8–15 and their importance in 6:1–6 (in 1, 2, 3b, and 5b), together with the notable shift in themes, indicates the independence of these sections from each other. There is a closer formal affinity between 6:1–6 and 6:7–7:2 (cf., the tristichs in 6:7, 10, and 7:1b) than between 5:8–15 and 6:1–6. The adversative והמה in 6:7 links also the preceding and the following sections.

Of course, there are no absolute breaks anywhere in 5:8–7:2 (some would say in 5:8–7:16). Whatever may have been the original status of the smaller units, there is now a considerable measure of continuity, even though it may be editorial.

H osea 6 bristles with problems that have long intrigued the interpreters. Does the revival on the third day mean resurrection? Of whom? Is it a notion derived from the cults of the dying-and-rising vegetation gods? Is the people's confession sincere and acceptable to God? Is it morally adequate? What sort of power does Hosea attribute here to the prophetic utterance? Does he deny the value of ritual in religion?

First, we will study the content of the popular confession in part I of this oracle. It begins with an acknowledgment that the people are afflicted and that Yahweh is the cause, but also the cure. No concrete malady is named; therefore, one is immediately disposed to regard this confession as a standard liturgical form that could be used in many situations. The scene is certainly the sanctuary, a conclusion confirmed by the closing remark in the prophet's response to the confession (vs. 6). So, the people's return to Yahweh (vs. 1) is a quest for his healing by means of a sacrifice that is accompanied by a lamentation and an affirmation of trust in God's ability and readiness to save.

The people's confidence is high. They count on being healed two days after their appeal. The healing is as predictable as the dawn and will be as welcome as rain. This assurance has been called cheap by some modern critics and the confession condemned as superficial ritualism, based on a belief in the automatic power of sacrifice. However, other expositors have thought better of the appeal, regarding it as an honest, though insufficient, act of repentance and as a means of restoration, morally helpful to some extent.

Why are the people so sure that their healing will be accomplished on the third day? What will this healing be, and the new life that follows it? The poems will tolerate several answers to these questions and will guarantee none. With that qualification, here is the interpretation I consider most probable. This communal lamentation with its confession of trust is a pilgrimage song for the occasion of a public ceremony in time of crisis, or for one of the annual pilgrimage festivals. The three-day period is a conventional one associated with the sacral traditions of the Sinaitic covenant. The revival is not from a physical disease or even from the scars of war—though at a given time such things might have been in the minds of the confessors—but it is the moral and religious renewal of the people, of their covenantal loyalties, of their sense of the presence of Yahweh, and of their hope for the social and economic well-being of the community. In short, the new life is a renewal of faith and of the sense of blessedness in relationship to God. The former is the knowledge of God (vs. 3), which is Israel's response to the blessing. The latter is the new life that God gives (vss. 1–2), not least in the sacred celebrations of the worshipping community.

The meaning of this song is not determined by the genesis of its images. Much attention has been devoted to the question of nature-cult parallels to the dawn and rain images in vs. 3 and to the revival on the third day in vs. 2; thus, it has been sometimes inferred that this song is "nothing but" a borrowing from one of the vegetation cults. Had this been the case, we may be sure Hosea would have denounced it as such. He was quick to point out Baalism and idolatry in Israel's cultus, as we have repeatedly seen. But no hint of such an accusation is made in the prophetic response to this popular liturgy. The similes of the dawn and the rain describe God's trustworthiness and the people's joy in his coming to them. They do not denote the content of the blessing they expect from him. The content of this blessing is defined only as healing (binding, lifting up), on the one hand, and as knowledge of God, on the other. These terms place the confession at the very pinnacle of biblical faith, unsurpassed by the words of Hosea himself.

Hans Schmidt has shown the close affinity between the liturgical confession in 6:1–3 and the communal lamentations elsewhere in the Old Testament.[2] This song would have been completely appropriate for a public ritual of atonement. Furthermore, the expectation (6:1) that the healing will take place on the third day implies that the occasion is a pilgrimage festival at the central sanctuary (which,

2 "Hosea 6, 1–6," *Sellin–Festschrift* (Leipzig, 1927), pp. 111–26. The communal lamentations in the Book of Psalms to which Schmidt refers are Pss. 12, 44, 60, 74, 79, 80, 83, 89, and especially 90. Other atonement prayers are to be found in Jer. 14:1–10; 14:19–15:4; and Isa. 63:15–64:11 (with a response in 64:1–25). Weiser also treats Hos. 6:1–6 as a penitential liturgy. Cf., also, Wolff's discussion.

for the northern kingdom, was at Bethel). The standard period of time allowed for the Israelites to assemble at the ritual center of the tribal confederacy was three days. This is indicated by a variety of references in the Old Testament (2 Sam. 20:4; Ezra 10:8–9; Josh. 9:16–17; Exod. 3:18; 5:3; and 8:27). The tradition incorporated in the last three of these passages, that the journey from Egypt to the mountain of God was a three-days' journey, might have arisen from the fact that this was the period required for the tribes to assemble at the ritual center in Palestine for the annual celebration of the Exodus–Sinai events. This feature of liturgical usage would then have been reflected in the literary tradition that described the original "pilgrimage" from Egypt to the desert. It is improbable that the earliest tribal memory of the event was already responsible for this otherwise unimportant datum. It has become embedded in the literary tradition because pilgrims to the annual liturgy of covenant-renewal have come to know the three days as the prelude to the event for which they journey, namely God's coming again to his people to renew their power and their health.[3]

Some such formal expectation is indicated by the careful statement that the renewal will occur on the third day.[4] The only other theory seriously proposed to explain the formula liturgically derives it from the cult of a dying-and-rising vegetation deity, which allegedly arose

[3] The time of preparation for Yahweh's appearance at the mountain, in Exod. 19:11 and 16, is also three days. Purifications were made on the third day after certain kinds of ritual defilement (Num. 19:12; 31:19) and this may explain why Isaiah promised Hezekiah that he would be able to go to the temple three days after his disease was cured (1 Kings 20:5, 8). Since Hos. 6:1–3 speaks of Yahweh's wounding and healing, it is interesting to note the three-day pestilence from Yahweh mentioned in 2 Sam. 24:13. Peters has argued that Hos. 6:1–3 refers to Yahweh's theophany to the people on the third day, as in Exod. 19:15 f. (*op. cit.*, p. 23), whereas Schmidt (*op. cit.*, pp. 120 f.), and Weiser have suggested the possibility that 6:1–3 was a liturgy for a pilgrimage festival.

[4] The statement may, of course, merely mean a short period of time, as many commentators believe (e.g., Harper, Brown, and Mauchline). It does not say "two or three days," i.e., a short period of indeterminate length, as is often claimed (e.g., Harper and Mauchline). Vs. 2a, like vs. 1b, contains a synonymous parallel. "After two days" is identical with "on the third day." Both mean the day after tomorrow, since today is the first day in such reckonings in the Bible. The three-day period is commonly employed in the OT as a designation of the next longer period than that of one single day (cf., Gen. 30:36; Judg. 19:4; Neh. 2:11; 1 Sam. 20:5; etc.). Jonah was in the fish's belly for three days and three nights (Jonah 1:17), or seventy-two hours, a different period from the one in Hos. 6:2.

on the third day.[5] If this formula did originate in such a setting, the only feature that has survived in Hosea's version is "the third day," for in Hosea's liturgy it is the people who revive and not God. However, very little evidence has been found to indicate that the formula of the third day had currency in the fertility rituals of Hosea's time (or before), and what little there is has been variously interpreted.[6] The probability is extremely low therefore that this hypothesis is correct.[7]

This lamentation of affliction and song of trust gives way in part II to an oracular response delivered by the prophet. No question is answered, because none was asked. But the divine word has the form of an oracular answer to a ritual petition. Surprisingly, the people's exalted affirmation of faith does not evoke divine acceptance and forgiveness. Instead, the oracle contains the most brilliant proclamation of the judging demand of God in the entire literature of ancient Israel: "Your devotion is like a morning cloud. . . . Therefore I have hewn by the prophets. . . . Because I crave sure love and not sacrifice, the knowledge of God, rather than burnt offerings."

Is the people's faith a delusion, then, and their quest vain? Not at all. Hosea does not reject their confession. On the contrary, he affirms that the knowledge of God, the very goal of their endeavor (vs. 3), is precisely what God desires of them (vs. 6). Nor does he negate their confidence in the certainty of God's healing and gift of

---

[5] Among those who have espoused this view are W. W. Baudissin (*Adonis und Esmun*, 1911, pp. 403–40), Sellin, Robinson, May (*AJSL* 48 [1931/32], 75–77), and Weiser.

[6] See, F. Nötscher, "Die Auferstehung nach drei Tagen," *Biblica* 35 (1954), 313–19, where the fragmentary evidence is examined, with a negative estimate of its bearing on Hos. 6:2 and on the NT accounts of Jesus' resurrection. Further opponents of the theory in question are Peters (*Osee*, p. 23), Budde (JBL 53 [1934], 118–33), H. Schmidt (*Sellin-Festschrift*, 1927, pp. 111–26), E. König (*ZKT* 70 [1948], 94–100), and G. Fohrer (*TZ* 11 [1955], 166–67).

[7] The terminology of this confession would be appropriate to a ritual for physical healing. Many of the individual complaint psalms in the Psalter (e.g., Ps. 88) were probably employed for this purpose. Hos. 6:1–3 is a communal lament, however, and the malady would have been general therefore and not private. The question has been debated whether "revive" and "lift up" in vs. 2 (like "heal" and "bind up" in vs. 1) are best interpreted as recovery from disease or as resurrection from death. Sellin, for instance, defends the latter interpretation, whereas Franz König has denied its validity ("Die Auferstehungshoffnung bei Osee 6:1–3," *ZKT* 70 [1948], 94–100). See, further, C. Barth, *Die Errettung vom Tode in den individuellen Klage- und Dankliedern des Alten Testaments* (Zollikon, 1947).

life. He does not even doubt the sincerity of their confession, that is the earnestness of their desire to be renewed in the presence of God, and their determination to "press on" to know God. But he laments the inconstancy of their desire. Their covenantal loyalty is a fleeting thing and therefore no loyalty at all.

When this oracle is interpreted in relationship to the others of Hosea, it is evident that the people's quest is one device among others to meet the crisis of their corporate life. It is unmatched by a zeal for obedience in routine affairs and in times of prosperity. Thus, while Yahweh is the ultimate healer, the healing that they seek is not available, because they have not met its conditions. This is not to say that covenantal righteousness would have guaranteed the entire healing they sought. In so far as they sought the reversal of material adversity, it was futile in any case. God is Lord of nature, to be sure, and every natural blessing comes ultimately from him. But Hosea never proposes a relationship between God and Israel, be it moral or cultic, by which Israel could secure special favors from God in the material order of nature. The healing that is assured to the community that practices *hesed*—devotion, mercy, covenant-love— toward God and neighbor, is the renewal of *hesed,* with God and man. The rituals of public worship are means of seeking this renewal and appropriating it. The torn relationships with men and with God can be essentially healed in this way. The cult is a legitimate, perhaps an indispensable, means of grace. Here faith can be strengthened or revived and the moral vitality of the people renewed.

Israel had not understood the cult in quite this way. Hosea's climactic line, which contrasts the efficacy of *hesed* with that of burnt offerings, implies that the cult has been distorted into a mechanism for exploiting God's power. As such, it fails not only to achieve its objective, but actually jeopardizes the faith and moral integrity of the participants. We may go perhaps even further than this and take Hosea's declaration to be a denial of the value of animal sacrifice.

One of the great debates among Old Testament scholars during the twentieth century centered on the question whether the canonical prophets denied the legitimacy of a formal cultus. In recent years a near consensus has emerged that they did not condemn the cult in itself but only a baalized cult, or one that was unaccompanied by a concern for morality and justice. This conclusion is virtually inevitable if the terms of the debate are broadly defined, because a corporate religion is inconceivable without a cultus. The narrower question of the status of animal sacrifice in prophetic teaching is not so easily settled, however. Indeed, I believe the evidence supports the conclusion that at least Amos, Hosea, and Isaiah denied the validity of animal sacrifice in Yahwism.

Isa. 1:10–17 condemns sacrificial offerings absolutely, as an abomination to the Lord. The force of this denunciation cannot be mitigated by appealing to Isa. 6, as is often done. Chapter 6 does indeed prove the importance of the temple and formal acts of atonement in Isaiah's own experience and faith, but it does not constitute an endorsement of animal sacrifices. Historically, the ritual of the temple had always involved sacrifice, and the imagery of Isaiah's description in chapter 6 is partly associated with such rites (i.e., the smoke that filled the temple, vs. 4, and the burning coals upon the altar, vs. 6). Nevertheless, no justification of sacrifice itself may be deduced from this report. That Isaiah had a visionary experience of decisive moment for his prophetic career, in which images were called up, out of his lifelong association with the established practices of the Jerusalem temple, does not imply that he subsequently approved of all these practices. Again, it is not convincing to argue that public worship without animal sacrifice would have been inconceivable to Isaiah and that he could not have favored therefore one without the other. If this argument were valid, we would have to conclude that Isaiah, in at least one moment of his public ministry, disapproved of the whole enterprise. If we must believe either that he accepted both the cult in general and sacrifice in particular, or that he rejected them both, then we must conclude that he did reject them both; for the force of his explicit denunciation of sacrifice in 1:10–17 outweighs any implied approval of the cult-in-general that might be inferred from other passages.

However, this argument need not be accepted. Isaiah could perfectly well have rejected animal sacrifice and not the total practice of public worship. He could have done this, even though he did not and was not able to propose a new system of worship that excluded sacrifice. Prophets constantly point out evils in the established order without proposing concrete alternatives. The evidence indicates that Isaiah did just this in the case of the Judean system of sacrifices.

It seems to me that the condemnation of sacrifice by Amos was as absolute as that by Isaiah. Amos 4:4–5, and especially 5:21–27, may hardly be read in any other way. There is not a shred of evidence, on the other hand, that he denied the legitimacy of sacrifice for the morally unrighteous but conceded its legitimacy for those who obeyed the covenantal law and strove for social justice. He might have conceded the legitimacy of a cultus without sacrifice under such conditions, but even on that point his oracles are silent. He left us in no doubt, however, about his opinion of the practice of animal sacrifice as he actually found it in Israel.

Hosea shared this negative estimate. Every allusion to sacrifice in his poems is a denunciation. We have already examined those in 4:8, 13, 15; and 5:6. Subsequent chapters of this volume will treat the ones in 8:11–13; 9:1–6; 10:1–2; 12:11; and 14:2. The overwhelming burden of these passages taken together is that Hosea regarded the sacrificial system as a vicious thing, an instrument of immorality and idolatry. Yahweh desired *hesed* and not sacrifice, he said, the knowledge of God rather than burnt offerings. The sacrifices, far from mediating *hesed* and faith, bred selfishness and idolatry, the opposites of the covenantal virtues. The people's confession in 6:1–3 is not in itself spurned by Hosea. It contains some of the essential ingredients of true Yahwism. He spurns the burnt offerings that accompanied the confession and that undermined the good that this confession contained by being taken as a means to coerce the power of God for the people's chosen ends.

"Therefore I have hewn by the prophets, I have slain them with the words of my mouth. And my judgment goes forth as the light." A prophetic oracle plays a crucial role in the execution of divine justice. This role is not a semimagical one wherein the word spoken has the power of bringing about the event it describes, merely by virtue of its being uttered. In many cultures, blessings and curses have been believed to have this power, but this is not the power of the prophetic word.[8] This word has two functions, to judge and to

---

[8] Several of the symbolic actions performed by Ezekiel (cf., Ezek. 4–5) seem to involve a similar conception. In pure magic, the act or word is powerful in itself, quite apart from any connection with a supernatural will. In fact, in many of the religious texts from the ancient Near East it is said that the gods themselves are subject to magic. Magic, there, is an impersonal force that transcends the individual deities. Ezekiel's acts were not magical in this sense. God commanded him to perform them as signs of the events that God himself was going to bring to pass. Because God was in control of the events, his symbolic announcements were certain to be fulfilled. Nevertheless, some of Ezekiel's actions appear to have been performed in private. They could have played no prophetic role therefore in the usual sense,

redeem. Both functions require the people's hearing, if thoroughgoing chastisement and renewal are to be accomplished.

If the punitive judgments of God were simply external, it would be unnecessary for them to be announced by a prophet. A transcendent divine justice could punish a sinful mankind with natural catastrophes, regardless whether they were recognized as just or as divinely sent. Even this sort of judgment would be a better vindication of divine justice, however, if the recipient were informed of the full dimensions of his affliction and were thus enabled, however reluctantly, to acknowledge the sovereignty of the Judge. There are occasions in the Old Testament when this is the last discernible purpose of the prophetic announcement; for instance, in Amos 8:1–9:8a. Yet the terms of Yahweh's covenant with Israel were primarily moral, not material. The interior dimensions of this relationship were the prophets' first interest. Their task was peculiarly human, that is, they addressed man as man, as a rational, moral being. They spoke for a God who knew them in freedom, obedience, and love—not as slaves or machines to be manipulated while useful and discarded when intractable.

In the prophetic writings, and especially in Hosea, we discover a view of human life in which the paramount values are existential, moral, intellectual, emotional, and social. Salvation is therefore faith, love, hope, and joy; and damnation is faithlessness, lovelessness, hopelessness, and despair. It is true that the order of redemption is continuous with the order of creation, since God is Lord of both orders. Therefore, the wholeness of man, that is his salvation, involves his physical well-being. But, this well-being serves humane ends. The saving prophetic word is therefore supremely the word that provides the occasion for faith, strengthens the faithful in love, and inspires his joy. Conversely, the supremely judging word is the one that provides the occasion for unfaith, disobedience, and despair. The saving word and the judging word may be one. The word of God's gracious demand is the occasion for man to choose obedience or damnation, faith or despair. Thus, one word may destroy or redeem, depending on man's response.

God craved steadfast love and faithful knowledge from Israel. The

---

namely making known to Israel what God was doing. Once the narrative of the action was published, of course, the act would have been prophetic, even though the original performance had been private.

slaying words he spoke through the prophets were intended to augment that knowledge and confirm that faith. However, failing in this objective, they were the instruments of moral death. They could not be empty. They were bound to bear fruit. In the situation described in Hos. 6:1–6, they bore bitter fruit, because of Israel's faithless response. The material consequences of Israel's failure were the dissolution of her society, and the loss of the land and of its material culture. For that reason, it might be fair to say that the prophetic word slew by announcing a visible death that was still to come. By the same token, if Israel's response had been the reverse of what it was, it would have been fair to say that the prophetic word had saved by leading Israel to repent and thus avoid the outer calamity. Such an interpretation is not adequate, however. The prophetic word slays, first of all, when men reject its demand and its gift, and choose the death of unfaith. It saves, first of all, when men accept its gift and its demand, and live by faith. It was precisely in failing to comprehend this as the nature of the covenant that Israel erred. By seeking another revival than this renewal of faith and *ḥesed* (vs. 2), she actually died.

In the light of my last comments, it might seem as though we should now reverse the judgment made at the beginning of the exposition of chapter 6 and declare false and insincere the faith expressed in the popular confession quoted by Hosea (6:1–3). But such a conclusion is not justified, for the words themselves *are* valid. If one were to imagine these same words spoken by the participants in the new covenant of the future (Hos. 2:18–23), he would have no difficulty in acknowledging their worth. It is not because of the words that Hosea reprimands the people, but because of the inconstancy of their behavior. Are the words, then, hypocritical and unacceptable to God? Perhaps. But what of the words to be spoken by the new covenanters (14:2)? Will they be matched by an inflexible firmness of devotion and an unfailing rectitude of behavior? Hosea does not make a prediction about that. Yet, we who know the history of the post-exilic Jewish community and the later Christian church, may say that the confession of every man is hypocritical if judged by the constancy of his deeds. There is no reason to exalt the prayers of later generations above those of Hosea's contemporaries. The idolatries and follies of the later generations were different from those of eighth-century Israel, but hardly less evil.

Hosea's oracles of denunciation would have been as relevant to them as they were to his own countrymen, though some of the details would have had to be changed.

The perfect devotion of the bride of Yahweh is never achieved by the historical Israel, in any age. Her needs and disposition never fully match her words, at least not for long. "What shall I do with you, O Ephraim? . . . Your devotion is like a morning cloud," can always be asked, and a new slaying by the prophets is always required. The cycle of faith – apostasy – faith is everlasting. This fact does not put covenantal experience on the same level as the cults of nature, however. The cycle experienced in those cults is the cycle of life – death – life in the physical order. The power of the gods waxes and wanes and must be ritually stimulated to wax again. In covenantal theology the terms are quite different. God's power is constant and so is his will. What requires renewal is not the vitality of nature but the people's love and faith. The cycle is a moral one. The *feelings* of exhilaration and depression experienced in the ancient rituals celebrating the cycle of nature would be probably impossible to distinguish from those known in rituals of the people of Yahweh. But the objective bases and the moral correspondents of those emotions are entirely different in the two types of worship. It is not in their form that they differ so much as in their substance.

8 A CATALOGUE OF CRIMES: HOSEA 6:7−7:16

I. *Treachery*

7 (At) Adam they broke a covenant;
    they dealt treacherously with me there.
8 Gilead was like a city full of criminals,
    tracked with blood.
9 Like a gang in ambush
    was the band of priests.
    They murdered habitually in Shechem;
    yes, they practiced abominations.
10 In (Bethel) I have seen disgusting things;
    there is the whoredom of Ephraim.
    Israel has been defiled.
11a [Also, Judah, a harvest is set for you.]

II. *Perversity*

11b When I would reverse the captivity of my people,
7:1   when I would heal Israel,
    Then Ephraim's guilt becomes clear,
    and the evils of Samaria.
    For they have behaved perversely
    —a thief breaking in,
    a gang attacking in the street—
2 And they do not lay to heart
    all their evil that I remember.
    Even now their deeds surround them,
    right before my face!

III. *Conspiracy*

3 They anoint a king in their iniquity,
    and princes in their corruption.

4   They are all (enraged),
        like an oven heated by a baker;
    He ceases stoking (the fire)
        from the kneading of the dough until it is leavened.

5   They make the king sick,
        and princes, with the heat of wine.
    He joins hands with impostors,

6   for their hearts burn like ovens with their treachery.
    All night their anger smolders;
        at dawn it burns like a flaming fire.

7   They are all hot like an oven,
        and they devour their rulers.
    All of their kings have fallen.
    Not one of them calls upon me!

IV. *Stupidity*

8   Ephraim mixes himself with the peoples;
        Ephraim is a cake not turned.

9   Strangers consume his strength,
        but he does not know it.
    White hairs are scattered upon him,
        but he does not know it.

10   Israel's pride will testify against him;
        for they turn not to Yahweh their God,
        and they seek him not in all this.

11   Ephraim behaves like a dove,
        silly and without sense.
    They cry to Egypt,
        they run to Assyria.

12   As they run,
        I will throw my net over them.
    I will bring them down like a bird from the sky;
        I will punish them according to. . . .

13   Woe to them,
        for they have strayed from me!
    Ruin upon them,
        for they have rebelled against me!

V. *Duplicity*

It is I who would redeem them;
    but it is they who tell me lies.

14 They do not cry to me from their hearts,
　　but they howl upon their beds.
　　They slash themselves for grain and grapes;
　　　they rebel against me.
15 I trained them and strengthened their arms,
　　but they plot against me.
16 They turn to (Baal);
　　they are like a slack bow.
　　Their princes will fall by the sword
　　　for the arrogance of their tongues.
　　Thus will they be derided in the land of Egypt.

NOTES ON THE TEXT

Verse 7. Read בָּאָדָם ("at Adam," with nearly all recent critics) for the MT, כְּאָדָם ("like Adam"), on the basis of 7b, "there." בְּרִית is often rendered "*the* covenant" (*KJV, ASV, RSV, JPS,* Brown, Harper, and others), but the Hebrew has no article. No indication is given which covenant was broken or who broke it. Hosea may have been thinking of the Mosaic covenant, but what he said was vague. The place *Adam* is near the place where Joshua led the Israelites across the Jordan (Josh. 3:9–17). Sellin suggested that Hos. 6:7 contains an implicit word play on the verb עָבַר, "cross over." Thus, at Adam, where Israel crossed over the Jordan, they also crossed over (i.e., transgressed) a covenant.

Verse 8. "Gilead" usually denotes the territory east of Ephraim. However, Nowack, Harper, and Wolff (following Noth) regard it in this passage as the name of the city. It could also be an allusion to some such city as Ramoth-Gilead, or it could be an error for "Gilgal" (cf., the Greek text of Lucian). Budde (*JBL* 53 [1934], 122) thinks of a sacred heap "gilgal" near Shechem, rather than that of Joshua at the Jordan. I have taken "city" as a metaphor here, like the "gang" (of robbers) in 9a. Vss. 6:7–9a deal with the segment of the northern Israelite kingdom that was east of the Jordan, and vss. 6:9b–10a deal with the portion west of that river. The first passage mentions one particular place (Adam), the second, two places (Shechem and Bethel). The first calls the principal territory "Gilead," the second calls the corresponding territory "Ephraim." Finally, both are comprehended in the totality "Israel" (10b).

Verse 9. The text is difficult, but the translation given here represents the current consensus in all but one paticular. I believe דרך has here the meaning "behavior, custom, habit" (see *BDB,* p. 203a, and Köhler, *Lexicon,* p. 218). The word is separated from "Shechem" by the verb and therefore seems to modify the verb rather than the noun. Had the poet intended to say "road to Shechem," as many scholars believe, he would more likely have put דרך in a construct phrase with שכמה. The localic ending of שכמה can, of course, denote "the place where" as well as "the place to which" (cf., *G.K.* 90d).

Verse 10. The MT has "Beth('House of')-Israel" but most commentators prefer a place-name because of the parallel "there." "Israel" in 10a may be an assimilation to the second clause in 10b. Indeed, the latter may be itself an editor's afterthought. Wolff deletes the third as well as the second clause, whereas Sellin deletes the second.

Verse 11. "Also, Judah, a harvest is set for you" (MT) can only be a Judean editor's comment. The passage has nothing to do with Judah and lacks any parallel threat of coming doom. It is deleted, with or without 11b, by *Jerusalem,* Harper, Weiser, Wolff, Mauchline, Nötscher, Scott (*op. cit.,* pp. 51 f.), and Lindblom (*op. cit.,* p. 86).

Vs. 11b forms a fine parallel to the first clause in 7:1, and I have retained it, with some misgivings, in spite of the suspicious שוב שבות ("turn the captivity"), which many regard as an exilic phrase. It is deleted by Wellhausen, Sellin, Nötscher, and Lindblom (*loc. cit.*). It is joined to 7:1 by the *LXX, RSV, Moffatt, Chicago, BH, JPS,* Harper, Brown, Cheyne, Mauchline, and Wolff.

Verse 7:1. Wellhausen, Lindblom, and Nötscher delete the first two words, along with 11b, as an exilic gloss. I have rendered most verbs in this strophe in the past tense. The first verb in 7:1b and the first one in 2a are imperfects. The clause "a thief breaks in" should be taken, together with the clause "a gang attacking in the street" (vocalizing פשט, with *BH* and Sellin), as illustrative of the past action in the preceding clause ("have behaved"). They may be even interpreted metaphorically, as I have done. The verb in vs. 2a is paralleled by a perfect ("I have remembered") and I have rendered them both as if perfect, although the sense is not seriously affected by reading "they do not lay to heart" and "I have remembered," or even "I remember" (*RSV* and others).

When 6:11a is removed, 6:7–7:2 falls into two strophes of five lines, with tristichs at the end of the first and the center of the second. The last part of 7:1, "a thief breaking in, a gang attacking in the street," is metaphorical, suggesting the instability, corruption, and danger that prevail in both internal and external affairs.

7:3–7. Verse 7 is the only part of this section that may be translated with some assurance, but its meaning is uncertain, nevertheless. The rest seems hopeless. Vss. 6 and 7 imply conspiracies to commit regicide. These were common in Hosea's time (2 Kings 15:10, 14, 25). Hosea's picture recalls Zimri's murder of the drunken king Asa (1 Kings 16:8–10).

Verse 3. The last line of 7b ("not one of them calls upon me") recalls 8:4, 10 and suggests that the original beginning of this section may have been "they anoint a king in their iniquity . . ." (מָשַׁח for

שָׁמַח, *BH*, Wellhauser, Sellin, Weiser, Robinson, Nötscher, and

others). The MT has "they cause a king to rejoice," but without the sign of the direct object, which this verb usually takes.

Verse 4. If the MT's "adulterers" (מְנָאֲפִים) is correct, its meaning is opaque. "Angry, enraged" (אֲנֵפִים; Sellin, Robinson, Nötscher, Mauchline, Weiser, and others) requires only a slight change.

The oven image is ambiguous. Once again calling on vs. 7 for help, we may take vs. 4b to mean that the people, after destroying one king and anointing another, delay the destruction of the new one only long enough to plot the conspiracy. Alternatively, it may be taken to mean that they conceal their plot until it is ready to be carried out. This seems to be the point conveyed by the second oven image in vs. 6.

Verse 5. The MT is literally "the day our king they make sick princes the heat of wine." Among the reasonable efforts to make sense of this are: (1) "On the day of our king the princes become sick with the heat of wine" (*RSV, ASV*). The king's day might be his coronation, or his anniversary, or the feast of Tabernacles, or an annual enthronement festival. (2) "As soon as the king is fallen sick, and the princes, with the heat of wine," which is completed by the following line, "they join hands with robbers" (*G.R. Driver, JTS*

39, 156–57). (3) "On the day of our king (or, "From the day he became king," *Chicago*) the princes made him sick with the heat of wine" (*JPS;* cf., *KJV*). (4) "They make their king weak, they set their princes aglow with wine" (Nötscher; cf., *Jerusalem*). Each of these versions requires minor changes in the Hebrew text.

"Impostors" is Gaster's reading of a rare Hebrew word (לצצים), based on an Arabic cognate (*VT* 4 [1954], 78). It conveys the idea of conspiring better than "scoffers/scorners/mockers" (*KJV, ASV, RSV, JPS*, etc.). Some sort of rebel is meant (Weiser, Mauchline, Sellin, Robinson, and others).

Guthe's proposal to change "he joins his hand with" (משך ידו את־) to "they (i.e., the rebels) make him drunk" (השכירו אתו) has been accepted by Robinson, Sellin, and *Chicago*. It suits the parallel nicely.

Verse 6. The translation adopted here follows the *LXX* and Syriac. The simplest route to this version is to change קרב to קדח (Sellin, Robinson, Nötscher, Nowack, Wolff, and others).

Verse 12b. The MT is "I will punish them according to the report to their congregation" (*KJV, ASV, JPS*). There are almost as many conjectural emendations of this line as there are commentators. Wellhausen was correct: the line is hopeless. "According to their wickedness" (*Chicago, RSV, Moffatt*, and others) is less a consensus than a counsel of despair.

Verse 14. "Slash themselves" (יתגודדו) for the MT's (יתגוררו) is now the standard translation.

Verse 16. "To Baal," for the MT version "not upwards" (אל בעל or לבעל for לא על), is widely adopted, although some scholars prefer "to what is not" (על לא) or "to what accomplishes nothing" (לא יועיל אל). Nyberg (*Studien zum Hoseabuch*, p. 114) takes 'al as the name of one of the baals, and reads "to '*Al*'" (לעל).

IT IS IMPOSSIBLE to separate independent oracles in this part of the Book of Hosea. One poem flows into another, and the continuity of substance is greater than the formal discontinuities among the strophes. The major theme of the preceding section (6:1–7) also appears prominently here, namely the impossibility of God's fulfilling his wish to heal the people, because of their disloyalty and hypocrisy. Therefore, the whole complex of poems in 6:1–7:16 could be treated together, if it were not cumbersome to do so.[1] Nearly all of this material is invective, the enumeration of Israel's corporate crimes. No overt threat of punishment appears until 7:10, and the major threats are confined to the closing lines of the last two parts (7:12–13; 7:16). Although the prophetic pattern of invective-plus-threat is not always found in Hosea's poems, its appearance here may be used as a criterion for determining the limits of the poem.

One may only guess at the concrete nature of the actions mentioned in part I (6:7–10). They may have been cultic, since priests are accused (vs. 9), and since Bethel, the location of Israel's chief sanctuary, is described as "whorish" (vs. 10). This is Hosea's favorite term for ritual perversity. If this guess is correct, the blood, ambush, and murder (vss. 8–9), are not literal but figurative. The idea of cultic murder by the priests complements the other notion of Hosea that Ephraim "became guilty through Baal and died" (13:1). This is not a physical death but a moral one. Viewed as a whole, the nation has committed religious suicide. Viewed from the angle of the quality of their leadership, the people have been murdered. This treachery among the official servants of the covenant is against the people, but it is simultaneously against God (6:7).

There are several ways of explaining Hosea's choice of place-names in this poem, but all of them are speculative. One may assume that they were associated with certain contemporary events, known to Hosea's audience but unknown to us, in which national leaders behaved criminally. The juxtaposition of references might be then due to the similarity in character of these deeds; and, it might be that actual killing was involved. To this theory, one might add the further hypotheses that the crimes were part of a royal conspiracy and that the conspiracy originated in Gilead.[2] Or again, one might surmise that the sequence of places points to a pilgrimage route from Gilead to Bethel by way of Adam (on the Jordan) and Shechem.[3] The merit of this alternative is that it accords with the cultic aspect of the crimes catalogued here. Still another possible explanation is that

[1] Wolff treats 5:8–7:16 together. The specific historical background of 5:8–15, which is not implied in the remainder, justifies dealing with that poem separately, however.

[2] Cf., Sellin and Alt (*op. cit.,* p. 186).

[3] Cf., Weiser and Mauchline. This theory presupposes the emendation of "Beth-Israel" to "Bethel" in vs. 10. See the textual note.

the sequence follows the line of progress of the original Ephraimite settlement in Palestine, as marked by successive locations of the central sanctuary.[4] The point of the accusation, according to this hypothesis, is that Israel was treacherous and corrupt, already at the beginning of her migration to the land, and that she had never ceased to be so. Each of these theories has merit and each is about as probable as the others.

The second bill of overt particulars (7:3–7) is less ambiguous. It concerns crimes close to the throne. Older commentators preferred to regard the evil as debauchery with its attendant outbursts of violence. However, few kings have fallen because of debauchery (cf., vs. 7). On the other hand, several kings in Hosea's time fell, and the thrones of others were jeopardized, by conspiracy. The imagery of the piece is more consistent and more elegant if taken in this way. Therefore, the current consensus is correct, namely, that this part of the poem scores the rash of regicides that marked the period 745–737 B.C. (Zechariah in 745 B.C., Shallum in the same year, and Pekahiah in 737 B.C.). Here then is another variation on the theme of treachery in Israel. The priests were not the only artists talented in this line.

A third kind of manifest crime in national affairs is the subject of part IV of this long poem. It is the desperate flight to the shadow of the major powers for international security. Little detailed information is given us here about the conditions and consequences of such efforts. We infer from Hosea's brief strictures that there was vacillation in policy (7:11). It could have been caused by fluctuations in power between pro-Egyptian and pro-Assyrian parties at the court, or by changes of dynasty, or merely by weakness and indecision on the part of the kings. Regardless of the short-range purposes of these policies, Hosea described two lasting results, the immediate waste of resources (vss. 8–9) and the final loss of national identity (vss. 12–13). The first might mean perennial tribute payments, but the statement that Israel does not know what is happening makes it more likely that Hosea was thinking of gradual moral attrition. Indeed, these lines might simply mean that Israel failed to realize that the policies themselves had entangled her in a web of relations that would end by strangling her. She would know it only when it was too late to prevent it.

[4] Cf., Lindblom, *op. cit.*, pp. 84–89.

Parts II and V move on another level than the rest of the poem. Their subject is the subjective side of the policies alluded to elsewhere: more specifically, it is the influence of these policies upon Israel's covenantal relationship with Yahweh. The extent of decay in this bond was revealed in the fact that Israel chose to pursue her current policy even when confronted with an alternative (6:11b–7:2). She refused to acknowledge the viciousness of her objectives, even though this was manifest to the prophet (vs. 2). We are forced to think, concretely, of the public disdain for prophetic instruction. Verse 6:11b implies a prophetic confrontation with the state concerning alternative courses of action. It could be merely a reference to the hidden alternatives that lie unconsciously at hand in the making of national decisions, but this possibility seems remote. In any case, Israel's perversion of policy affects both domestic and foreign affairs (vs. 1b, interpreting the "thief" and "gang" metaphorically.) He has surrounded himself with this network of policy and has cut himself off from God. God remains in the situation, though unknown to Israel, as the keen observer and ultimate judge.

Part V is covenantal but also cultic. Israel was not atheistic, after all. She did not know the realities of her predicament, but she continued to support the traditional ritual service of Yahweh. She had overlaid it with baalistic accretions (7:14, 16), however, so that it had become a lie (vs. 13b). It was therefore no longer a means of redemption. This cultic duplicity was the formal center of a pervasive disease that corrupted the body politic. The final destruction of the government and deportation of the people (vs. 16) were, consequently, not punishments for non-political crimes imposed from the outside. They were only the last visible signs of a total social collapse that had both cultic and civil causes as well as cultic and civil consequences.

A fundamental ethical question is raised by Hosea's invective, which is relevant to many other prophetic oracles in the Old Testament. In condemning Israel's foreign alliances, did Hosea mean to say that faith in Yahweh was the one legitimate choice among alternative national policies? If this is what he meant, would it be just to describe him as a political isolationist? Is the issue really "faith or politics"?

The sections of the present oracle that are directly relevant to this discussion are parts III and IV. Part III concludes with "They are

all hot like an oven,/and they devour their rulers./ All of their kings
have fallen./ Not one of them calls upon Me!" (7:7). The interpretation of this passage depends on the identity of "them" in the last
line. Two considerations make it imperative that we regard "them" as
referring to the conspirators described in the poem and not to the
kings. The first is that "they" are the subject of the action throughout
the section, except in one line, where the subject is the king ("He
joins hands with impostors"). "They" are the devourers of kings.
The second is that the final two lines are chiastic, ABBA. The
parallel pairs are "They devour their rulers" // "All of their kings
have fallen," and "They are all hot like an oven" // "Not one of
them calls upon Me."

The alternative to this interpretation of vs. 7, while formally possible, suggests a meaning of faith that I find incompatible with the
rest of Hosea's teaching. It is based on the assumption that the last
two lines comprise a synonymous poetic parallelism: "All of their
kings have fallen" // "Not one of them calls upon Me." Such an
affirmation could have several meanings. It might mean, first of all,
that the kings have fallen because they failed to exploit Yahweh's
name as a means for securing special favor and extraordinary power
for themselves. Such a semimagical notion of faith, however, is an
obvious perversion of Hosea's message.

A less objectionable paraphrase of the statement would be to say
that the kings have fallen because they rejected faith (quietism) as
one among several political policies, and chose instead to levy armies
and conclude international alliances. This is probably the most common interpretation of the passage. It is less suitable, in my opinion,
to the total thrust of Hosea's oracles, and it presupposes a less adequate view of the structure of the present poem (7:3–7) than the
one described above.

One last possibility may be suggested, though it seems improbable.
The last sentence ("Not one of them calls upon Me") might be
allowed to stand apart from the rest of the strophe, without any
direct connection to the statements immediately preceding. Its meaning then would be that "they," that is, the kings, or the conspirators,
or both, are unfaithful to Yahweh, in *addition* to being agents of
political anarchy. Their two faults are thus distinct. The difficulty
with this line of argument is that it makes the former assertion an
afterthought, important in itself but irrelevant to the social situation

with which the poem deals. The second course is to relate the last sentence to the poem as a whole in the manner I initially proposed. The men without faith are the king-makers who destroy rulers as fast as they create them.

How, then, is their failure to "call upon" Yahweh related to their political behavior? Surely, there is no implication here that faith and politics are alternative forms of behavior. The meaning is simply that these men are faithless toward God as well as toward their fellow citizens. They have no loyalties. They are treacherous men. This does not mean that men of faith would not be engaged in state affairs, but that these particular men, who are disloyal to God, are also disloyal to the kings whom they have established. There is undoubtedly an intimate connection between the two kinds of disloyalty, but it is the result of the unity of human personality and not the result of an inherent contradiction between faith and political action.

In ancient Israel, there was a further connection between loyalty to God and loyalty to the king, which arose from the fact that the anointing of a king was a sacred act. The sovereign was God's vicegerent. It is true that Hosea did not regard the current kings as God's acceptable servants (cf., 8:4, for example). Yet the people, and especially the courtiers who were most directly involved in royal affairs, ostensibly regarded them as such. They maintained the sacral aspects of monarchial rule under the traditional sanction of Yahwism. Therefore, their political treachery was a violation of their covenant with Yahweh, as they themselves understood it.

Part IV of this oracle is even more important than part III, from the point of view of providing answers to the questions I have asked above. Ephraim is depicted in it as a stupid bird flying here and there in search of a safe perch, making appeals to Egypt and Assyria in turn, but refusing to seek the Lord. The point seems to be that trust in Yahweh is incompatible with alliances with foreign powers. Furthermore, Hosea adds that Israel will perish by Yahweh's hand for having chosen to rely on foreign powers. Such, at least, is a conventional interpretation of this and of similar prophetic oracles. Within limits, this interpretation is justified. This statement of the prophetic ethic needs a careful qualification, however, and should not be given the status of a universal directive for political action by men who believe in the God of the prophets.

Hosea said that the Israelite kingdom's relations with the two major powers in its world, in the middle of the eighth century B.C., constituted a rebellion against Yahweh. This kingdom was both a national state and a religious community. The conduct of government and the conduct of the cult were specialized functions in the hands of distinct groups, but they were interdependent and, in some things, synonymous. Both were under the control of an absolute and hereditary monarch, whose authority derived from a doctrine of divine rule and whose actual power resided in a standing, mercenary army. Under these circumstances, both justice and religion were easily corrupted. The cult was readily made the servant of the king as well as of any social objectives that he and his court wished to pursue. The system permitted a huge expenditure of national resources for the maintenance of the king's power. The prevailing competition among the kings of the Middle Eastern world for widening spheres of sovereignty required such expenditures as the price of participation. The cults of the foreign nations were focused upon the worship of the state itself, personified as a high god, such as Horus in Egypt or Asshur in Assyria. International affairs involved therefore relations with these tutelary deities, at least to the extent that they were formally acknowledged. It was an easy step to the introduction of foreign cult-objects and sacred notions into Israelite religious practice. Inevitably, Yahweh was regarded by the other powers as nothing more than the god of Israel, and Israel must have been constantly tempted to do likewise. The relativizing of Yahwism, of course, meant the relativizing of the principles of justice that were traditionally sanctioned by the Yahwistic covenant. The consequences of this process may be summarized by saying that respect for the freedom, dignity, and integrity of individual men, and for the personal loyalties of family and small group life, were increasingly sacrificed, and the vast, impersonal, and dehumanizing forces of nature and of the state were exalted.

The fundamental evil in all this was that God was no longer worshipped as transcendent creator and loving Lord. Israel lost therefore her ultimate loyalty, in the light of which all her proximate loyalties could be evaluated and corrected. She lost also the final sanction of her universal and personal covenantal ethic, in the light of which the justice of her political and economic institutions could be measured. It was not that all international alliances and governmental programs of social control were necessarily evil, but that in conditions of Israel's existence at that time their pursuit was inevitably idolatrous and, therefore, tyrannical and destructive.

There is no modern equivalent to Hosea's Israel. The religious communities that share the prophet's faith in God, and bear the responsibility for defending their ultimate allegiance from perversion and idolatry, are not the institutional bearers of political authority and power. Under these circumstances, it is much easier to maintain the recognition of God as the sole, ultimate Lord, and to maintain also national loyalties. In ancient Israel, the effective preservation of Yahwistic faith and covenantal morality depended upon the disavowal of political responsibility, because of the identity of leadership in the ecclesiastical and political realms. Most modern priests and prophets do not bear political responsibility and most modern statesmen are not cult functionaries or commissioned defenders of the faith.

Modern churchmen are no less subject to syncretism and apostasy than Hosea's contemporaries, and modern states are no less subject to idolatry and tyranny than ancient Israel. However, international relations do not entail nowadays an immediate compromise of religious loyalties as they did in the old world of absolute despots and state cults. The simple choice between politics and faith is neither necessary for the modern defender of the faith nor possible for the modern leader of state. Hosea's confrontation of Israel with that choice was not a universal demand. It was conditioned by the particular circumstances of his time.

This great oracle moves not only on the plane of international events; it also contains several keen psychological observations. We have come to expect these from Hosea. The moral dishonesty that he described in parts II, IV, and V, illustrates the infinite capacity of man for self-deception. Israel's guilt was not that she had made a straightforward choice of evil, in conscious disdain of the good. Her pride required that she justify her behavior to herself and that she rationalize it as good. Indeed, it may have been a partial good, but her pride prevented her from seeing its partial evil, and thus she corrupted the good. Deceived by herself, she was ignorant of her real situation and was unable therefore to correct it. Thus, her pride was a principal factor in her ultimate condemnation (7:9–10). Israel pretended to be faithful to Yahweh and was persuaded by her own pretense. As a consequence, she did not know, or could not admit, that her prayers to God were lies (7:13b–14). Her arrogance and self-delusion had to lead to her eventual fall, because they insulated her from self-criticism, which is the prerequisite of renewal.

A modern reader may object that Hosea's analysis of Israel's affairs involved the confusion of individual psychology with the far more complex and largely impersonal dynamics of state policy. This objection is undeniably valid. Hosea, like the rest of the writers of the Old Testament, represented Israel as a person, and thus, from our point of view, considerably oversimplified, partly even falsified, the realities of the social process. This feature of Hebraic mentality makes it often difficult for us to appreciate the ethical insights of the prophets. It should be remembered, on the other hand, that the dynamics of polities and society were a good deal more personalistic in ancient Israel than they are in a typical modern state. The chief reason for this, naturally, was that absolute monarchy placed the power of decision in one person. There were many other factors as well. Indeed, the entire political and economic life of Israel was far simpler and more personal than that of a huge, urban, industrial society. These qualifications do not make the application of prophetic ethics easier for us; they simply make the difficulty more understandable.

We have observed now that the discussion in chapter 7 alternates between an analysis of the psychology of sin and a description of Israel's current diplomacy. The chapter closes by returning once more to the second level. Hosea says quite simply that the diplomats will be slain and Israel will be derided in Egypt. This last remark could mean that Israel's Egyptian allies will laugh at her fate,[5] and thus, incidentally, give the final proof of the folly of Israel's reliance on such fickle friends. It could also mean that those who flee to Egypt from the invading Assyrians will be greeted in Egypt with scorn. Their fate in this case will resemble that of their forefathers before the exodus. This association with the exodus tradition may even be the principal intention of the line, for it echoes other predictions by Hosea of a return to Egypt (literal or figurative) as a symbol both of punishment and of the possibility of covenant-renewal (cf., 8:13; 9:3; 12:9; 11:5, 11; 2:14–15).

[5] Cf., Weiser.

9 ROYAL POLICY IN SAMARIA: HOSEA 8

1   Blow the Shophar!
        For the Eagle is over the house of Yahweh,
      Because they have transgressed my covenant
        and rebelled against my law.
2   They cry to me, "My God!"
        "We, Israel, have known thee."
3   Israel has loathed the good.
        Let the enemy pursue him.

4   They have set up kings, but not by me;
        created princes, but without my acknowledgment.
    Of their silver and their gold
        they have made themselves idols
          —in order to be destroyed!
5   I have loathed your calf, O Samaria.
        My anger rages against it!
    [How long till they can be free from punishment?]

6   "Because it comes from Israel,
        an expert made it!"
    But this is not God.
        For the calf of Samaria
          will be (smashed) to pieces.
7   "For they sow the wind,
        but they reap the whirlwind."
    "If the stalk has no grain
        it yields no flour."
    And if it does yield,
        strangers will swallow it.

8   Israel is swallowed up.
        They are now among the nations
        as a useless tool.
9   For they went off to Assyria;

>   Ephraim is a wild ass all alone;
>   they have hired lovers.
> 10   Though they hire among the nations,
>   I am about to gather them up,
>   And they will cease for a little while
>   from the tribute of king and princes.
>
> 11   Because Ephraim multiplied altars for sin,
>   they became for him altars for sinning.
> 12   For, though I wrote my teachings by myriads,
>   he would count them in alien thing.
> 13   Let them slaughter their precious sacrifices!
>   Let them eat flesh!
>   Yahweh takes no pleasure in them.
>   But he will remember their guilt
>   and punish them for their sin:
>   they will return to Egypt.
>
> 14   Israel has forgotten his maker.
>   He has built palaces
>   and multiplied walled cities.
>   But I will spread fire through his cities
>   to consume his fortresses.

NOTES ON THE TEXT

Verse 1. "For the Eagle" (כי נשר, *RSV,* Wellhausen, Harper) differs slightly from the MT's "as the eagle" (כנשר), but obviates the need of injecting another verb ("He comes as an eagle," *KJV, ASV, JPS;* cf., *Moffatt).* Wolff observes rightly that the common emendation to "like a watchman" (כנצר, *Chicago,* Sellin, Weiser, and others) deprives the warning of its basis. The eagle was a familiar Assyrian state symbol. Since Assyria was the obvious threat to Israel's sovereignty in the eighth century B.C., there is every reason to conclude that the eagle symbolizes Assyria here. "House of Yahweh" apparently means the land of Israel in this line. See the discussion of 9:3–4 (p. 164) and 9:15 (pp. 167–68), below.

Verse 2. The English versions translate both verbs in the present tense. However, the second verb in Hebrew is in the perfect, and is better taken as a statement of previous knowledge, i.e., covenantal relationship, to which Israel in her extremity now appeals as the ground of her hope.

Verse 4. G. R. Driver has proposed to interpret הִמְלִיךְ (following Haupt) in the sense of the Aramaic אמלך, "counselled," and הֵשִׂירוּ in the sense of the Arabic *'ašâra*, "gave advice," though as denominative rather than transitive verbs. Thus, "They have taken counsel, but not of me; they have got advice, and I know not (of it)," i.e., they have resorted to idols. This reading would unify the theme of 8:4–5, but it lacks the support of parallel usage in the OT. The recurrence of the king-prince motif in vs. 10, on the other hand, as well as the sense of the poem as a whole, supports the standard translation.

Verse 5. The initial Hebrew verb (זנח) is in the third person. Most modern translators suppose that the original was in the first person. It may have been assimilated to the verb in the second line and to זנח in vs. 3. As an alternative, the Hebrew might be repointed as an imperative: "Cast away your calf, O Samaria" (*LXX;* Wolff; Scott, *The Message of Hosea,* p. 135).

The statement in 5b spoils the climax of the second strophe, which parallels that of the first strophe: "Israel has loathed. . . . I have loathed. . . ." It is deleted by *Jerusalem,* Sellin, Harper, Weiser, and others.

Verse 6. Some scholars link the first two words with 5b, although this entails a textual change from "for from Israel" (כי מישראל) to "in Israel" (בישראל, *RSV)* or "the sons of Israel" (בני ישראל, *Jerusalem,* Robinson, Nötscher). I prefer retaining the MT (with *ASV, Chicago,* Harper, Brown, and others) and interpreting it as Hosea's ridicule of an Israelite boast.

Verse 7. The first two statements sound like popular adages that Hosea has quoted, with an added threat. The second proverb rhymes in Hebrew (*ṣemaḥ, qemaḥ*), and the first contains a double assonance. These features are difficult to imitate in English without changing the meaning, although G. A. Smith's "Stalk without shoot shall never yield fruit" is quite good (cf., *Moffatt).*

Verse 8. Several of the components of chapter 8 have apparently been brought together because of catchword similarities. Vss. 5 and 6 share "calf of Samaria," while vss. 7 and 8 share "swallow." There is a tolerable continuity of themes in these short poems, but the poems are perhaps best understood as independent variations on these themes.

Verses 9–10. The confusing mixture of metaphors in 8–10 makes these verses difficult to interpret. Furthermore, the precise meaning of אתנן is uncertain, though it seems to mean "to give or take gifts," especially for prostitution (cf., אתנה, 2:14, and אתנן, 9:1: "harlot's hire"). The Masoretic pointing makes Ephraim the subject of a plural verb. Rather than emend the verb ("Ephraim has hired lovers," *KJV, RSV, Chicago,* etc.), I take "Ephraim" with the preceding phrase. This division is also called for by the pun on Ephraim and *pere'* (wild ass).

Verse 10. My rendition of the last clause is based upon the MT. "Burden" *(ASV,* Mauchline) is an acceptable alternative to "tribute" (Harper and many others). The "hiring among the nations" certainly justifies this meaning. Many modern translators follow the *LXX,* however, and read "from anointing" (ממשח for ממשא). "Become sick" (חלה,ויחלו Pi.) is a possibility for the MT's "begin" (חלל,ויחלו Hi.); cf., the concordant idea in 11:7. The line could then be translated, "They will become sick in a little while of the burden of king and princes." The translation I have adopted, however, provides a better sequel to the previous sentence. Thus, the cessation of tribute is a consequence of exile.

Verse 11. Many commentators follow the *LXX,* which lacks "sin" in the first clause (e.g., *Moffatt, Chicago,* Weiser, Brown), and some also delete "altars" in the second, to give, "Because Ephraim has multiplied altars, they have become sin for him" (e.g., *BH* and Weiser). The paronomasia is worth preserving, however, whoever was responsible for it. The poetic form is perhaps improved by dividing the line into three stichs: "Because Ephraim has multiplied altars, /they have become sin for him,/ altars for sinning!" (Buber and Wolff). This procedure destroys the play on "sin," however, and drastically weakens therefore the force of the statement. The sense is that Ephraim's elaborate cultus, devised as a means for expiating sin, has become a means of sinning.

Verse 13. The LXX understood הבהבי, which occurs only here, as an adjective (ἠγαπημένα, beloved), and I have incorporated this interpretation into the translation ("precious").

The final sentence makes the line a tristich. This situation in itself is unobjectionable, but the assertion is abrupt and might be a marginal comment, based on 9:3, 6; 11:5, 11. Lindblom *(Hosea,* p. 92), Scott *(op. cit.,* p. 57), Marti, Robinson, and Weiser delete it.

Verse 14. Many scholars (e.g., Wellhausen, G. A. Smith, Lindblom, Scott, and Harper) have deleted this verse as a late, editorial expansion, because of the mention of Judah (MT: "Judah has multiplied walled cities"), the unique reference to God as Israel's "maker" (allegedly a late idea), and the supposedly un-Hosean condemnation of fortified cities. I prefer deleting "Judah" (with Sellin and Weiser, among others) and retaining the rest.

THE PREVIOUS ORACLE spoke of unobserved atrophy in Israel (7:8–10), alluding either to the loss of moral vitality and cultural integrity through the adoption of alien policies and ideals, or to the dissipation of economic wealth through tribute. In the oracle before us, references to such subtle forms of national death give away to a picture of the most evident form of all—military conquest. Here and in the chapters that follow, Hosea returns again and again to the violent scene of Israel's final travail. The Assyrian spectre, which brooded over the previous chapters, now materializes, disclosed in its terrible reality as the definite instrument of Ephraim's death.

Two causes of death are adduced, idolatry in the sacrificial cult, as epitomized by the calf image at Bethel, and apostasy in the choice of national goals, as epitomized by the sacral kingship. We have already encountered strictures against sacrifice (8:11–13; cf., 4:8 and 6:6) and against the conduct of national affairs (8:8–10; cf., 1:4; 5:8–15; 7:3–13). The special attention given here to the cult image and the anointed king represents a further development in Hosea's oracles, however. Thus, we may properly focus the discussion of chapter 8 on these themes.

Official use of calf images in the cult of Yahweh in the northern kingdom dates back to Jeroboam I (*ca.* 922–901 B.C.). This first king of the northern state erected such images in two national sanctuaries, one in Dan in the north and the other in Bethel in the south (1 Kings 12:26–33). His action is described in 1 Kings as simple idolatry, that is, the representation of a god in plastic form. If this charge were correct, the deity worshipped would have been a bull god of the Canaanite nature cult. However, modern critics have recognized a strong Judean bias in the account in 1 Kings, and reconstructed a less vicious picture of the calves of Jeroboam. Even in Canaanite iconography the bull was not necessarily a representation of the high-god himself, but was often the symbol of his power. The god in these cases was shown in human form, standing upon the back of the bull.[1] Correspondingly, Jeroboam's calves were probably symbols of Yahweh's power as well as of his presence in the sanctuary; and, they were doubtless riderless, in accordance with the aniconic character of Yahweh. In all probability, these calves were comparable to the ark in the temple of Jerusalem, upon which Yahweh was believed to be invisibly enthroned, Jeroboam erected the images in order to provide pilgrimage centers that would displace the Jerusalem temple in the affections of his subjects. Since, traditionally, there had been only one ark, he could not duplicate the one in Jerusalem but had to provide an alternative symbol. One cannot create genuine religious symbols by fiat, and so he chose what must have been the best one available. It did, indeed, have a well-established place in the imagination and cultic practice of the Palestinian populace.

Unfortunately, the theological liabilities of the bull image were as great as its assets, and eventually they proved to be far greater. As a plastic image it was easily idolized. Incidentally, similar reverence was accorded to the ark by the Judeans, and Jeremiah's disdain for it matched that of Hosea for the calf of Bethel (Jer. 3:16). The most pernicious corollary of this reverence was the conviction that the cult object guaranteed the presence of God in the sanctuary and therefore made him permanently available for exploitation (cf., Jer. 7:1–4). Hosea's rejection of this comfortable notion is already familiar to us (5:6, 15). The calf of Bethel carried a further liability, from which the ark of Jerusalem was happily free. It was an animal image, forming an intrinsic part of the worship of nature since immemorial times, and inevitably subject to all the abuses of the fertility cult.

In Hos. 8, the calf of Samaria symbolizes all that the prophet found wrong with Israelite public worship, and the Lord's rage against the image (vs. 5) is matched by his scorn for their sacrifices (vs. 13), as much as for the whole expiatory ritual of the altar (vs. 11). Whether this "calf of Samaria" was identical with the one in the temple of Bethel is an interesting historical question, though it is not one that affects the substance of Hosea's teaching. The only biblical references to a sanctuary in Samaria relate to the temple built by

[1] See, for example, *IDB*, A–D, pp. 488–89, where there is a picture of Baal-Hadad standing upon the back of a bull, and also a general discussion of Jeroboam's calves and of their relationship to the golden-calf episode in Exod. 32.

Ahab for Jezebel's worship of the Baal of Sidon (1 Kings 16:32). Jehu razed that temple and "made it a latrine to this day" (2 Kings 10:27; cf., 10:21–6), but modern excavation of Samaria has produced no evidence of it or of any other Israelite temple.[2] The natural conclusion, therefore, is that there was none in Samaria in Hosea's time. What he meant by the phrase "calf of Samaria" was the bull image in the temple of Yahweh in Bethel, which was the principal sanctuary of the royal house of Samaria. Hosea 10:5–6 supports this conclusion. There, the image that interests the Samarians and that is referred to as *the* idol of Ephraim/Israel (vs. 6), is called the "calf of Beth-aven ('Beth-evil')," i.e., Bethel. As in chapter 8, the discussion in chapter 10 revolves around two foci, the Samarian king and the "Samarian" idol. The latter, then, was the official image in the national sanctuary at Bethel.[3]

Here is the trademark of the Ephraimite cult: "Made in Israel! By an expert!" Both the cult and the calf. Although to the people it was a symbol, not of Yahweh himself, but of divine power, to Hosea the calf was the symbol of a whole system of worship that had reduced the transcendent mystery of God to measurable certainty and manageable size. Yet, calf and cult were both doomed, along with the state that subsidized them. In their extinction, Israel would be brought once more before the mystery of God. Whether the confrontation would lead to hope or despair depended, of course, on other factors in the inner environment of Israel.

Hosea's oracle was formerly considered to be the earliest denunciation of images of Yahweh, or of images in general, in the Old Testament.[4] During recent decades the number of scholars who believe that the Mosaic religion was aniconic has grown. If their judgment is correct, the literary prophets were conservatives in this respect and not innovators. The question is tied up with that of the date of the Decalogue and Covenant Code (Exod. 20–23). Since this question—

[2] See the article on Samaria in *IDB*.

[3] A dissenting opinion has been given by Harper, Robinson (who follows O. Eissfeldt, *Archiv fur Religionswissenschaft* 28 [1930], 16), and Noth (*The History of Israel*, 1960, p. 232). "Samaria" is synonymous with the Ephraimite kingdom in Hos. 7:1, also. There were originally two "calves of Samaria," in Bethel and in Dan (1 Kings 12:29); it is possible that Hosea mentioned only that in Bethel because Dan had already been lost to Assyria by the time Hosea wrote these oracles (cf., Weiser).

[4] See, Harper and Brown, respectively.

not of the final fixation of the literary tradition as it appears in the canon, but of the convictions embodied in it—is unlikely to be settled absolutely, it is futile to try to establish Hosea's precise relationship to this tradition. However, the judgment cannot be far wrong that the orthodox view of Yahweh presented in the Yahwist–Elohist narrative in the Pentateuch (as well as in the Decalogue and Covenant Code, which are associated with it) had been given definitive form by the time Hosea completed his work.[5] Hosea's protest, in any case, is much more than a mere statute prohibiting idolatry. It is a skillful exposé of the politics of idolatry.

The cult of Israel, like its central image, was the creation of the state. Regardless of the motives that lay behind this work, it was the servant of the court in Hosea's time. Chapter 8 scornfully parades before us a series of such servants that have been corrupted by the monarchy and that have corrupted it in turn. In addition to the cult image, which was inherently corrupting, there were the propitiatory system of sacrifice (vss. 11–13), the policy of tributary alliances (vss. 8 and 10), and the program of royal building (14).

A principal motive in the sacrificial system of Israel was the eradication of the taint caused by sin, through presentation of sin offerings and the manipulation of the atoning blood of animals. These rites were used in instances of violation both of moral and of ritual standards, although in the codes that have survived in the Old Testament far more space is devoted to atonement for ritual than for moral impurity. Ephraimite practice may not have been identical with what is legislated in the extant (Judean) canon, but it was probably similar. Old Testament sin offerings are perhaps better dubbed expiatory than propitiatory. They aimed more at removing the evil effects of sin than at placating an angry God. After all, it was God himself, according to the tradition, who had graciously ordained the service of the altar as the means of atonement. Nevertheless, in a cult devoted

---

[5] On the aniconic character of Mosaic Yahwism, see J. Muilenburg, *The Interpreter's Bible*, Vol. 1, pp. 302 f.; H. H. Rowley, "Moses and the Decalogue," *BJRL* 34 (1951), 81–118; S. R. Driver, *The Book of Exodus* (Cambridge, 1911), pp. 413–17; and the articles on the Ten Commandments and on Idolatry in *IDB*. The opinions expressed in these works are not uniform, by any means. Because of the uncertainty concerning the relationship between the Decalogue and Covenant Code, as well as the surrounding narrative, it is impossible to be confident about the high antiquity of the former on the basis of the date of the latter. M. Noth's cautious analysis is therefore a good model (*Exodus*, Philadelphia, 1962, pp. 13, 153–55).

to a personal deity it must have been impossible to avoid the feeling that such rites forestalled the wrath of the Holy One or turned back a wrath already aroused.[6]

Hosea's indictment of the religious establishment was that it lavished attention on the rituals of atonement but totally disregarded "the weightier matters of the law," i.e., Yahweh's *torah* (teaching) (8:11–12). This *torah* was diverse and it included cultic instructions. As the infinitely instructive expression of God's will (vs. 12), however, it extended beyond the cult to every corner of Israel's corporate life. It could be said to comprehend the whole of covenantal obedience. Sin and guilt (vs. 13) were to be understood therefore in the context of a universal and radical obligation to God. Hosea's implication is that Israel had narrowed the sphere of obedience and atonement to the sacred meal and the blood sacrifice. The irony in this delusion was that their feasts effected no communion with God and their sin offerings did not touch their real guilt. This remained to be atoned for in an unwonted way (vs. 13). We are left with the ludicrous picture of Ephraim merrily indulging himself in the unblemished flesh of consecrated beasts and sanctimoniously purifying himself with their warm blood, while Armageddon was drawing near all unnoticed.

The final tool of the tyrants mentioned in this oracle is the building program of the state, especially the urban fortifications (vs. 14). Too little is said in these short lines to give us a clear understanding of Hosea's negative attitude toward these fortresses and palaces. The word translated as "palaces" also means "temples" and has frequently been taken here to mean baalized cult places.[7] It is more consistent with the rest of vs. 14, however, to think of buildings used for administrative or military purposes.[8] In this connection, there comes to mind immediately the account of Solomon's elaborate expenditures on royal buildings (1 Kings 7:1–14), as well as the bitter

---

[6] A pertinent discussion of sacrifices in general and sin offerings in particular, together with a full listing of relevant Old Testament passages and a good bibliography, may be found in the article "Sacrifices and Offerings, OT," in *IDB*, R–Z, pp. 147–59. Unfortunately, the comments made there about prophetic attitudes are superficial and likely to be misleading; the rest is helpful.

[7] Cf., Wellhausen, Sellin, and the translations of *KJV, Moffatt,* and Weiser.

[8] Cf., *ASV, Chicago, RSV, Jerusalem* Cheyne, Harper, Robinson, Wolff, and Nötscher.

catalogue of royal excesses put on the lips of Samuel by a writer of the opposition party (1 Sam. 8:11–18). The establishment cost dearly, and there was an ancient dislike for it among the northern tribes (1 Kings 12). These tribes, however, which rebelled against the Davidic dynasty, soon found themselves saddled with a royal establishment of their own. So, it is not surprising that among conservative Israelites the spirit of opposition persisted.

There is no reason to conclude from Hos. 8:14, however, that the prophet was merely a tribal conservative who longed for the simple old ways and was irrationally repelled by the life of large cities. He may not have been opposed to the cities and their fortifications at all. What he said was that Israel had forgotten God, though they had taken great pains to protect their elaborate cities and, further, that this effort was wasted, because the cities were merely going to be ruined in the coming holocaust. This was a prediction of what was about to happen and not a moral judgment of the worth of fortified cities. Israel had devoted much attention to urban protection and none to covenantal obedience. Israel's preoccupation did not make urban protection evil; it merely demonstrated where her special interests lay. Hosea's prediction showed his disdain for Israel's preoccupation with self-protection and self-aggrandizement, but it was not a condemnation either of urban civilization or of self-protection.

In the competition among Near Eastern nations, the royal state of Israel had employed many tools of self-preservation. To Hosea, she had meanwhile ceased to be the servant of the Lord and become a mere tool of larger powers, unconsciously serving their interests while consciously aping their cultures. "Israel is swallowed up . . . as a useless tool" (8:8). Did Hosea deny therefore the validity for Israel of the very principle of monarchy? This is the most vexing question raised by the oracle in chapter 8. Discussion of the problem centers naturally on vs. 4: "They have set up kings, but not by me; created princes, but without my acknowlegment." This brilliant but ambiguous condemnation has been variously referred by the interpreters to the usurper-kings of the northern kingdom in the eighth century B.C., to the schismatic northern kingdom from Jeroboam I on down, and to the institution of kingship itself. Still another theory is that the kings and princes of this passage, and others in Hosea, are cult images representative of a Canaanite king-god and his heavenly court. A well-known god of this type was Milcom (cf., Hebrew *melek,* king) of Ammon, i.e., "the King," whose proper name was probably Athtar.[9]

If Hos. 8 were concerned only with the cult and its central image, this last theory would be attractive, as it would be also for 10:1–8. However, other aspects of official life in Israel are considered in both of these oracles, especially in chapter 8. Verses 8–10, in which the same "king and princes" are mentioned, have as their subject Israel's disastrous international policy, which has made her an impotent tributary of Assyria.[10] Furthermore, vs. 14 adds a word about the national building program. It may be that chapter 8 is not a single poem, as many commentators contend, and our reference to vss. 8–10, 14 might seem to be weakened by this consideration. Yet it is precisely the alternation of cultic and political themes, throughout this chapter (be it original or editorial), that prevents us from taking the king and princes in vs. 4 as cult images.

The point of the juxtaposition of king and idol in vs. 4 is not that the idol was called "king," but that the two were similar human creations which, taken together, represented Israel's whole national life in its current degradation. Israel set up kings as she set up idols—tailor-made to her purposes. Then, paradoxically, she revered her handiwork as the embodiment of superhuman power! Her perseverance in this folly—of whose outcome Hosea was certain—made it appear as though she purposed her own destruction (vs. 4). Under the conditions of society in eighth-century Israel, the public life of the people was nearly comprehended by the few activities controlled by the king, which were largely military, plus those controlled by the

[9] For the view that only the usurpers were denounced by Hosea, see, e.g., Sellin (who cites others in his support), Robinson, and Lindblom (*op. cit.,* p. 90). For the broader theory that it was the northern kingship as a whole, see Harper (who gives a long list of like-minded scholars) and Cheyne. For the position that monarchy as such is rejected here, see Cornill (*The Prophets,* 1913, p. 57), H. W. Robinson (*Two Hebrew Prophets,* pp. 36 f.), and Cheyne (in W. R. Smith, *The Prophets of Israel,* 1895, pp. xviii f.). Nyberg is the principal advocate of the king-god interpretation (*Studien zum Hoseabuch*), but it has also been supported by H. Cazelles (*CBQ* 11 [1949], 14–25) and, with respect to some of the references in Hosea, by Danell (*op. cit.,* pp. 150 ff.), Mauchline (*The Interpreter's Bible,* Vol. 6, pp. 555–56; only in 10:3–7), and Buber (*The Prophetic Faith,* p. 122; only in 10:3–7). See the article on Molech (Moloch) in *IDB,* K–Q, pp. 422–23, for a discussion of Milcom of Ammon.

[10] If the emended text of vs. 10 ("anointing king and princes") is correct (see textual note), the political character of these offices becomes more obvious.

priesthood. The king was invested with sacred dignity, which often threatened to become idolatrous, and the cult was supported and controlled by the crown. In other words, the two creatures, king and cult image, signified the major functions of a single establishment.

In Judah, the temptation to an idolatrous regard for the king was fostered by the successful establishment of the dynastic principle and the ability of the Davidic line to keep the throne for four hundred years. In turn, success was aided by the sacral features of the royal office, which the Jerusalem court borrowed from older Semitic monarchies. Fragments of the Judean royal theology survive in the Old Testament, notably in Psalms 2, 45, 72, 89, and 110. Among the important claims of this theology were that God had granted vicegerency on earth to one family, David's, and would guarantee it forever: that this guarantee would not be rescinded on account of the sins of the incumbent: that the sovereignty granted was ultimately coextensive with the sphere of Israel's national interests: and, that the office of the king was both political and priestly. In other words, the king was Israel's protector on earth and mediator in heaven.[11]

Although the everlasting appointment could not be forfeited by breaches of office or morality, the royal house could be chastened in other ways (2 Sam. 7:14; Ps. 89:30–32). In this way, the royal covenant was made to conform, albeit superficially, to the Yahwistic tradition of a morally conditioned relationship to God. Unfortunately, chastisements short of divestiture of office, such as military invasions, were likely to be harder on the people than on the king, and nothing less than divestiture or the threat of it could effectively discipline a king, as Israel's sad experience proved. The fragmentary Old Testament record of the northern Israelite monarchy indicates, however, that its kings did not enjoy the same exaltation as their Davidic counterparts. It is impossible for us to determine which of the operative factors was the cause and which was the effect, but the facts were, first, that no northern king was able to establish a permanent, sacral dynasty and, second, that the Yahwistic, charismatic prophets played a significant role in political affairs.[12] To our knowledge, the second fact distinguished Israel from Judah as much as the first.

[11] See, especially, the following passages: 2 Sam. 7:8–16; Pss. 2:7–11; 45:2–8; 72:8–11; 89:19–37; 110.

[12] The northern revolt against Rehoboam was prophetically inspired (1 Kings 11:29–39; 12:15), as was that of Jehu against the house of Omri (2 Kings, 9:1 ff.). The role of Jehu ben Hanani in the demise of Baasha's house is less clear, though it was perhaps significant (1 Kings 16:1–3).

Hosea's protest that Yahweh had had nothing to do with the enthronement of Israel's kings could perhaps mean that the charismatic prophets had not been consulted in selecting them.[13] However, the mere fact of selection by a prophet of Yahweh did not prevent Jehu's condemnation by Hosea (1:4). It is therefore most unlikely that Hosea's appraisal of the kings in 8:4 was based on the manner of their choice. This conclusion applies just as much to selection by direct charismatic inspiration (Saul) as to selection by a prophet.[14] Control of the choice of kings by Yahwistic prophets might prevent the perpetuation of one king's policies into the reign of his successors. It could not check the policies of a king during his own lifetime, however. Samuel's eventual prophetic opposition to Saul, for instance, had no notable effect on the course of Saul's administration.

There is no question but that Hosea's ringing cry, "They have set up kings, but not by me!" is an indictment of the Israelite kingship as an opponent of the will of God. We may certainly assume that he wholly repudiated the means by which the current kings were created and destroyed. But the context of this cry makes clear that his objections went far deeper than the electoral process. On the one hand, Hosea describes the king-making people as rebels against God's covenant and law (vs. 1). They claim to be bearers of the ancient tradition: "We, Israel, have known thee" (vs. 2); that is, they are the people known by God, the ones with whom he has covenanted. But their claim is a lie. By this repudiation Hosea can only mean that they have rejected the traditional aims of the covenant, namely service of God and loyalty to the neighbor. On the other hand, Hosea links the making of kings directly to the making of idols (vs. 4). Encompassed as it is by these devastating remarks, the cry concerning the kings and princes (8:4) is as radical a repudiation of kingship as one could utter. To be sure, Hosea's words are not, "I decry the institution of kingship per se, because I believe it to be totally incompatible with convenantal ethics and faith in Yahweh." His impassioned outburst was not made to satisfy the analytical curiosity of

[13] Robinson hints at such an interpretation when he says that Hosea opposed the contemporary kings because they did not rule by God's will, and he uses Jehu as an example of one who did (in spite of Hosea's opinion of him).

[14] Wolff accepts Alt's opinion that Hos. 8:4 was spoken in behalf of a charismatic rule in opposition to a dynastic one. See Alt, *Kleine Schriften* II, p. 126. If Hosea opposed the dynastic monarchy simply because it was dynastic he did not say so in his extant oracles. The dynastic principle did not prevail in his time, anyway; quite the contrary!

modern commentators. Its thrust, however, is every bit as thorough as this other statement. What difference does it make if it leaves open the bare theoretical possibility that a king might be a proper servant of the covenant? It damns the kingship as it was known in Israel. And, this kingship was no worse than the other monarchies; so, they all stand condemned by these words. Monarchy did never prove itself a fit covenantal institution in the entire history of the people of God. Hosea denounced it in so far as he knew it. Why should any reader of Hosea seek a loophole in the prophet's reasoning to slip in a good word for the theoretical possibilities of kingship? Hosea's oracle may be rightly used as a classical instance of prophetic insight into the fundamental contradiction between covenantal community based on faith in God, and the practice of kingship.

Having taken this position with respect to the impact of Hosea's words, it is idle for us to speculate about his relative estimate of the various kings of Israel and Judah. The editors of the Books of Kings were quick to engage in this kind of analysis, and they rated all the monarchs on their purity scale. But Hosea did not share the two presuppositions of their appraisal, namely acceptance of the Davidic claim to universal hegemony in Israel and the belief in the sole legitimacy of the Jerusalem temple. Hosea's estimate of the Israelite kingship was based on its practical function as an agent of covenantal loyalty and the knowledge of Yahweh. His negative evaluation of it on this basis was not confined to single kings, but extended to the entire practice of kingship in his time. This practice was the natural fruit of the institution. Given its inherent weaknesses, it inevitably produced the policies witnessed by Hosea.

A few Judean kings were able to perform a better service to the covenant than the majority. Chief among these were Hezekiah and Josiah (2 Kings 18; 22–23). But Hezekiah failed to check the course of monarchial history even in his own lifetime, and Josiah's reform died with him. It is questionable also whether Josiah's reform may be rated as an unalloyed promotion of covenantal ethics, since it involved a widespread blood purge of nonconformists. Josiah was orthodox and he restored the cult therefore to traditional Yahwistic standards; but, he was a tyrant like all ancient kings and made use of the customary repressive measures of the absolute monarch. Ultimately, therefore, Hosea's strictures against the kings of his era apply in some measure to all the kings of Israel and Judah, and constitute, by implication, a repudiation of monarchy as a true instrument of covenantal justice.

This judgment of the force of Hosea's proclamation is confirmed, I believe, by two references to Israel's iniquity as originating "in the days of Gibeah." In 9:9, Hosea compares the current hostility between prophet and establishment to the days of Gibeah. The most natural interpretation of this comparison is that it refers to the hostility between Saul and Samuel. In other words, the monarchy from its very beginning, in Gibeah under Saul, had been corrupt in its relationship to the prophets, the defenders of Yahwism. Again, in 10:9, Hosea traces the besetting sins of the contemporary kingship back to the days of Gibeah. The context, in which he predicts the end of the Samarian monarchy (vss. 7 and 15), together with its military establishment (vss. 13–15), shows that this phrase refers to the beginning of kingship in Israel. Saul's capital, Gibeah, is thus the prototype of Samaria, or, put another way, the bad seed of a poisonous plant. Hosea was disposed to see the essential character of an institution through its particular historical embodiments, latent already in its beginning. He did this, as we have just observed, in the case of monarchy, and he did it also in the case of Israel's Palestinian cultus. He believed that it, too, had been evil from the time of Israel's settlement (cf., 9:10; 13:5–6).

If the end of a human action is already contained in its beginning, what hope is there for a community that makes a bad start? When the wind is sown, must the whirlwind always be reaped? It seems clear that Hosea believed this to be true of the major actions of Israel's national history. There was simply no escape from the consequences of these actions. We should be careful, however, not to extend this observation too far, to include areas of human experience to which it does not apply. Nevertheless, this theme recurs in Hosea's poems and is quite fundamental to his understanding of human life. If he were right, then the only hope for release from the consequences of sin would lie in forgiveness. If the chain of action cannot be broken until it has run out, then the destructive outcome of an evil action cannot be prevented, nor can it be undone, even though it can be sometimes compensated for. It can be only forgotten, that is, forgiven, if it is to be followed by creative action. Divine justice, therefore, must be rooted in love, if it is to be an instrument of creation and not of destruction. Thus, the shape of Hosea's vision of restoration (2:14–3:5; 14:2–7) is fully consonant with the profundity of his moral analysis.

10 DEATH AND DEPORTATION:
HOSEA 9

I

1   Rejoice not, O Israel;
        exult not like the peoples;
            for you have gone whoring from your God.
    You have loved a harlot's hire
        upon every threshing-floor of Dagon.
2   Threshing-floor and wine press will not feed them,
        and new wine will fail them.
3   They will not remain in Yahweh's land;
        but Ephraim will return to Egypt,
        and in Assyria they will eat unclean food.

4   They will pour out no wine to Yahweh
        nor ply him with their sacrifices,
    (Which will be) for them like mourners' bread;
        whoever eats it will be defiled.
    For their bread will be only for food;
        it will not come to the house of Yahweh.
5   (Then) what will you do on the festival day,
        on the day of the feast of Yahweh?

6   For though they flee from the desolation,
        Egypt will gather them up;
        Memphis will bury them.
    The pedestal for their silver (idol)
        the weeds will inherit.
        Thorns in their tents!
7   The days of retribution have come;
        the days of recompense are here.
        Israel will know it!

II

(The People:)
"The prophet is a fool;
    the inspired one is mad!"

(*The Prophet:*)
As great as your guilt,
    so great is your hatred.

8   The prophet is a watchman of Ephraim with my God,
    (but) a fowler's snare is on all his paths;
    there is hostility in the house of his God.

9   They have gone deep in corruption,
    as in the days of Gibeah.
    He will remember their perversion;
    he will punish their sin.

III

(*The Lord:*)
10   "Like grapes in the wilderness
    I found Israel.
    Like first figs on a young tree
    I saw your fathers.
    They came to Baal-Peor
    and consecrated themselves to Baal.
    They became loathsome
    like Ephraim's lover.

11   Their glory will fly away like a bird:
    No birth. No Pregnancy. No conception.

12   Should they bring up their sons,
    I will bereave them to a man.
    Woe to them
    when I abandon them!

13   Ephraim, as I have seen,
    has made his sons a prey.
    Ephraim must bring forth
    his sons to slaughter."

(*The Prophet:*)
14   Give them, O Yahweh—
    what will you give?
    Give them a miscarrying womb
    and dry breasts!

(*The Lord:*)
15   "All their evil was in Gilgal;
    yea, there I learned to hate them.

For the iniquity of their deeds
    I will drive them from my house.
I will no longer love them;
    all their princes are rebels.
16   Ephraim is stricken;
      their root is shrivelled;
        they can bear no fruit.
Even though they bear,
    I will kill their precious babies."

(The Prophet:)
17   My God will reject them,
      because they heed him not,
        and they will be fugitives among the nations.

NOTES ON THE TEXT

Verse 1. "Dagon" was both the grain and the Canaanite grain-god. In this context a reference to the popular worship of Dagon is quite reasonable.

Verse 4. I have taken the analogy of the mourners' bread to apply to all food that might have been used ritually, as indicated by the wine and sacrifices in the first part of this verse (cf., Wolff). An alternative is to emend לחם to לחמם (or insert לחמם in addition to להם) and translate "their bread shall be like mourners' bread (to them)" (so, e.g., *RSV, Chicago,* Sellin, Robinson, and Weiser).

Marti and Sellin regarded the last sentence in vs. 4 as a post-exilic gloss, which presupposed the fall of the Jerusalem temple (cf., Lindblom, *op. cit.,* p. 93). Robinson, however, claimed that it was written while the temple was still standing, and Harper denied that the phrase "house of Yahweh" could be restricted to the Jerusalem sanctuary at all. The grounds for deletion thus appear to be weak. Formal considerations support the retention of the line, for the first and second strophes of this section are constructed chiastically, ABBA.

Verse 5. This verse is synthetically parallel to the first line of this strophe (4a), as well as to the first line of the previous one (1a). It is better therefore to read it as the climactic line, followed by a pause, rather than put it at the head of the next strophe (as was done in *RSV* and *Chicago,* for instance).

Verse 6. This and the following verses comprise a strophe of three

160 : HOSEA: THEOLOGICAL COMMENTARY

tristichs. The fourth clause has occasioned widely divergent interpretations because of the awkward phrase "the precious thing for their silver" (מחמד לכספם). Rather than delete "their silver" (Sellin and *Chicago*), or change the text to מחמדי כספם, "their precious things of silver" (*RSV*, Wellhausen, Harper, and others), I have substituted one laryngeal for another to get מעמד ("station, standing place"; cf., Ps. 69:3, Isa. 22:19; 2 Chron. 35:15). This makes much better sense. The weeds would inherit the deserted sanctuary but certainly not its silver treasures. These would be taken as booty. There is a marked assonance among the Hebrew verbs for "gather," "bury," and "inherit," in this verse.

Verse 8. Numerous emendations of the first line have been proposed but none is required, since the MT makes sense.

Verse 10. "Baal" in the third line has been restored (along with most commentators), in place of the euphemistic "shame" (MT), which is probably editorial.

The last line of this verse consists of only three words in the MT and is too short therefore to be an independent poetic line (which requires at least four words, 2+2). Something may be lost. Alternatively, the first word of vs. 11 may be read with vs. 10, provided that the pronoun *they* is deleted (from כאהבם): "like Ephraim's lover" (*BH*, Sellin, and Mauchline). The next line would then be, "Their glory will fly away like a bird." The MT is literally, "They became loathsome like what they loved. Ephraim, their glory will fly away like a bird."

Verse 13. The MT is, "Ephraim, as I look toward Tyre, is planted in a pleasant place" (cf., *KJV, ASV, JPS*). The translation I have adopted (cf., *Chicago, Moffatt, RSV*, and most of the commentaries) follows the *LXX*. It presupposes a parallelism with the next line and involves no radical change in the text (לציד שתו לה בניה or לציד שתולה בנה for שתולה בניו).

Verse 15. The assonance in the final clause *(sarehem, sorrim)* is lost in translation.

Two SEGMENTS of chapter 9 provide the nearest thing we have to a report on Hosea's public ministry and the people's response to him. Part I concerns Israel's harvest festival and the prophet's prediction of the imminent cessation of such ritual celebrations. Because the oracle is addressed to the worshippers, it has been reasonably concluded that Hosea was present at the festival and spoke this oracle on the occasion.[1] Part II describes the public opposition to the prophet in Israel. It has been generally thought to be autobiographical and even to be the record of a heated dialogue between Hosea and the worshippers, on the occasion of the feast described in part I.[2] However uncertain these conclusions are, they seem justified by the sense of immediacy conveyed by the poems. In their turn, these inferences help to explain why the subsequent oracle is so bitter, especially the cruel petition interjected in the middle of it: "Give them a miscarrying womb and dry breasts!"

Hosea's vicious curse against a public who ridiculed him was more than a personal retaliation. According to Yahwistic belief, he filled a sacred office to which God himself had commissioned him, and public laughter at this "insane fool" (vs. 7b) was tantamount to blasphemy. His prayer was therefore partly a wish for the vindication of his vocation and the awful truths he proclaimed. Yet it is impossible to deny a measure of injured pride manifest in his curse. This illustrates the chief weakness in the Yahwistic conception of the prophetic office. The divine spokesman was so closely identified with God himself that he constantly ran the risk of confusing his personal sentiments and convictions with the will of God. Indeed, one of the remarkable facts about the canonical prophets is that their oracles contain so few private pleadings, in spite of the hazardous vocation they fulfilled.

Amos understood the prophet's responsibility as consisting in the prior disclosure of the great judgments of God in Israel's history (Amos 3:3–8). He understood his announcement as the people's opportunity to repent and thus check their headlong rush toward disaster (Amos 5:6, 14–15). In this way, the prophet exercised a kind of pastoral function, because his efforts were directed toward the people's ultimate welfare. The lofty oracles of Amos may seem to have more of a ring of righteous indignation about them, however, than a note of compassion. Thus, one is likely to think of Amos as the exemplar of moral criticism. The pastoral implications of the office emerge more fully in Hosea. His oracles of covenant-renewal represent his serious desire to support his people's faith in the constructive

---

[1] See, e.g., Sellin, Lindblom (*Hosea*, pp. 93–94), and Weiser.
[2] Cf., Wellhausen, Sellin, Weiser, and Mauchline.

love of God—a concern that may well be the supreme pastoral responsibility. His acted parable of the ransomed bride (chap. 3) is an expression of the healing office of the prophet.

Hosea's lone explicit statement about the meaning of the prophet's role is the sentence "The prophet is a watchman of Ephraim with my God" (9:8). We could wish for much more, but even this one word is extremely important. Hosea was appalled at Israel's self-betrayal in repudiating her own best hope, a hope that was latent in the words he spoke. But the people took the watchman for a spy and laughed him to impotency, to their own misfortune. The notion of the prophet as watchman is expounded with fuller logic by Ezekiel (Ezek. 3:16–21; 33:1–20). The coldness of his analysis of the ratio of prophetic to popular responsibilities demonstrates the inadequacy of the watchman-image to describe the total prophetic office. It is too impersonal, too mechanical. Nevertheless, Ezekiel's famous statement of the motive of the watchman's duty demonstrates the power of this image. It is fully consonant with the spirit of Hosea. "Say to them, 'As I live, says the Lord God, I have no pleasure in the death of the wicked, but that the wicked turn from his way and live; turn back, turn back from your evil ways; for why will you die, O house of Israel?' " (Ezek. 33:11). Other dimensions of the pastoral responsibility of the prophet remained for Jeremiah, Deutero-Isaiah, and Jesus to discover and expound. Hosea made only a beginning in this direction. Nevertheless, it was a crucial moment in the history of the idea of the covenantal mediator.

The harvest rite that provided the occasion for these oracles of Hosea was perhaps the autumnal feast of Tabernacles. This pilgrimage festival was the feast of Yahweh par excellence from the time of the settlement in Palestine. Lev. 23:43 sanctions this feast as a memorial of the exodus—wilderness era, marking the creation of Israel as the people of Yahweh. This interpretation of the event may have been much older than the Priestly Code, in which this text appears, although it is not given in the Covenant Code (Exod. 23:16) or Deuteronomy (Deut. 16:13–15).[3] A septennial renewal of the covenant

---

[3] Exod. 23:14 associates the spring feast of unleavened bread with the Exodus tradition, and Deut. 16:12 does the same with the feast of weeks. Thus, all the national festivals were celebrated at one time or another as memorials of Israel's covenantal history under Yahweh. The chances are that this was regular practice at all three feasts from an early date, in spite of the irregularity of the legal notices in the extant codes.

was enjoined upon Israel, according to Deut. 31:9–13, to take place at the feast of Tabernacles; it is clear, therefore, that it had a decisive place in Yahwism. Under the monarchy it may have had the character of a new-year festival, in which the kingship of Yahweh over creation was celebrated, together with the kingship of his vicegerent over Israel.[4] Furthermore, this festival probably played a formative role in the development and transmission of the covenantal traditions of the Pentateuch.[5] At the same time, it was a harvest festival. Whether or not the Israelite tribal confederacy adopted it from the indigenous Canaanites, as seems likely, it was subject to the usual perversions of harvest celebrations.

Hosea did not give a bill of particulars. He said in a general way that the rejoicing was harlotrous and the harlotry universal (vs. 1). However, if *Dagon* is here both a common and a proper noun, he did name one of the harlot's lovers. It is a simple matter to imagine the details. Hosea was more interested in relating the consequences than in describing the symptoms.

Israel (vss. 1 and 7) was the people who were created for Yahweh by the exodus from Egypt and the gift of the land, both of which were traditionally celebrated in the feast of Tabernacles. However, Israel had turned the feast around. The authentic motive of thanksgiving to God for land and covenant had been displaced by sensual and selfish motives and the rites degraded to the status of a bribe. In consequence, Israel's history was to be turned around as well. They would be thrown out of Yahweh's sanctuary (vs. 4), out of Yahweh's land (vs. 3), and enslaved once more (or killed) in "Egypt" (vss. 3 and 6). Bereft of the land and of the deliverance from Egypt, they could no longer celebrate the feast of Yahweh (vs. 5), by which their authentic existence ought to have been sustained. Their lives would be entirely de-sacralized (vs. 4), and their idolatrous national

---

[4] See, S. Mowinckel, *Psalmenstudien II: Das Thronbesteigungsfest Jahwäs und der Ursprung der Eschatologie* (Kristiania, 1922); A. R. Johnson, *Sacral Kingship in Ancient Israel* (Cardiff, 1955); H.-J. Kraus, *Gottesdienst in Israel: Studien zur Geschichte des Laubhüttenfestes* (Munich, 1954); H. Schmid, "Jahwe und die Kulttraditionen von Jerusalem," *ZAW* 67 (1955), 168–97.

[5] See, especially, G. von Rad, *Das formgeschichtliche Problem des Hexateuchs*, and M. Noth, *Überlieferungsgeschichte des Pentateuchs* (Stuttgart, 1948). A summary of recent studies of this and related problems, together with bibliographical references, may be found in A. Weiser, *The Old Testament: Its Formation and Development* (New York, 1961), pp. 81–99.

sanctuary, together with the pilgrims' tents at the annual festival (vs. 6), would be left to the weeds. Then Israel would know what Hosea already saw, that the days of retribution had come (vs. 7).

In calling the land of Israel "Yahweh's land," Hosea was not endorsing the popular conviction that Palestine alone was Yahweh's land and the only place where he could be properly worshipped.[6] He regarded everything that had happened on Palestinian soil as a moral disaster, and he had no desire whatever for the Palestinian cultus of Israel to continue. Even in his oracles of the new era, the land merely served as a symbol of the natural basis of communal existence. Hosea promised a second "settlement," but he did so in the same sense in which he threatened a second "captivity in Egypt." Possession of land was necessary for any people, including Yahweh's new people. Hosea did not anticipate the possibility that a religious community would go on existing permanently without a country. The historical fact that Yahweh had been worshipped only by the people who dwelt in the land of Israel gave that land a special significance. But this de facto "sanctity" of the land was not matched by any attribution of de jure sanctity on Hosea's part. Yahweh's "house" was first of all his people and only secondarily the land of their habitation, the place where their covenantal service of God was rendered. Therefore, the cessation of the Israelite cult during the exile was not an evil that had to be borne because Canaan was the only legitimate cult-place. It was a positive good, the purging of a debauched system. Hosea regarded the exile primarily as the result of the cult's corruption and not as the mere occasion of its cessation, although it was that, too.

These remarks bring us directly to the question of the relationship between sin and punishment in this oracle. Older commentators interpreted the failure of the threshing-floor and the wine press (vs. 2) as the result of a drought, and thus attributed to Hosea the conviction that moral evil was punishable by physical means.[7] I would not deny that Hosea held the same voluntaristic conception of nature that was generally held by ancient man. Presumably he believed, as Amos did,

[6] Cf., Ps. 137, for example. Jeremiah's contemporaries disbelieved his teaching that they could worship Yahweh in Babylonia (Jer. 29). Like Naaman the Syrian (2 Kings 5:17), they believed they needed Palestinian soil on which to worship him.

[7] See Harper's comment on the older consensus. Weiser supports this interpretation, essentially, when he says in his comment on 9:2 that, since God orders nature, nature turns against him who sins against God.

for instance, that natural phenomena conformed to the will of God, and that God could, and did, use them to punish sin.[8] Yet nowhere in the Book of Hosea is there a simple natural phenomenon put forward as a direct divine punishment for Israel's sin. Examples of this sort of voluntarism, which a modern man might call an interventionist view of God's reationship to the physical world, are not found in Hosea's oracles. Therefore, although he may well have shared the ancient perspective in this instance, it was not important in his preaching.

Throughout his oracles, Hosea describes social results of social causes. He does not introduce non-moral factors into his analysis of the justice of God. The coming desolation of the land is the result of military invasion, deportation, and the cessation of national institutions, such as state maintenance of the sanctuaries and urban defenses. These were the immediate causes of harvest failure, the cessation of pilgrimage feasts, and the despoiling of the sanctuaries. The ultimate causes were the corporate behavior of Israel and the righteous will of God, whose justice was executed within the dynamics of human history. Israel's invasion and collapse were the consequence, and therefore the punishment, of her political policies. The end of her public worship was the fitting reward for a decadent ritual system. Her loss of the land was the appropriate result of her misuse of its opportunities. To interpret Hosea's meaning in this way is not to say that he believed all human behavior was justly rewarded within the historical process. Nothing so general is suggested in his oracles; they treat only the particular situation of Israel in his own epoch and presuppose the existence of Israel's covenantal relationship with God. Similar analyses may be made of other communities in other times and circumstances, but the task of formulating a general ethical theory lies beyond the scope of exegesis, and it is not legitimate to read one into Hosea's oracles.

Part II of the chapter contains another of Hosea's remarkable psychological insights. It is that the people's hatred of him was a manifestation of their guilt (vs. 7b). This is a highly suggestive statement, which may mean at least two things. The more obvious of the two is that the people's hateful persecution of Hosea and their spurning of his message were themselves great evils, since he was

---

[8] See, Amos 4:6, 7, 9, 10. Even here, the prophet describes the natural catastrophe more as an occasion for repentance than as a punishment for sin.

the mediator of God's word to them. The other is that their hatred was the product of their guilt. In their effort to hide their bad conscience, the people placed the onus of their heedlessness on Hosea, by accusing him of being mentally unbalanced. Thus, they saved themselves from having to reckon with his proclamation. He was dismissed as insane and irrelevant. Their responsibility under the covenant was thus set aside, together with their former guilt. Hosea's response included the observation that God would not forget as easily as they did (vs. 9)! What Hosea did not say here was that this need to hide their guilt, while it complicated the problem of their reformation enormously and even compounded their guilt, was an evidence, nevertheless, of their residual moral sensitivity. A completely immoral man, if such a man could exist, would not need to hide his guilt behind this sort of attack. The necessity that Hosea's hearers felt of justifying their neglect of his preaching was, therefore, both a perversion and a testimony to the moral vitality still latent within them. Might not their forthcoming punishment then be both a divine judgment upon their perversion as well as a means of their redemption? The answer, of course, depended on what happened to this residual morality when the mask of self-deceit was finally stripped away.

Ernst Sellin made the interesting suggestion in connection with 9:7b–9 that it was the people's refusal to allow Hosea access to the temple and its assemblies that made him a *writer* of oracles. His persecution consisted chiefly in being denied a prophet's right to speak. Sellin's thesis is quite attractive. Amos was expelled from the vicinity of the national cult-center in Bethel during Jeroboam's reign (Amos 7:10–13), and Hosea's reception there (and elsewhere) would surely have been no warmer during the reigns of Jeroboam's wretched successors. Futhermore, many of Hosea's poems seem too carefully fashioned and too long to have originated in oral address. If this theory is correct, we may owe the creation of much of the Book of Hosea, and the preservation of it all, to the hostility encountered by the prophet "in the house of his God" (9:8). Isaiah's public rejection led him to "bind up the testimony" in writing (Isa. 8:16), and Jeremiah's persecution by the later officials of Judah made him resort to the scroll as a vehicle of prophecy (Jer. 36). Thus a great good entered the history of Yahwistic tradition on the back of evil.

Hosea was preoccupied by the continuities of Israel's history. He constantly sought analogies to the present in the past and the roots of present behavior in that of former times, especially in case of evil. It was is if Israel had not changed for generations. This rhetorical use of historical memories is an effective means of ethical criticism. It is easier to recognize the sins of one's ancestors than one's own but, having acknowledged those of the ancestors and his own solidarity with them, one can the better recognize his own follies.

There are four historical allusions in chapter 9: one in part II and three in part III. Since the last three are less problematical than the first, I will speak about part III first. It is a grisly prophecy of the slaughter and deportation of Ephraimites in the coming day of punishment. It is a description of the end of the nation's life. In the last line, Hosea predicts that the exiles will be fugitives among the nations (vs. 17). Thus, Israel's history, which began with the creation of a covenant people out of wandering tribes, will have come full circle. This will be a return to the "wilderness," where Yahweh first found them, in the events recalled by the opening lines of the oracle (vs. 10).[9] Hosea's recollection of the wilderness meeting between God and Israel is followed immediately by another, the worshipping of Baal of Peor, which marked the next phase of Israel's history (Num. 25:1–5). Here was the sign of Israel's abiding infidelity, the mark of the apostate people. Her end was already in her beginning. The death and deportation of the eighth century were the harvest of the seeds sown then.

This historical analogy in the first part of the oracle is complemented toward the end by another allusion to the past: "All their evil was in Gilgal, for there I learned to hate them" (vs. 15) (because "they became loathsome like Ephraim's lover," vs. 10). Gilgal can only mean the point of entry into western Palestine, which marked the beginning of Ephraim's permanent settlement in the land (Josh. 4). Any other interpretation is excluded by the next line, "I will drive them from my house." Ephraim will be driven from the land, and the evil that began in Gilgal will be justly punished. This designation of the land as Yahweh's house is also found in 8:1, where an alarm is raised for the approaching invasion. On the other hand, the same phrase is used in a narrower sense in 9:4, where it means the

[9] It makes no difference here whether the people were to be forcibly exiled or were to flee voluntarily before the invaders. Hosea seems to have assumed that both kinds of departure would take place (vs. 6).

sanctuary. At first glance, 9:8 seems also to refer to the temple. Yet, perhaps a double meaning is intended here (and even in 9:4). Israel's land was the place of God's covenantal presence, his "sanctuary" (cf., Exod. 15:17), for it was there that he condescended to be with his people. This presence was symbolically concentrated upon the sanctuary, so that the latter became the house of God in a derivative way. Either of these meanings will make sense in 9:4 and 9:8; but, in 9:15-17 Hosea prophesies expulsion from the land, that is, the reversal of the settlement that took place in Joshua's time.[10]

Gilgal played another role in Israel's early history, which is also brought to mind by Hosea's remark. According to one of the traditions incorporated in 1 Samuel, Saul was made king at Gilgal (1 Sam. 11:14–15), and it was there that he was rejected by Samuel for disobedience to the Lord (1 Sam. 13:8–15; 15:10–29). Samuel's famous speech on the day when "the Lord tore the kingdom of Israel" from Saul (15:28) is so much like Hosea's oracle in 6:6 that one suspects literary dependence between the two texts. Samuel said to Saul, "Has the Lord as great delight in burnt offerings and sacrifices, as in obeying the voice of the Lord? Behold, to obey is better than sacrifice, and to hearken than the fat of rams" (1 Sam. 15:22). Hosea said to Israel, "I crave sure love and not sacrifice, the knowledge of God, rather than burnt offerings." When Hosea says in the oracle before us that "all their evil was in Gilgal," and continues, "I will no longer love them; all their princes are rebels" (9:15), the inference is almost inevitable that he was pointing to the fulfilment in his own day of the royal apostasy begun by Saul.[11]

To trace the evils of the present time to their roots in the time of national beginnings is to reject the very institutions that characterize

[10] Cf., Harper and Knight. The theory that 9:15 refers to particular ritual crimes in Gilgal (Wellhausen) gives an esoteric meaning to the passage, though if "my house" meant the temple of Yahweh, this interpretation would not be unreasonable. Scott (*op. cit.*, pp. 61–62) thought the sin must have been child sacrifice, and Lindblom (*op. cit.*, pp. 95–96), the regicides of Hosea's time (Gilgal, he said, was not at the Jordan, but near Shechem, citing 6:8–9, where he reads Gilgal for Gilead, and 12:11). In answer to the first, we may ask whether the slaughter of Ephraim's children in the invasion (vs. 16) would have been, for Hosea, a fitting punishment for child sacrifice? Was Hosea that callous? In reply to the second, we may doubt whether such an obscure allusion is as probable as the one advocated above.

[11] See, Cheyne, Sellin, and Weiser. Robinson cannot decide between the entry into Canaan and the coronation of Saul as the intended meaning of this allusion, and Mauchline believes it points to both.

the nation. If all the evil of their Palestinian system of worship was adumbrated in its initial phases, then the system itself was evil. If *all their evil* was already present, in principle and prototype, in the kingship of Saul, then the monarchy itself was evil.

If we move now from these considerations back to part II of the chapter, we are in a position of interpreting the difficult phrase "in the days of Gibeah" (9:9). Two historical occasions command our attention, the intertribal war over Benjamin's rape of the Levite's concubine, described in Judg. 19–20, and the establishment of Saul's capital in Gibeah (1 Sam. 10:26; 14:2, 22:6; etc.). There are three reasons why the second is a better choice than the first as the object of Hosea's reference. The first is that it provides a better analogy to the corruption with which the oracle is concerned. The second is that it is far more likely to have been a matter of common knowledge among Hosea's audience. The third is that it conforms to Hosea's habit of tracing institutionalized evil back to the historical beginning of the institution.

The evil that this oracle decries is Ephraim's hostility toward the prophet, a hatred that is the expression of guilt. And, although the poem does not say it, it is understood that prophets are persecuted because of their proclamations—the covenantal teaching they defend and the divine acts they announce. Neither of the situations that made Gibeah notorious, according to the extant traditions, is identical with that of Hosea, for neither involves the persecution of a prophet by his compatriots. Nevertheless, the account of Saul's conflict with Samuel provides an excellent analogy. The essence of that story is that the charismatic, prophetic, covenantal tradition in Israel, represented by Samuel, had come into conflict with the monarchy, embodied in Saul, and had become subordinated to the new kingship and its needs. In the story as we have it, Saul surrenders to Samuel, even though it is too late. This, however, is a doubtful feature of the tradition. Hosea may have known quite another version, in which the details varied considerably (there are at least two different versions combined in the narrative as it is). Yet we can be fairly sure that whatever version he might have known would have preserved the recollection of the fundamental conflict between the two orders represented by Saul and Samuel respectively. This conflict was the same that Hosea experienced in his time.[12]

There is no parallel to this conflict in the story of the Levite and

[12] Incidentally, Samuel was an Ephraimite (1 Sam. 1:1)!

his concubine and the ensuing tribal war. The Levite was merely passing through Gibeah and became the private victim of lawless men. He was not a prophet and he made no public pronouncements. Nor can we find an analogy to Hosea's experience if we look at the narrative of Judg. 19–20 from the perspective of the war between Benjamin and the avenging tribes. That war was a great evil, to be sure, a terrible breakdown of covenantal loyalty among the tribes. However, unlike the story of Samuel and Saul, it provides no specific parallel to Hosea's situation.

Secondly, it is much more likely that Hosea's audience was acquainted with the tradition about Saul and Samuel, rather than with the one about the Levite's concubine, because the former was more recent and was concerned with a matter far more relevant to the affairs of the eighth century. If his audience had known both of these traditions, they probably would have thought at once of Saul in this connection, again because of the story's pertinence. Finally, if neither of these stories were known to Hosea's audience, the phrase "days of Gibeah" would certainly have meant to them the time when the center of the kingdom was at Gibeah, for the people would have had at least that much knowledge of Israel's history.

The third consideration is related to the first but is somewhat different. Hosea's historical allusions do not merely illustrate a contemporary episode by comparing it with another episode from the past. Rather, they point to the continuity of social institutions and corporate practices, backward through history to their origins in the past. The rape of the Levite's concubine and the resulting war of vengeance were isolated, unique incidents. They illustrate the wickedness of man as man, as well as the horrors of ancient tribal justice. They do not illuminate, however, the particular corporate evils that Hosea found in his own community. On the other hand, Saul's kingship was the historical antecedent of the current state in Israel, and the problems with which Hosea and his contemporaries had to cope were first set on foot in Saul's days at Gibeah.

Hosea's dreadful picture of the slaughter of Ephraimite children in part III, is an amalagam of historical realism and moral outrage, held together by the conviction that Yahweh was the Lord of nations, as well as the Lord of the covenant people. Hosea's realism was based on knowledge of what happened to the populations of conquered nations in his time. Such a disaster would surely descend upon the people of Israel when the nation fell to the coming invader. Hosea's outrage was a response to the baalization of Israel's life, which he discerned in every significant quarter. He may have been wrong—at least we are repelled by the thought that he could have been right—when he described the murder of Israelite babies as the direct act of a wrathful God. We may avoid the repugnant attribution of those deaths to God, and we may apologize for Hosea's intemperate cry of indignation: yet, ultimately, we must reckon with the fact that if God is the Lord of history, in some way he must be the Lord of such dreadful things as Hosea's oracles describe, even though he is not the one who wills them to happen. The struggle between Yahweh and Israel on the stage of history was a total contest the terms of which were the actualities of corporate existence and the issue of which was life or death.

The last line of chapter 9 comes as an anticlimax to the absolute terror of the previous acts of the drama, but it is a welcome anticlimax. It is the prophecy of deportation from the land of Israel. This is welcome in that it shows that Hosea's prophecy of the annihilation of Ephraim was exaggerated. Small comfort to those who would perish under Assyrian swords! But it was a realistic appraisal of the probabilities, just the same. It stands formally somewhat apart from the preceding strophe, and its mood is entirely different. It is a somber reflection on the last phase of the tragedy of the kingdom of Israel, and it sums up the prophet's entire estimate of the kingdom's history and character. This kingdom had been a violation of the covenant with Yahweh, and so it was rejected as his instrument in the world. Therefore, it would come to an end in the scattered fragments of a disintegrated people.

CHAPTER

11 THE IMMINENT DESTRUCTION
OF BETHEL AND SAMARIA:
HOSEA 10

I

1   Israel is a luxuriant vine
         and luscious is his fruit.
     So rich his fruit,
         so many his altars.
     So good his land,
         so great his sacred pillars.
2   Their heart is divided;
         now they must pay the penalty:
     He will level their altars
         and smash their pillars.

3   But now they are saying,
         "We have no king.
     "For we don't fear Yahweh;
         and the king, what does he do for us?"
4   They mouth words,
         swearing empty oaths,
             making covenants.
     But judgment will sprout like deadly weeds
         along the furrows of a field.

5   They tremble for the calf of "Beth-evil,"
         those Samaritans.
     So lament him, O his people,
         and you, his priestlings!
     Let them chant over his glory,
         when he is carted away.
6   The thing itself will be carried to Asshur,
         as an offering to the "Great King!"

     Shame will Ephraim garner,
         shame for Israel's rebellion.

7 Samaria's king is silenced
      like a chip on the waves.
8 The high places of Aven will be ruined,
      the sin of Israel.
   Thorn and thistle
      will go up onto their altars!
   And they will say to the mountains, "Cover us!"
      and to the hills, "Fall on us!"

II

(The Indictment and Threat:)
9 From the days of Gibeah
      Israel has sinned.
   Then they thought that war
      would not reach them in Gibeah!
   I will punish the sons of iniquity
10   when I please;
   And peoples will be gathered against them,
      when I punish them for their double guilt.

11 Ephraim is a trained heifer
      who loves to thresh;
   But I have mounted
      upon her fair neck.
   I will ride Ephraim;
      Israel will plow;
         Jacob will harrow for himself!

(The Wish:)
12 "Sow justice for yourselves;
      reap the fruit of loyalty;
         till your fallow ground;
   For it is time to seek Yahweh,
      until he comes
         to teach you justice."

(The Fact:)
13 You have sown rebellion!
      you have reaped injustice!
         you have eaten the fruit of lies!
   For you have trusted in your chariots,
      in the host of your mighty men.

14   And a tumult is rising among your people,
      and all of your fortresses will be ruined.

(The Result:)
      As Shalman destroyed Beth-arbel
        on the day of battle
          —mothers were dashed against their children!—
15   So will he do to you, O Bethel,
      because of your wretched sin.
      At dawn the king of Israel
        will be utterly put to silence!

NOTES ON THE TEXT

Verse 1. The adjective בּוֹקֵק means either "sending out shoots wantonly" (*ASV, Moffatt, Chicago, RSV,* and many commentators) or "stripped bare" (Torczyner, *BZAW* 41 [1925], 278; and Knight). *Köhler* suggests "degenerating." The second line is literally "the fruit was equal to it." The image seems to be that of a lush vine running to rankness. The following lines militate against the meaning "empty" or "stripped," even though this is a reasonable deduction from the root בקק.

Verse 2. "Yahweh" (יהוה) should perhaps be substituted for "he" (הוא) (Lindblom, *Hosea,* p. 97, and *RSV).* In any case, this is what the pronoun means.

Verse 5. The MT has "calves," but the antecedent of the following pronouns is properly singular. On "Beth-evil," see the textual note to 4:15.

Verse 6b. Reading עצה ("disobedience, rebellion"), with G. R. Driver (*Nötscher Festschrift,* Bonn, 1950), p. 54, and not עצה ("counsel"). "Of his idol" (מעצבו) is a common emendation (*Moffatt, Chicago, RSV,* Wellhausen, Sellin, Weiser, and others).

Verse 8. "Go up" (עלה) is the verb generally used for the presentation of offerings upon the altar. The irony is less obvious in English.

"Aven" (i.e., "Evil") and "sin" may be the products of later scribal pedantry (thus, Wellhausen, Cheyne, Robinson, Sellin, Nowack, Marti, and Harper). Their removal leaves "The high places of Israel will be ruined." See the textual note to 4:15.

Verse 9. The MT reads, "There they stood" (עמדו). The relatively simple change to "they said" (אמרו) is made by *Chicago*. This expedient makes the best sense of the line. The more usual translation, "There they have stood (stayed, continued). Shall not war overtake them in Gibeah" (*Moffatt, RSV,* Nötscher, Sellin, and others) also entails a textual change (הלא for לא). שם is usually translated "there" in this passage. The reference is to the "days of Gibeah," however, and this is better conveyed in English by "then" (cf., Harper). The point is that the kingdom of Israel felt militarily secure during the time when its center was at Gibeah, i.e., under Saul. When שם is translated "there," as a reference to the place, the sentence becomes redundant: "There (i.e., in Gibeah) they thought that war would not reach them in Gibeah." For a general discussion of the phrase "days of Gibeah," see the treatment of 9:9, above.

Verse 10. The first two words are literally, "when I desire, I will bind them" (באותי ואסרם). This clause is joined to the last phrase of vs. 9 (*RSV, Chicago,* Duhm, Sellin, Mauchline, Wolff), with ואסרם emended to ואיסרם (*Köhler, Moffatt, RSV, Chicago,* Harper, and others). Many scholars also emend the preceding verb to "when I come" (באתי) (*RSV, Chicago, LXX,* Wolff, Robinson, and others).

Verse 11. Literally, "I have passed over upon her fair neck." "Mounted" goes well with the following sentence. "I have placed a yoke upon her fair neck" (*Moffatt,* Sellin, Weiser, Mauchline and others) and "I spared her fair neck" (*RSV,* Harper, Cheyne, Brown, and others) require textual changes and yield a poorer meaning. The question is not whether riding on a heifer was a common practice (presumably it was not) but merely what the Hebrew says and whether it makes sense. It does. Gods rode animals in ancient iconography, incidentally. What we have in Hosea's image is a far cry, however, from the popular models of Baal-on-a-bull.

The MT reads "Judah" in the next-to-last clause, but the parallel, "Jacob," shows that originally it must have been "Israel" (thus, *Jerusalem,* Nowack, and Harper). Some scholars merely delete "Judah must plow" (Weiser, Nötscher, Robinson, Sellin, Mauchline, and others). But "Israel" must have stood in the text before the Jacob-clause was written, because "Jacob" is not simply parallel to "Ephraim." For the parallelism "Ephraim//Israel//Jacob," cf. Isa. 9:8–9. The Judean editor of Hosea has apparently changed "Israel" to "Judah." Compare, however, Ephraim//House of Israel//Judah, in 11:12, and Judah//Jacob, in 12:2.

Verse 12. The Hebrew verb (וירה) in the last clause has been interpreted to mean either "to rain" (*Chicago, Jerusalem, RSV*, Sellin,
Brown, and others) or "to teach" (Syriac, Targum, Vulgate, Robinson, Weiser, Nötscher, and others). The former is less appropriate in
this passage and also requires a slight textual alteration (to וירוה).
Some scholars have accepted the *LXX*'s reading: "Until the fruit
(פרי) of righteousness comes to you" (Wellhausen, Nowack, Harper,
and Wolff, among others). In the last sentence, צדק may mean "one's
right," and thus "victory" or "salvation" (*Moffatt, RSV*, Brown, and
Cheyne), rather than "justice." But "righteousness" (*KJV, ASV,
Chicago,* and many others) or "justice" (Köhler, *Lexicon,* p. 794) is
certainly the meaning in the first sentence of the verse, and probably
in the repetition at the end as well. If the Masoretic verb is ירה
("instruct"), the choice is a clear one.

Verse 13. Read "chariots" (רכביך), with the *LXX* (*Moffatt, Chicago, RSV,* Harper, Brown, Wolff, Sellin, and many others), instead
of "way" (דרכך), with the MT.

Verse 14. Although there is no versional support for the change,
some commentators emend "your people" (עמך) to "your cities"
(עריך) (Wellhausen, Sellin, Nötscher, and Robinson). This forms a
far better parallel to "fortresses" and is therefore an attractive suggestion.

A few ancient witnesses substitute "Jeroboam" for "Arbel" (cf.,
Ziegler, *Septuaginta,* p. 171), a reading that is accepted by *BH,*
Procksch (*Theologie,* p. 152), Cheyne, and Sellin. These men also
take the Hebrew as a reference to Shallum (reading שלום for שלמן).
It would be convenient to have such a citation of a contemporary
event (cf., 2 Kings 15:10), but it is difficult to imagine how such a
simple text could have been changed to the cryptic reference to
Shalman and Beth-arbel.

Verse 15. "Beth ('House of')-Israel" is preferred by many scholars
to "Bethel." The *LXX* supports this reading, but one wonders
whether the Greek translator did not accommodate this word to
"people" in the first line. If "cities" were correct for vs. 14, "Bethel"
would be clearly better in vs. 15.

The Hebrew of the second clause is literally, "because of the
wickedness of your wickedness." Wolff follows the *LXX* in omit-
ting the repetition, but this sort of superlative is characteristic of
Hosea (cf., 7:2; 9:7, 15).

"At dawn" (בשחר) has been emended to "in the storm" (בשער,
e.g., *RSV*, Wellhausen, Weiser, Robinson), or "in the gate" (בשער,
BH), or "with soldiers" בשכיר, Riessler, cited by Sellin), or "as
through magic" (כשחר, Sellin). None of these commends itself
especially.

A PRETENTIOUS CULT, a futile kingship, and a pathetic idol are
the themes of the two oracles in Hos. 10. We have long since come to
know these as the prophet's preoccupying concerns; they recur over
and over in the book. Part I of the present chapter combines the three
in splendid fashion. A strophe is given to each of them in turn, and
a fourth strophe combines all three. The first three strophes are
identically constructed, with several lines of invective followed by
a single line of threat. The closing strophe is appropriately threatening throughout. Note that the four consist of five, four, four, and
five lines, respectively.

Part II opens and closes with prophecies of military defeat for the
kingdom (9–10 and 14b–15). In the middle are two brief metaphorical strophes. Their images are related: the working heifer (11) and
the farmer (12). The first is a self-contained oracle, since it includes
both an accusation and a threat of punishment. The second could
also stand alone as a prophetic saying or *torah* (instruction) It is one
of the most quotable sayings in the prophetic literature. What follows
is a bitter parody of this saying, which leads into the final prediction
of disaster (13–14a).

I

Looked at naively, Israel's ecclesiastical development in Palestine
was a noble thing. Theistic Yahwism was built on man's grateful response to the free gifts of God, and the multiplication of altars was
the logical means of providing the universal opportunity for frequent
ritual expressions of Israel's gratitude to God for the land. The
land's fruits were not merely physical; they included the opportunity
of creating a just social order and of pursuing the highest arts of
man. Therefore, the advancement of the cult, which accompanied the
exploitation of the land, made it possible to keep the whole culture
oriented toward Yahwistic objectives. Indeed, this orientation could

not have been achieved for the society as a whole or long maintained, without an extensive and diversified system of worship. Still,
Hosea finds nothing to commend in the actual Israelite system.

In the present oracle (10:1–8), he forces us to guess at the substantive grounds of his opposition. Were the sacred pillars *maṣṣe-
both*, vs. 1) being used as fetishes? Were all the high places (vs. 8)
baalized? He does not say. Has he condemned the entire system
because of the aberrations at the national center in Bethel? One
infers as much from his special mention of this place, derogatively
called Beth-aven ("House of Evil"), and Aven ("Evil"), in the last
two strophes (vss. 5 and 8), and from his combination of royal and
cultic motifs in the oracle.

One of the cultic aberrations was the idolatry of the calf, to which
we were introduced in Hos. 8. But the image alone can hardly account for Hosea's sweeping dismissal of the whole cultic edifice.
Therefore, we turn to the only other clue that he provides in the
poem before us: "Their heart is divided; now they must pay the
penalty" (vs. 2a).[1] This word does not give us sufficient descriptive
information about Israel's ritual practices to judge their validity for
ourselves, but it gives us something that no amount of descriptive
information could provide. It diagnoses the hidden malady of the
contemporary cultus and declares it to be a disease of the will. This
is a judgment that cannot be made at second hand. It requires direct
participation. Thus, even if Hosea had supplied us with a full account
of the phenomena of public worship, we would still have had to rely
upon his opinion about the motives that inspired it. He said they
were false.

His accusation recalls statements by other radical monotheists
such as "No one can serve two masters" (Matt. 6:24), or "Purity
of heart is to will one thing."[2] The falsity of Israel's worship lay in
the absence of a dominating, unifying will to serve God and to
recognize his lordship in every act. Worship pursued for any other
objective is futile, self-defeating, and finally unacceptable to God.

---

[1] The last word is אשם, which might be here translated "atone" (cf.,
Chicago). The sense of the line is that a penalty must be paid for the sin
committed. See, T. H. Gaster's discussion of אשם in *IDB*, R–Z, p. 152.
Some English versions render the verb here "be found guilty" (cf., *KJV,
ASV*). This is not adequate. "Bear their guilt" (*JPS, RSV*) is better, though
ambiguous. *Moffatt*'s "suffer for it" is good.

[2] Kierkegaard, S., *Purity of Heart is to Will One Thing* (New York, 1938).

Hosea promised the definite end of Israel's cult, because it was not single-minded. Under the circumstances of his time, this outward destruction was the likely result of duplicity of heart, because ritual and politics were interdependent. Under most other circumstances, the consequences would be far less obvious. Nevertheless, Hosea's insight is perhaps universally valid, in a more subtle and inward way.

Is any worshipper's heart undivided? If not, is there any legitimate worship? Is it possible to make atonement by confession and contrition and thus to neutralize the evil, even though one worships with a divided heart? Are there no legitimate secondary motives for worship, either moral or aesthetic? It is a pity that the compact oracles of the prophets do not give us a "biblical" solution to such perennial problems of the covenant community.

The second strophe of this oracle (vss. 3–4) contains no clearly useful, additional data for an exposition of Hosea's theology and ethics. If the current consensus of the interpreters is correct, these lines merely reaffirm what we have learned of his view of the monarchy from previous oracles. If it is not, then the meaning is too obscure, or the material is too un-Hosean to be used with any confidence. The leading theory about 10:3–4 at the present time is that it presupposes the general state of dynastic confusion that prevailed in the Israelite kingdom during its last two decades.[3] The people are quoted as repudiating their trust in either Yahweh or the temporal king and are accused, apparently, of seeking security in whatever momentary alliance is expedient, instead. The outcome is, naturally, disastrous (vs. 4).

Another treatment of the passage makes the people's word an affirmation of the temporal king and not a repudiation: "But now they are saying, 'Have we not a king?'" The Hebrew mark of interrogation is absent here, but it is often omitted (especially in poetry) in lines that are nevertheless interrogatory. If this translation is preferred, one of two further courses is open. One may take the next lines as Hosea's reply, namely, "But they don't fear Yahweh.

[3] See, Sellin, Robinson, Weiser, Knight, and Mauchline. Some commentators believe this passage comes from the time when Israel's withholding of tribute to Assyria (i.e., Israel's "false oaths," vs. 4) led to the imprisonment of king Hoshea (2 Kings 17:3–4). Cf., Scott, *The Message of Hosea,* p. 63; Brown; and Knight. This interpretation makes the false oaths and alliances the cause of the people's being without a king. Alternatively, the former may represent the intrigue that undermined a given king's control. I prefer the former view for reasons given below (pp. 185 f. and notes).

And the king, what can he do for them?" Here the text must be altered to yield third-person pronouns.[4] Or, on the other hand, one may delete these lines as a later editor's comment.[5] The simplest exegetical solution, as always, is to throw out the whole passage.[6]

In none of these cases do we encounter any obstacle to our previous explication of the theology of Hosea's poems. One other theory ought to be mentioned, however, which would cast doubt on what I have already said about Hosea's estimate of the monarchy. According to many older commentators, the statement "We have no king" does not mean simply that there is no one on the throne; rather, it means a repudiation of the schismatic northern kingdom.[7] Had the people properly feared God they would have remained loyal to their true, Davidic, king and not incurred their just punishment in the present chaos and impotency (vs. 3b). This interpretation requires that we understand the people's words as a confession to which they have been forced by the failure of the Israelite kingship.[8] Even if the statement meant this, however, we would be hard pressed to find endorsement of the opinion in Hosea's following words. For this reason, and because of the general exegetical confusion that surrounds the whole passage, there is nothing here that could legitimately alter our previous interpretation of Hosea's oracles concerning the monarchy. So many constructions of 10:3–4 can be produced by means of combinations of alternative translations and emendations of the text, that we could prove anything from it, and therefore nothing.

The last two strophes of the oracle explain themselves. I merely wish to call attention to the ironies in Hosea's picture of the futile cult of Bethel. He shows us its adherents, led by their priests in an absurd procession, lamenting the removal of the golden image after the fashion of popular laments for the dead vegetation god, Tammuz (vss. 5–6). At the end, he describes the silent altars in the abandoned ruins, with no offering upon them but the climbing weeds (vs. 8). A pathetic end for a pretentious kingdom and its sacred institutions.

---

[4] See, *Moffatt*, for example.
[5] Cf., Sellin.
[6] Thus, Nowack, Marti, and Harper.
[7] Harper cites Hitzig, Pusey, Keil, and others.
[8] Harper contended that all eighth-century Israelites would have thought themselves fearers of Yahweh and that this statement must therefore be exilic in date. Since we know nothing about the thoughts of most Israelites of the eighth century, or of those of the exile for that matter, this argument is not especially forceful.

II

Saul's kingdom was little more than an armed camp with an obligation to defend the victims of Philistine aggression in central Palestine. Saul failed even in this limited mission, but the three hundred years that intervened between the tragic career of the son of Kish, the Benjaminite, and the last kings of Ephraim, brought larger goals and notable successes to the kingdom of Israel, both under the united monarchy of David and Solomon, and under the separate hegemony of the northern kings. The historian, reading between the lines of the Old Testament, and the archaeologist, drawing upon extra-biblical sources, are able to describe positive contributions of the Israelite kingdom to the welfare of its citizens during three centuries; but the writings of the son of Beeri, the only ones of known Israelite origin to survive the kingdom's fall, do not contain a single word of appreciation or one note of gratitude for its achievements. Hosea's silence is the measure of his uncompromising zeal for Yahweh. He reduced the three-hundred-year-old history of the kingdom to a syllogism: "From the days of Gibeah Israel has sinned . . . (God) will punish the sons of iniquity when (he) pleases . . . Therefore, . . . at dawn the king of Israel will be utterly put to silence!" (10:9–10, 14–15). Thus the destiny of the last Israelite king would repeat the fate of the first. But in his death, the kingdom, too, would die, and so the tragic experiment with "a king . . . like . . . the nations" (1 Sam. 8:5) would be finished. The kingship that had begun as an effort to preserve the integrity of Israel by preventing her military conquest destroyed her integrity and then lost her independence. A tolerable military security was maintained throughout much of her history, but her integrity was ultimately compromised to that security. After the moral and religious accommodations had been made to the nations, under the exigencies of diplomacy, it was a matter of indifference for the preservation of the covenantal community whether Israel's national independence was maintained. As it turned out, that too was lost in the international power struggles of the eighth century.

Hosea interpreted the final destruction of the kingdom by military conquest as the just punishment for the compromise of Israel's religious integrity and for the misconceived effort to preserve "Israel" by competing in the military and diplomatic plots of the monarchs.

The very effort to engage in the struggle presupposed a misunderstanding of what it meant to be Israel. We may ask, however, whether this insight was available at the time the monarchy was established in Israel, or whether it came only to men like Hosea and only by hindsight at that? Many who study Israel's history and the development of her theology will be inclined to consider the second conclusion more probable. If this is the case, any indictment of the creators of the Israelite kingship is unfair. Even an indictment of subsequent generations is unfair, because it wrongly assumes that they could have reversed the course of history and rid themselves of the monarchial institutions if they had wished to do so. However, the prophet is not detained by such considerations. His unitary characterization of the Israelite kingdom from Saul to Hoshea (or whoever was king when he wrote this oracle) as a thing of rebellion, iniquity, and lies (vs. 13), is based on the assumption that her leaders, from the first to the last, were morally responsible for the decisions they made, and that their decisions shaped the course of her life more than they were shaped by forces beyond their control.

I have used Hosea's allusion to the days of Gibeah as a symbol of the kingdom's beginning under Saul.[9] This view is not particularly popular today and so I must comment on the one that is, namely, that the reference is to the murder of the Levite's concubine and to the retaliatory war against the tribe of Benjamin in Judg. 19–20.[10] Let us admit at once that Hosea could have been thinking of that event (or some other we know nothing about). Had he been, then the point of the comment was that Israel's life had been marked by grievous breaches of covenantal (nay, common human) morality, like the sex-murder of the Levite's woman and the civil war that followed. Further, that as the brother tribes had gathered in this event to punish the guilty Benjaminites, so God would gather other nations to execute his ultimate punishment of the long-guilty kingdom of Israel (vs. 10). My objection to this interpretation of 10:9 (as in the case of 9:9) is that the alleged analogy is not really analogous to the crimes of the eighth century, with which Hosea was concerned, unless all crimes are analogous to all others. Secondly, the phrase

---

[9] Cf., Wellhausen and Nowack. Mauchline and Weiser consider this interpretation possible. See also the discussion of 9:9 above.

[10] Cf., Cheyne, Robinson, Weiser, Mauchline, Nötscher, and Wolff, among others.

"days of Gibeah" suggests an epoch in the development of Israel's life and institutions more than a particular act, however notorious that act may have been.[11]

Some of the commentators who endorse this theory seem to do so as a last resort, because of the alleged unacceptability of the view that Hosea meant Saul's kingdom. By beginning their discussion with the denial that Hosea meant that, they virtually concede that it is the most natural explanation, the one that comes first to mind. But why can it not be right? Because the kingship of Saul began at Gilgal or Mizpah (depending on which tradition in 1 Samuel is correct) not at Gibeah.[12] This is a weak objection. Hosea may have known nothing of the coronation-traditions associated with Gilgal and Mizpah. Far from our looking to the Bible (that is, to the final written compilation of surviving traditions) for a particular text with which to explain Hosea's allusion, we should rely on the context and the general probabilities of the case. Hosea had no Bible! Even the extant sources of the Bible are in disagreement over the place where the ceremonial beginning of the kingship occurred.[13] Besides, Hos. 10:9 says "days," and so is not intended to point to a single act or ceremony. There is no reason not to read the phrase as a designation of the initial phase of the monarchial era in Israel and the poetic complement to the description of the last phase in 10:13b–15.[14]

This difficult but important poem describes the great reversal in Israel's history, the "change of destiny" beyond the imagining of a populace whose religious attention was focused upon the changes of the agricultural year. A people who had been blessed by the use of

[11] Sellin turns the proper exegetical method upside down by assuming that Gibeah means the event referred to in Judg. 19–20 and then insisting that the crime Hosea is denouncing in this oracle must be as concrete an event as that one was. He thus interprets the better known, i.e., what is described in Hosea's poem, by the lesser known, i.e., what is only alluded to.

[12] See, Wolff and Mauchline.

[13] Cf., 1 Sam. 10:17–27 (Mizpah) and 11:14–15 (Gilgal). 1 Sam. 9:27–10:2 contains yet another account of Saul's anointing, though the place is unnamed (it is merely described as a city of Zuph, 9:5). The relationships among these traditions are unclear.

[14] It must be admitted that 10:9–15 is not an indisputable unity. Vs. 11 in particular seems to disturb the flow of ideas. If vss. 9–15 were broken up, therefore, into separate pieces, it would be illegitimate to use the reference to the king in vs. 15 in the discussion of vs. 9. There are real marks of unity in 9–15, however. The military motif is the dominant one in 9–10 and in 13–15. Vss. 13–15 are bound to vs. 12 by the play on sowing/reaping in 12 and 13. Vs. 11 also uses a farming image.

a good land and who were protected by a spendid military establishment were faced with the loss of both the economic means and the political freedom for self-determination. Ephraim would exchange the comfortable, well-fed lot of the threshing ox for the harder role of the plow beast (vs. 11). So much for idolent self-assurance in a green and pleasant land!

Why? Because the farmer (to change the metaphor) had sown the wrong seed. Eschewing covenantal virtues, he had sown rebellion for justice and reaped unrighteousness instead of *hesed*. Therefore, he was bound to eat the fruit of lies (vss. 12–13a). Obedience to God and covenantal morality were the conditions of "threshing" in the land of promise. However, instead of relying upon justice and loyalty (*hesed*) to preserve the fundamental welfare of the community—the only security they could rightly expect in a hazardous world—Israel had sacrificed her true obedience for a spurious security. Having lost her soul, she was about to lose the world as well.

It is a mistake to argue on the basis of this oracle that Hosea was a pacifist, but it is equally mistaken to argue that he was not. We do not know whether he had a general view of the legitimacy of military establishments. The oracle at hand merely suggests that *Israel's* military policy under the monarchy had proved to be futile. Because it had undermined covenantal justice and devotion to God, it was about to produce revolts that the monarchs richly deserved.

The crucial lines in the second half of this oracle may be distributed in two ways, with significantly different implications. First, vs. 13b may be read as the complement to 13a, explaining the concrete substance of the situation described metaphorically in the latter:

13a   You have sown rebellion;
        you have reaped iniquity;
            you have eaten the fruit of lies,
13b   In that you have trusted in your chariots,
        in the host of your mighty men.

In other words, rebellion, iniquity, and the fruit of lies are synonymous, and they refer to Israel's militarism. Vs. 14, on this view, describes the punishment that God will bring upon the wicked nation:

14   Therefore a tumult will arise among your people,
        and all of your fortresses will be ruined,
    As Shalman destroyed Beth-arbel . . . .

This is the interpretation suggested by many of the English versions.[15]

However, the three lines of 13a are not synonymous. They are sequential: planting, harvesting, eating. Trusting in chariots, Israel has planted a poisonous crop. Already chaos and panic are spreading across the nation, as the initial harvest of their policy, and the final fruit is soon to be eaten, when the destruction of their fortified cities leaves them homeless. Vss. 13b–14a together are the complement to 13a.[16] The prophet has traced the internal logic of Israel's diplomacy. He has not merely predicted a punishment from without, even though he understands the whole process as a judgment upon the sinful kingship (vss. 10 and 15).

The full force of the fourth stanza is measured only when it is set antithetically beside the third. It is a prophetic *torah* that finely states the course of wisdom in Israel's cultural crisis, namely the revival of covenantal Yahwism. "Sow justice (*mishpaṭ*) for yourselves; reap the fruit of loyalty (*ḥesed*). . . ." Here is man's earnest obedience to the demands of God. "Until he comes to teach you justice (*mishpaṭ*)." Here is the divine gift of what is demanded. Out of the pursuit of justice, defined by the ancient law of Israel, will come a new justice and a new law. God will teach justice to Israel in her new historical circumstances, as he taught justice to the tribes of the ancient confederacy. This justice is always human, but it is also divine, because it is motivated by faith and by gratitude to God for the *ḥesed* he has shown. It is an ancient justice, but it is not static. God "comes" again and again to teach it, and it is always appropriate to the needs of a new age.

Israel's course has been different from this one. She has "sown rebellion." Accordingly, she has "reaped injustice" and "eaten the fruit of lies." Through this process of disobedience, God still comes to teach Israel justice. His justice is now punitive, however. Like the redemptive righteousness of God, which is given in the very act of seeking to the people that strive for it (vs. 12), God's chastening righteousness is also executed within the processes of decision in the life of the disloyal people.

Apropos of this last observation it is interesting to note that Hosea names Shalman and not God as the executioner of the Israelite king

---

[15] See, e.g., *KJV*, *ASV*, and *Chicago*.

[16] A better arrangement of the lines is given by *Moffatt* and *RSV* than by the versions cited in the previous note.

and his subjects (vss. 14b–15).[17] It is uncertain who Shalman was, but the best guess is Shalmaneser V of Assyria. After 745 B.C., and especially after 732 B.C., Assyria would have been the only serious military threat to Israel and surely the only power capable of conquering her outright. A common reason for concluding that Hosea did not refer to Shalmaneser is the scholarly reluctance to date any of Hosea's oracles as late as Shalmaneser's reign (727–22 B.C.), let alone as late as his siege of Samaria, which began sometime during the period 724–22 B.C.[18] Yet the standard reason for declining to date his oracles later than 735 B.C. has been the alleged absence of references to the Syro–Ephraimitic war and its aftermath. Since this objection is no longer forceful, as has been pointed out in the discussion of Hos. 5:8–15 (it never was a decisive consideration), the old prejudice is groundless. Hos. 10:9–15 may be set most naturally against the events of the last years of the Israelite kingdom. Perhaps the siege of Samaria had already begun. The complete assurance

---

[17] The *LXX* changes the subject to "I," i.e., God, and many translators follow the lead, e.g., *Moffatt, Chicago, RSV,* Wolff, and Robinson. It is better to do this than to settle for Bethel as the subject of the verb (*KJV, ASV,* and *JPS*), but one must go out of his way to construe the sentence in this fashion. If the two parts of 14b–15 are taken together, it is hard to understand how the parallelism could have been overlooked and the natural meaning of the MT missed. Thus:

כשד שלמן בית ארבאל
ביום מלחמה ...
ככה עשה לכם בית־אל ...
בשחר נדמה ...

As Shalman destroyed Beth-arbel
in the day of battle, . . .
So will he do to you, O Bethel . . .
At dawn . . . .

The verbs in vs. 15 are admittedly perfect (עשה and נדמה), but this will remain a problem regardless who their subject is. "So will he have done" and "will have been put to silence" are perhaps more accurate translations. Usage of this sort is often called the "prophetic perfect," i.e., denoting future action, which the prophet is so sure will come to pass that he describes it as if it were already done. Whatever the merits of this designation, the verbs in this passage are universally interpreted as pointing to a definite act in the future.

[18] Shalmaneser is referred to by name in 2 Kings 17:3 and 18:9. The Hebrew is שלמנאסר. The name in Hos. 10:14 is שלמן. Among those who regard Shalmaneser as the king referred to here are Harper, Weiser, Wellhausen, and Knight. The reference to Assyria in 10:6 strongly supports this interpretation. Beth-arbel is otherwise unknown in the Old Testament but is generally believed to have been in Gilead (see *IDB,* A–D, p. 388).

that Hosea displays regarding the imminent fall of Bethel and Samaria is most understandable if we suppose that this oracle was composed on the eve of the disaster. "Samaria's king is cut loose" (vs. 7) implies that the crisis has already begun. 2 Kings 17:3–6 tells of king Hoshea's imprisonment prior to Shalmaneser's siege of Samaria, and thus provides the best historical setting for the oracles in Hos. 10. Seldom are we given such a precise clue to contemporary events in the poems of the eighth-century prophets. The conclusion to which it points seems irresistible to me, though of course it makes no theological difference whether these oracles reflect the events of Hoshea's time or of those of some other king.[19]

Biblical exegesis is occasionally comic, and on these occasions it can also be properly humbling to the interpreter of Hosea's obscure, ancient poems. Witness the history of exegesis of Hos. 10:10 ("when I punish them for their double guilt"). The following are some of the pairs of sins that have been suggested to explain Hosea's allusions: (1) the cult and the kingship; (2) the calf of Dan and the calf of Bethel (1 Kings 12:27–32); (3) the cult and the schism of Jeroboam I; (4) apostasy and idolatry; (5) the cult-image of Micah (Judg. 17) and that of Jeroboam I; (6) spiritual unfaithfulness and political plotting; (7) the old sin and the new sin; (8) the Gibeah atrocity (Judg.

---

[19] Hos. 10:1–8 is dated in Hoshea's reign by Brown, Scott (*op. cit.*, p. 63), Lindblom (*op. cit.*, pp. 97 f.), Robinson, and Knight. Sellin and Wolff prefer the interregnum after the murder of Pekah (2 Kings 15:30). However, there was almost certainly no interregnum at that time. Hoshea's murder of Pekah simultaneously removed the one and established the other. Furthermore, the calf of Bethel was probably not delivered to Assyria as tribute at that time (Sellin) but was taken as booty in the final debacle. The passage in 2 Kings makes at least no reference to its prior removal. Hos. 10:5–6a represents the people's anxious concern over the calf. Of all their treasures, it would have been relinquished last. Hoshea was a grudging tributary after all (cf., 2 Kings 17:4). Hos. 10:5–8 threatens the loss of the calf at the time of the final destruction (vs. 8). Wolff says vs. 4a points to the revolt of Hoshea against Pekah. It might do so in a general sense, since every citizen was "under oath," as it were, to his king, and Hoshea's treachery was a violation of that "covenant." But Hoshea's violation of his covenant with Assyria (2 Kings 17:4) is a far better background for these lines. In short, every historical allusion in chapter 10 finds its best explanation in what we are told of Hoshea's reign. The only reference not clarified by 2 Kings 17:1–6 is the mention of Beth-arbel, but it remains a mystery in any case. Hosea simply cited a recent Assyrian conquest that he attributed to "Shalman" and that our fragmentary sources for the history of the period do not mention.

19–20) and the kingship; (9) the idols and the kings; and (10) the sin of Gibeah and the sin of the present.[20] One hesitates to add another voice to this clamor. Therefore, instead of advocating one of these pairs or proposing yet another slate of candidates, I shall merely raise two questions that bear on the issue. First, is it possible that the "double guilt" in vs. 10 is the same as the "wretched sin" in verse 15? The latter is, literally, "wicked wickedness" (רעת רעתכם), that is, *double* wickedness. Knight takes "double guilt" in vs. 10 to mean very great guilt. This is precisely parallel to the phrase in vs. 15. Israel's sin is described in various ways in the oracle, and the sum of the statements means that Israel has broken faith with God and substituted other goals for that relationship. "Idolatry," "rebellion," and other terms point to different aspects of this phenomenon, but faithlessness is probably the single best word for it. Second, is not the duality of Israel's sin here the same duality that Jeremiah described when he said, "My people have committed two evils: they have forsaken me, the fountain of living waters, and hewed out cisterns for themselves, broken cisterns that can hold no water (Jer. 2:13)"?

---

[20] See, e.g., (1) Harper, (2) Wellhausen, (3) Cheyne, (4) and (5) Harper, (citing Jerome), (6) Mauchline, (7) Sellin, (8) Weiser, (9) Brown, and (10) cited by Brown.

PART THREE

PROVIDENCE
AND HISTORY

12

FATHER AND SON:
HOSEA 11

I

1   When Israel was a child I loved him,
        and out of Egypt I called my son.
2   As I called them,
        so they left me.
    To Baals they sacrificed;
        to idols they burned offerings.

3   And it was I who taught Ephraim to walk,
        I that took them in my arms;
           but they did not know I cared for them.
4   I led them with cords of devotion,
        with bonds of love.
    And I was with them as one
        who lifts an infant to his cheek,
           and I bent down to give them food.

II

5   He will return to the land of Egypt,
        and Asshur will be his king,
           because they refused to return.
6   The sword will whirl in his cities,
        and destroy his gates,
           and wreck his fortresses.
7   And my people will weary of their apostasy:
        together they will call to Baal,
           but he can not raise them up.

III

8   How can I give you up, O Ephraim?
        How can I surrender you, O Israel?

How can I make you like Admah?
How can I treat you like Zeboiim?
My heart recoils within me;
all my compassion is stirred.
9   I will not execute my wrath;
I will not again destroy Ephraim.
For God am I and not man,
the Holy One in your midst,
and I will not come to destroy.

IV

10   After Yahweh they will go;
like a lion he will roar.
When he roars, the children
will come trembling from the sea.
11   They will hurry like birds out of Egypt,
like doves from the land of Asshur;
and I will restore them to their homes.

[Oracle of Yahweh]

NOTES ON THE TEXT

Verse 3. This version of the second line is almost universally adopted (אקחם על־זרועתי for קחם על־זרועתיו), although "taking him by his arms" (*JPS*) is an excellent complement to line 1 and is as close to the MT as the alternative.

Verse 4. "Devotion" (*RSV:* "compassion," for *ḥesed*) is widely adopted for the MT's אדם ("man"; cf., e.g., Sellin, Robinson, Well-hausen, and Nötscher), partly because of the parallel "love." However, many scholars prefer the MT ("human," or "of a man": *ASV, JPS, Moffatt, Chicago,* Weiser, Wolff, Harper, and Brown).

The present translation of the fourth line is more suitable than "who lifts the yoke upon their jaws" (*RSV, KJV, ASV, Chicago,* and others). It merely involves a different vocalization of one word (עוּל for עֹל). The alternative is extremely clumsy. Yokes are not known to have been placed on animals' jaws. The yoke-simile is also unsuitable to the rest of the strophe. When "infant" (literally, "suckling") is read, the imagery of the poem is completely consistent (cf., Weiser, Nötscher, Wolff, G. R. Driver [*JTS* 39, pp. 160 ff.], and others).

Most scholars agree that the meaning of the last clause is something like that I have adopted, although the text is uncertain in detail. *Verse 5*. MT: "He shall not return to the land of Egypt, but (and?) Asshur, he (is, will be) his king" (cf., *KJV, ASV,* and *Knox*). This denial is contradicted by 7:16; 8:13; and 9:3, 6, unless it be interpreted to mean the failure of a current alliance with Egypt or of a flight to Egypt, away from the invading Assyrians. Yet even scholars who have taken this reference to Egypt as a comment on current policy have regarded the "not" (לֹא), which is the first word in the line, as a scribal error for "to him" (לוֹ), which would have been the last word in the preceding line (e.g., *RSV, Chicago, Moffatt,* Sellin, Robinson, Wolff, and many others). For an alternative proposal, see the discussion of 11:5–7 below.

Verse 6. "Gates" is one of several popular guesses (others: "bars," "bars of his gates," "sons," and "fields") for the Hebrew בדים. בדים elsewhere means sticks or staves (*Köhler*), unless it be *II בַּד ("idle talk"; cf., "babbling seers," G. R. Driver, *Nötscher Festschrift,* p. 54).

"Fortresses" (מבצריהם) is a standard emendation (*Chicago, Jerusalem, Moffatt, RSV,* Harper, Brown, Robinson, Marti, and Sellin), although some scholars still prefer the "counsels" (מעצותיהם) of the MT (*ASV, JPS,* Weiser, and Wolff). Cf., G. R. Driver's "disobedience" (from *II עצה; *loc. cit.*).

Verse 7. Literally, "My people shall hang at my returning," or the like. Wellhausen and Nowack declared the text wholly corrupt. Dozens of improbable solutions have been proposed, one of which I have adopted (as have *Moffatt,* Sellin, Weiser, and, in part, Harper), reading some form of לאה for תלא. A good parallel to this emended text is found in Isa. 16:12, where the verb is לאה (Moab, wearying himself with Baalism). Compare, also, Hos. 8:10, where the verb is perhaps "become sick." A minor change is required to obtain the second sentence, namely בעל (Baal) for עַל **(up)** (*BH, Jerusalem,* Weiser, Wolff, May [*AJSL* 48, p. 83], Robinson, and Nötscher).

Verse 8. "Compassion" (either retaining the MT's נחומי, or emending to לחמי is popular (*RSV, Chicago,* Sellin, Wellhausen, Weiser, Robinson, and many others). However, "repentence" is probably more accurate. It forms a good parallel to the foregoing line and makes excellent sense in this one (*KJV, LXX, Vulgate,* and Wolff, citing Zech. 1:13 and Isa. 57:18).

Verse 9. בער ("to burn," either literally or figuratively) is generally adopted in place of בעיר ("in a city," MT).

Verse 12. This verse belongs with Hos. 12, with which it is numbered in the Hebrew Bible.

The Unity of Hosea 11. The integrity of the chapter has often been denied and vss. 10–11 set aside as an insertion from a later writer whose optimistic viewpoint contradicts that of Hosea. One formal inconsistency exists, namely, the lone use of the third person in vs. 10, but this kind of shift is fairly common in Hosea (cf., 5:3–4; 12:9–14; and 14:1–7) and is not necessarily a mark of diverse origins. Sellin deleted most of vs. 10 for this reason, but Wellhausen, Nowack, and Harper, all of whom considered 10b–11 to be a late expansion, retained 10a, in spite of the shift of persons! The transition from vs. 9 to 10 is abrupt, but so is that from vs. 4 to 5 and that from vs. 7 to 8. The poem comprises four highly impressionistic pieces, set one after another without narrative transitions. This feature is a stroke of genius and not a mark of its disunity (contrary to G. A. Smith, for instance). Again, the originality of the promise in this place has been doubted because of its brevity (Robinson) or its shift of metaphors (Duhm). However, vss. 10–11 correspond exactly in length and function to 5–7. Robinson chopped out vs. 10 and then found the remaining verse too short and too fragmentary to keep in this place. He did not, however, deny its Hosean origin. As for the shift of metaphors, there is none. There are children in vss. 10–11 as there are in 1–4. The simile of the birds in 10–11 hardly disturbs the integrity of the poem.

I have been at pains both in the exposition of chapter 11 and in other parts of this volume to show that Hosea's promises do not negate the substance of his threats. A repetition of this discussion is unnecessary here. If there is no fundamental theological or historical contradiction between the threats and the promises, only two arguments for the inauthenticity of the promises can be made. One is that all promises of felicity in the pre-exilic prophets are post-exilic interpolations. This old dogma has been abandoned in most manuals of Old Testament criticism published in recent decades, though at least one great, standard work continues to perpetuate it.[1] (We are now in danger of an uncritical adherence to the opposite prejudice; and

[1] Cf., Pfeiffer, *Introduction to the OT,* p. 573.

so the pendulum swings!) The other argument is relatively objective. It is that the presence of those characteristically Jewish hopes that mark the literature of the sixth and of the following centuries, such as the return from the Babylonian exile and the restoration of the temple of Zion (e.g., Isa. 27:13 and Jer. 3:13 f.), marks a passage in a pre-exilic writing as an interpolation. Amos 9:8b–15 is suspect on these grounds. Is Hos. 11:10–11 suspect, likewise? I believe it is not. Egypt and Assyria are often mentioned by Hosea as the places of Israel's exile, and it is not surprising, therefore, that he should name them as the points of departure for the new exodus. His mention of the sea in vs. 10 is reminiscent of Deutero-Isaiah's "coastlands" (Isa. 41:1, 5; 42:4; etc.: however, the Hebrew words are not the same), but it is entirely credible on the lips of an eighth-century prophet in northern Israel.

"Post-exilic" usually means post-587 B.C. The flight and deportation of Israelites took place in 733 (2 Kings 15:29) and 721 B.C. (2 Kings 17:6), however, and "post-exilic" is an adjective that applies therefore to the latter part of Hosea's own career. According to the indications of Hosea's oracles, he witnessed the last decade of the Israelite kingship. Therefore, when we find reflections in his oracles, on Israel's exile and its aftermath, we should not be surprised or suspect the authenticity of the passage. He was interpreting contemporary events. He may even have written after 721 B.C.[2] It is quite unnecessary, however, to assume that he did, in order to find a cogent and consistent perspective in his oracles, including the oracles of hope.

Hos. 11–14 is marked off from chapters 4–10 by a concentration upon the covenantal past and future. The oracles in chapters 4–10 are focused on the present, although they occasionally allude to the past, and especially point to the historical continuity of evil in Israel's institutions and practices. In the other direction, they look forward only to the imminent end of the Israelite kingdom. Thus their temporal orientation is identical with that of the Tract for the Times (1:2–9). In chapters 11–14 the poet is preoccupied with the larger

---

[2] The statement "I will not again destroy Ephraim," in vs. 9 has been cited as evidence that the first destruction had already *taken place* when the passage was written (Stinespring, *op. cit.*, p. 204). It merely shows, however, that the first destruction had already *been predicted*, as in fact it had in vss. 5–6.

history of Israel, especially the problematic character of the story of
the covenant taken as a whole. In this respect, the last chapters correspond to the Allegory of Covenantal History (1:10–2:23) and the
Sign of the Ransomed Bride (3:1–5). They probe repeatedly into the
remoter past and future in order to define the ultimate meaning of
Israel's history within the purpose of God.

IT IS NOT SURPRISING that the majority of Hosea's oracles deals
with the conditions and prospects of the present. The bulk of Old
Testament prophecy does this. The prophet attempts first of all to
instruct the religious community concerning its actual relationship to
God. Therefore, he analyzes the moral condition of the community
in the light of covenantal norms and describes the consequences of
communal attitudes and behavior. In so far as the present conditions
reach back into or are a product of the past, their antecendants are
also considered. Above all, the situation must be related to the actions of God and his intentions for the people, in so far as the prophet
is able to discern them.

It is not always clear what the practical intention of the prophet
was in publishing the word of God. Often it may have been the desire
to effect a change in the moral situation. Yet the prophets never
proposed programs of reconstruction, either public or private. So
that men of the covenant would act faithfully, they needed to understand the aims and modes of divine action. Yet, in order to act
freely, they needed to work out for themselves the practical consequences of that understanding. The prophet was commissioned to
declare what was and, in so far as he knew it, what was to be. He
was not sent to decide for other men what in particular they should
do about it. Nor was he supposed to guess the precise outcome of
the decisions men made.

A right understanding of God's activity within man's life includes a knowledge of the ultimate context within which all action
takes place. The prophets, therefore, often declared what they believed to be the primary motive of divine action, or, put another
way, its ultimate intention. Accordingly, they probed into the foundations of the natural and social orders and into the future, promising
what they believed God would ultimately bring to pass. What God
was determined to achieve in the future was completely relevant to
the issues men faced in the present. A man's decisions are affected

at least as profoundly by what he believes about the ultimate future as they are by the demands of the immediate future. Whenever natural necessity allows him a choice, his decision will be shaped by his ultimate expectations.

Christ's resurrection, for example, is for the Christian the source of his assurance of God's forgiveness, and is therefore a source of immediate moral renewal. It is not merely a promise of eternal life. Yet, if the resurrection did not mean for the Christian the promise of eternal life, it is doubtful that it would mean the assurance of forgiveness in the present. The sin occasioned by fear of death and annihilation is overcome simultaneously with the death of that fear. Neither is utterly vanquished in life, but in so far as either is conquered, it is conquered with the other.

To be sure, the Old Testament prophets often preached from a point of view different from the one I have described. Amos, for example, apparently hoped to usher in a national reformation by threatening divine punishments for Israel's crimes. Hosea however, had no such intention. He threatened divine judgments, but these threats were set within the framework of a broader view of God's motives and achievements. His belief in the final, creative triumph of God was presupposed in his proclamation of God's immediate, destructive judgments.

Hosea's fundamental image of God was not that of the judge or of the king but that of the parent. By adopting this metaphor, and that of the husband, Hosea was able to reduce the tension between the ideas of God's mercy and his wrath. In the judge, these qualities are usually contradictory, but in the parent they are both comprehended in love. Parental love seeks the ultimate welfare of the child within a harmonious community of children. Education, protection, and punishment find all a place in the parent's behavior toward the child. His attitude is a compassionate identification with the child in all its experiences, both of weal and woe. However, since life is often dangerous and terrible, and always subject to human corruption, existence is as much a battlefield as a family circle. The prophets had no romantic illusions about the nature of the conflict. Alongside the image of God, the father, therefore, they placed those of the zealous warrior and the righteous judge. Nevertheless, in the Book of Hosea these and similar metaphors serve to qualify the fundamental image of the husband–father and not to displace it.

Chapter 11 presents in oracular form, in a single, incandescent poem, the same schematic theology of Israel's history that is embodied in the sign-narrative in chapter 3. Here, for the first time, however, the temporal progression is from past to present to future, rather than from present to past to future. Here, as elsewhere, Hosea says little in detail about either the past or the future. Two things about the past are decisive: God's persistent nurture of Israel, motivated by his love, and Israel's equally persistent blindness to the providential basis of her life, as well as her corresponding propensity to idolatry (11:1–4).

It is remarkable that Hosea said so little about the particular events of Israel's history. He mentioned the exodus from Egypt (11:1), to be sure, but not as the great turning point in a long drama of salvation. For him, it simply marked the beginning of God's effective calling and of Israel's turning away.[3] This relative silence about the particular events of the past is consistently maintained in the Book of Hosea, and it is surprising in one for whom the general pattern of Israel's history was so important.

The patriarchal traditions are never employed as illustrations of God's redemptive activity, although the references to Jacob in 12:3–4, 12, show some acquaintance, at least, with those traditions.[4] The era of deliberate, divine activity within the corporate life of Israel began with the exodus–wilderness experiences and was symbolized by them. "I am the Lord your God from the land of Egypt" (13:4; 12:9; cf., 12:13). "Like grapes in the wilderness I found Israel" (9:10; cf., 2:14–15; 13:5). When Hosea promised the ruined people that they would return to the point of covenantal beginning, in order to be given a new beginning, he described it as a return to Egypt (7:16; 8:13; 9:3, 6; 11:5) or to the wilderness (2:14; 12:9).[5]

[3] G. A. Smith's translation of 11:1 ("I called Israel to be my son") gives to the line the implication that the exodus was the beginning of Israel's sonship, whereas another popular version ("I came to love him"; cf., Chicago, Harper, Sellin, Robinson, Weiser, and Wolff) implies that God did not love Israel prior to that time. I believe neither inference is supported by the text, which is entirely neutral on the issue.

[4] They are attributed to another writer by Harper (citing Wellhausen, Nowack, Volz, and Marti), among others.

[5] The Book of Deuteronomy, the ultimate origin of which some scholars would place in the prophetic–Levitical circles of northern Israel in the ninth to eighth centuries B.C., contains some notable parallels to Hosea's references to the first and second exodus–wilderness eras. Compare, Deut. 32:10 ff. with Hos. 11:1 ff. and Hos. 9:10; Deut. 28:68 with Hos. 8:13, etc.; Deut. 34:10 with Hos. 12:14; and Deut. 32:28 f. with Hos. 14:9.

That the exodus and the wilderness are virtually interchangeable symbols in the book shows that it was the total experience of Israel in the wilderness era that had primary theological significance for Hosea and not the event of the exodus from Egypt per se. We should not expect Hosea to refer explicitly to the external features of the event, of course. He would have presupposed in his hearers a knowledge of the relevant traditions. In his oracles he dealt only with the interior aspects of the relationship established by God with the fathers, since the character of that relationship in his own time was the proper subject of prophetic teaching. We should perhaps not draw any inferences, therefore, from Hosea's silence about the outward features of the exodus event.

Nevertheless, his treatment of the exodus tradition differs from that of the Book of Exodus in more than the omission of such features as the ten plagues and the passage through the sea. It also differs in the meaning it attributes to the event. In the Pentateuch, the exodus is the turning point in a great historical drama that begins with the promises to the patriarchs (Gen. 12:1–3; 15:13–16; 17:1–8; cf., 9:25–27) and ends with Israel's conquest of Canaan. It is the decisive battle in God's contest with the enemies of Israel. It is also the overwhelming demonstration of God's power over nature. In the Book of Hosea, the exodus from Egypt is never associated with the promises to the patriarchs. There is no implication that it was a tangible demonstration of God's power. Quite the contrary, it is acknowledged that it failed to impress even the Israelites (11:2–3). And it is never suggested, even indirectly, that the conquest of Canaan was the goal of the drama that centered in the exodus. The exodus, in Hosea, is significant only as the beginning of that epoch in Israel's history in which God has worked to create a faithful community the life of which centered in him. It is primarily an event in the history of worship. No attention whatever is called to the natural or political dimensions of the exodus tradition. It may be assumed that the popular image of the exodus was defined by these latter features—so prominent in the Pentateuch—that would have fed Israel's national aspirations. But this image and that of Hosea are so different that they may be said to reflect almost different events.

I am not suggesting that the Pentateuch makes nothing of the interior significance of the exodus, since it obviously makes a great deal of it. It reports also the stubbornness and blindness of the people while in the wilderness, as Hosea does. I am saying, rather, that much of the meaning attached to the exodus by the Pentateuch, especially in the Priestly narrative, but also in such traditions as Exod. 15, is simply disregarded by Hosea. The reason, I believe, is not that Hosea was ignorant of these features of the tradition, or that he merely considered them irrelevant to his preaching, but that he found they contributed to an interpretation of the exodus that was incompatible with his own. The task of exegesis, however, is not to guess the reasoning that produced the writer's statements but to expound the meaning of what he said. Whether or not Hosea himself was aware of the incompatibility of his conception with others that found their way into the Old Testament, the difference remains and is extremely important.

Hosea refers to the wilderness era of Israel's history, in general terms, as the time of providential leading and nurture (11:1, 3–4). At the same time, he characterizes the history of the nation as a story of apostasy (11:2). The reader is likely to infer from this poem that Hosea placed the beginning of Israel's infidelity at the same point in time as the beginning of God's redemption. The effect of such a dating is to eliminate from the story of God and Israel any period of unsullied "bridal" devotion, prior to the initial breach of faith. This conclusion, however, seems to contradict what Hosea said in 2:15 about the youthful devotion of Yahweh's bride. In 11:3, he says of Israel—now symbolized by the infant child—that Israel did not even know that it stood in relationship to Yahweh. How can these statements be reconciled?

One way of eliminating any inconsistency is to take 11:2 as an historical foreshortening. This seems to make the initial calling and the initial apostasy simultaneous, but it was actually not meant in this way. The actual time of apostasy would then have to be fixed by other statements in the book. Several other passages date the beginning of Israel's infidelity at the time of the settlement in Canaan (6:7; 9:15; and 13:6). One passage names specifically the unhappy incident of the worship of Baal-Peor (9:10), which occurred on the long march from Sinai to Canaan (Num. 25). Compared with these references to the temporal stages in Israel's religious regression, 11:2 may be viewed as a summary of the entire history of her worship, a history characterized largely by the baalizing of Israel's behavior and purpose.

This first approach to the problem presented by the historical judgment in 11:2 is legitimate on the level of institutional history. It threatens to obscure, however, an important implication of Hos. 11. The oracle does not merely expound the history of social institutions in Israel, from the first to the second exodus. It describes the relationship between God and Israel, the relationship between God and believing men. Seen from this interior perspective, Israel's response to God may be called unfaithful from the very beginning. Not only did the later generations of covenanters, who established Israel in Canaan and syncretized her culture, prove to be disloyal, but so did the first generation. The innocent bride in her desert honeymoon was already a woman of the world. She responded to her husband sufficiently to make a marriage and begin a family. Without that much bridal devotion the love of God would have passed unknown and unremembered. Israel became at least a community that bore witness, however fitfully, to the grace of God. In spite of her disloyalty, she was obedient enough to transmit the memory of her betrothal and marriage, and to preserve the cultic forms within which the memory could be renewed again and again, and which kept alive the possibility that the marriage devotion itself might be renewed. At no time in her history, however, did she put herself entirely at the disposal of her Lord in perfect devotion. This, to my mind, is the meaning of Hos. 2:15 and 11:2, if these passages are read together.

The prophets were not satisfied with a devotion that stopped with the preservation of traditional rites and confessions.[6] They demanded a faith that would constantly seek to overcome its own faithlessness, and a zeal for the renewal of obedience. Hosea's denunciation, in this oracle, was not evoked by Israel's imperfect or wavering devotion, but by her refusal to renew devotion (". . . because they refused to *return* . . ."), which led to the death of faith. Hosea depicts God as a patient father, and not as a military martinet, unable to tolerate a single act of insubordination. For Hosea, the providence of God offered many more than the "one moment to decide." Was there any limit to the number of offers? The answer is yes and no. No, because God does not stop being the patient father, working eternally to bring up faithful children. This is the lesson of 11:8–11. Yes, be-

---

[6] The implication of 4:4–10 is that the official religious establishment had failed even in transmitting the traditions properly. See the discussion of that passage.

cause the time for decision may run out on Israel, since Israel represents a particular set of social and economic institutions that structure the people's life in a given place and time. This is the lesson of 11:5–7.

In the face of love's failure to evoke a persistent devotion, a devotion aware of its own need for renewal, a more radical measure is required. This measure is the deprivation of Israel's state and cult, and her dispossession from the land that supported her. In other words, a return to the beginning, to "Egypt" (". . . because they refused to return. . . .").

If the translation I have adopted in 11:5 were beyond dispute, I could move on immediately to discuss the remainder of the poem, since I have already devoted considerable space to the theme of the return to Egypt. Since it is not beyond dispute, however, I will stop long enough for a defense of this translation.

The mooted point in the discussion of 11:5 is not whether "not" belongs at the head of the verse, since nearly everyone agrees that it does not.[7] It is the meaning of the "return to Egypt." At least three recent commentators have interpreted the return as an Israelite embassy to Egypt, in conspiracy against Assyria, like Hoshea's after the death of Tiglath-Pileser III (2 Kings 17:4).[8] There are at least three reasons, however, for preferring the interpretation I have adopted. First, in 8:13 and 9:3, "return to Egypt" is a future punishment and not a present policy, and similar references to a second enslavement in Egypt are made in 7:16; 9:6; and 12:9. Second, the last strophe of the oracle predicts a later return out of Egypt (11:11).[9] Third, Hosea's references to diplomatic entanglements with foreign nations are phrased quite differently from vs. 5. Israel "cries" for aid (7:11), sends gifts (8:9–10; 12:2), makes covenants (12:2), or "goes" to the great kings (7:11; 5:13), but she does not "return" to them for

---

[7] Norman Gottwald has interpreted the negative statement of 11:5 to be Hosea's correction of his hearers' literalistic misunderstanding of his prediction of a "return to Egypt." The second captivity, Hosea is saying here, will be actually in Assyria, and only symbolically in Egypt. See, *All the Kingdoms of the Earth*, pp. 134–35. Alternatively, one may see the work of a later scribe here, who mistook the *lô* ("to him") at the end of the preceding sentence for *lo'* ("not") at the beginning of this one, encouraged by his knowledge of the actual course of events in 721 B.C. and thereafter.

[8] Sellin, Robinson, and Wolff.

[9] All three scholars named regard vs. 11 as authentic, but Robinson and Wolff believe it was not originally in this poem.

political support,[10] at least not according to parallel texts in the book. It makes no great difference for Hosea's theology whether the event described in 11:5–7 is already happening or is about to happen, or whether 11:5 denotes policy or punishment. All possible combinations of these alternatives are covered by other oracles. One combination, however, seems to be demanded by the relevant literary data.

The clue to the received Hebrew text of 11:5 may lie in a strikingly similar prediction in 9:3, namely, "They will not remain (לא ישבו) in Yahweh's land,/but Ephraim will return (ושב) to Egypt/ and in Assyria they will eat unclean food." The original text of 11:5 might have been, *"He will not remain* (לא ישב) in Yahweh's land,/but he will return (ישוב) to the land of Egypt/and Asshur will be his king,/because he refused to return (לשוב)." The first clause, except for the initial "not," was inadvertently omitted when the copyist's eye jumped from the first verb to the second. This hypothesis explains the anomalous "not" in 11:5, and it provides for a fuller poetic line at a point where some critics have thought the present text incomplete.[11]

Just as 11:1–4 is to be taken as the summary characterization of an era, so 11:5–7 should be read as a series of impressions of a single phase of Israel's destiny, and not as a chronicle of separate events. Deportation, a ravaged homeland, and cultic frustration are three of the fruits of Israel's ignorance and rebellion (vss. 2–3). They do not stand in causal or chronological relationship to each other. They are simply different aspects of one judgment.

If my reconstruction of vs. 7 is correct, it contains one of the finest in a notable series of ironies in the Book of Hosea. Here is the image of a ruined people, at their wits' end, plaintively calling to God for help against their enemy. The god they imagine to be their

[10] "Return to the land of Egypt" implies deportation from one land to another, not communication between the heads of state.

[11] In *JTS* 39 (1938), 160–62, G. R. Driver argues that a clause is missing between vss. 4 and 5. Fragments from two different recensions of the line have been preserved in the MT, he says. One was originally "but he refused to eat it" (לאכלו), of which the לא (which seems to be "not") remains. The other is preserved in 5b, "but they refused to return." Robinson also sees a lacuna here, but his reconstruction is altogether different. The Greek of 5a ("Ephraim *dwelt* in Egypt") might be from an original ישב, as I have suggested, but it might be only an interpretation of ישוב in the light of 9:3.

god is their own creation—a Baal—and not Yahweh. Their true enemy is not the one they see, but themselves, and, therefore, God. Their cry is futile, for Baal cannot save them from themselves, from Assyria, or from God. This is the end of their "fox-hole" Baalism.

Hosea's oracles contain many inversions of conventional religious notions and popular hopes. His reinterpretation of the meaning of God's holiness is one of the most dramatic of these: "I am God and not man, the Holy One in your midst, and I will not come to destroy" (11:9). Mosaic and prophetic Yahwism had lifted the idea of holiness from the level of tribalistic mana, where the power of God was believed to be ritually available in support of the tribe against its enemies, to the level of a morally conditioned religion, where that power was understood to support only the just purposes of God against *his* enemies, both within Israel and without. Thus a semimagical doctrine of special privilege was displaced by an ethical doctrine of distributive justice. But this notion, too, was transcended by Hosea's conception of God's holiness as redemptive love. His conviction was not a return to the non-moral level, for he upheld the validity of covenantal justice and never doubted the majestic righteousness of God. He thought of God's justice, however, as comprehended in his fatherly zeal to bless and fulfill the life of his people. Therefore, the ultimate irony in the story of Israel and God, as presented in Hos. 11, is that Egypt and Assyria, whom Israel has sought as her saviors, have become her judges and executioners, while God, whom Hosea proclaimed as judge and executioner, has become her savior.

I have probably gone too far in saying that Hosea conceived of God's holiness as redemptive love. To put the matter this way is to minimize the opposition that Hosea himself acknowledged between God's love and God's wrath. In 11:5–11, which reaches a climax in vss. 8 and 9, wrath and love are set sharply against each other. All they have in common is their emotional depth; they stand at the extremes of the spectrum of personal sentiments. Hosea actually pictures a complete reversal of affections, a veritable repentance in the mind of God.[12] As emotions, love and wrath are of course incompatible. Therefore, it is only honest, in attributing such feelings

---

[12] "Repentance" is perhaps the right translation in vs. 8, and not "compassion." See the textual note.

to God, to let them stand in opposition to each other. Ultimately, however, these attributions are only symbolic efforts at describing in finite terms the transcendent purposes of God.

God's radical change of heart (vss. 8–9) is not to be taken as a suspension of judgment against the sinful nation. The national disaster will take place. God's love is not proof against that. His love is rather the ground of hope beyond the disaster. Vss. 8–9 do not express the substance of that hope any more than they do the dismissal of judgment. They proclaim the changeless love of God, who purposed once to create a people for himself (11:1–4), and who will not change his mind about that, even though he is forced by his love to repent of the impulse toward retributive justice (11:8–9).[13] Neither the folly of Israel nor any human standard of retribution could deter him from his fundamental intention. In that purpose he would finally prevail. His triumph would not be a cheap one for Israel. It would be a victory of life out of death, and not an averting of death. The empirical kingdom of Israel was doomed, but the people of God were not, although they would suffer grievously in the tragedy of the state.

God's wrath was his response to Israel's persistent rejection of his love. But a permanent rejection of the godless could eventually frustrate the creative purposes of God. The rekindling of God's zeal to create a devoted people marked therefore the transition from Israel's time of rejection to the time of her new acceptance. In his picture of this new exodus from Egypt, from Assyria, and from the coastlands of the Mediterranean (11:10–11), Hosea pointed once again to the essential features of the new epoch, without chronicling its

---

[13] It is a mistake, I believe, to make too much of the idea that it costs God something to forgive his sinful children (as H. W. Robinson asserts, for instance, in his book on Hosea). It may cost a *man* something to condescend to forgiveness, but the point of Hos. 11 is precisely that *God's* love is not like that of a man. A loving father does not suffer from the son's evil because the father is offended by it, but because he sees his son choosing what is inimical to the son. No parent worthy of the name would hesitate for a moment to extend his love and all his resources to his sinful child. Surely, God is at least as ungrudging in his love. The parent will discipline the child in order to help him become responsible, that is, he will not merely indulge the wayward child. To ask the child to accept responsibility, however, is not to withhold love, or to ask the child to repay the parent for what it "costs" the parent to forgive. It costs him nothing; rather, it is the glad privilege of fulfilling his very nature as a parent.

particular events.[14] The sons of Israel would return to the place of their rejection and dwell once more—or finally—as the people of God. They would recognize Yahweh as the one who called and restored them to their homes, but they would acknowledge his transcendent power with awe, like birds fearfully answering the roaring summons of a lion. The prophet made no effort to predict the forms of the community's life. It would be a community of faith. This was the only prediction that he was called upon to make.

Who were the children who would come to the Lord when he called a new people to himself? They were whoever would respond when he called. Were they the survivors of the dying kingdom, given another chance to be faithful? Were they their descendants? Hosea did not say, of course, and we should not force an answer. The children of God are those who respond, whoever they may be, whenever he calls. It was Yahweh who would call, that is, the Lord of the ancient covenant, the savior known from the first exodus. Therefore, his call would be mediated by men who stood in the covenantal tradition and who *knew* him from what he had done. The voice of the prophet, speaking out of that tradition, was the only necessary condition for the fulfilment of Hosea's promise. Only the future could tell who would respond in faith to the prophet's speaking.

14 The returnees will come therefore from the west (the sea), the north (Assyria, via the upper Euphrates), and the south (Egypt), but not from the east, i.e., the relatively uninhabitable Arabian desert. These references, like the one to Egypt in vs. 5, are probably symbolic and not literal.

CHAPTER

13 ANALOGIES FROM ISRAEL'S HISTORY: HOSEA 12

I

11:12 Ephraim surrounds me with lies,
 the House of Israel, with treachery;
 And (Jacob) again strays with *'El,*
 and is faithful with "holy ones."
12:1 Ephraim herds a wind,
 chases an east wind all day.
 He compounds lies with violence.
 They make a covenant with Asshur,
 and oil is carried to Egypt.

2 So Yahweh has a controversy with (Israel)
 to punish Jacob for his ways,
 and requite him for his deeds.

II

3 In the womb he seized his brother's heel,
 and in his manhood he struggled with God.
4 He fought with an angel and prevailed;
 he wept and begged his favor.
 "(*'El-*) *Bethel* will find us,
 and there he will speak with us."

5 But Yahweh, God of hosts,
 Yahweh is his name.
6 So you shall (dwell in your tents),
 maintaining loyalty and justice,
 and waiting continually for your God.

III

7 A merchant with crooked scales,
 he loved to cheat.

8   Yet Ephraim declared,
        "See, I have become rich.
        I have found myself wealth.
        "(In) all my gain they will not find in me
          any crookedness that is a sin."

9   But I am Yahweh your God
        from the land of Egypt.
     I will again make you dwell in tents,
        as in the days of assembly.

IV

10   I spoke by the prophets;
        I multiplied visions;
          I inspired prophetic signs.
11   But the heap of witness was a fraud!
        How empty it became:
          in Gilgal they sacrifice bulls!

     But their altars (will) be like piles of rocks
        along the furrows of a field.

V

12   Jacob fled to the plain of Aram;
        Israel served for a wife;
        for a wife he tended (flocks).
13   But by a prophet Yahweh brought up
        Israel from Egypt,
        and by a prophet was he tended.

14   Ephraim has bitterly provoked (His) anger.
        His Lord will leave his blood (guilt) upon him,
        and turn his reproaches against him.

NOTES ON THE TEXT

Verse 11:12 (Heb. 12:1). The Hebrew chapter division is obviously correct. Chapter 11 concludes with vs. 11, and vs. 12 begins a new section. The text reads "Judah" in 11:12 and 12:2 (Heb. 12:3). The parallel to Jacob in the second must be "Israel," however. In the first, "Judah" is formally possible as a complement to Ephraim/House of Israel. But the chapter is solely concerned with Ephraim and his ancestor Jacob, so "Israel" should be substituted here as well, to remove the marks of the Judean edition. Neither Hosea nor the Judean editors made favorable references to Judah elsewhere in chapters 4–14, and there are no compelling reasons for interpreting this line in that way, as was done in the English versions as well as by Harper, Brown, and others. The line is ironic.

The "holy ones" are either sacred prostitutes (Cornill, Wellhausen, Weiser, Nötscher) or familiar deities of popular religion, past and present. Nötscher may be right in supposing that the original parallel to "holy ones" (*qᵉdhoshim*) was *'elim*, "gods," rather than *'el*. *Qᵉdhoshim* could conceivably be a plural of majesty (so *ASV, RSV, Chicago,* etc.), but it is rarely used elsewhere in this sense (only Prov. 9:10 and, possibly, 30:3). More commonly it designates heavenly beings (Ps. 89:6, 8; Deut. 8:13; Job 5:1; 15:15; Zech. 14:5). Jacob's *'el* is also the subject of vs. 4, where once again the popular understanding of this power is derided (vs. 5).

The verb רד is here taken to be from רוד (with *JPS, Moffatt,* Cheyne, Mauchline (?), Weiser, Nötscher, Sellin, and others). Some scholars read "Judah is still known by God" (e.g., *RSV,* Harper, and Brown), under the influence of the *LXX.* But the *LXX* cannot be used to support this translation. It reads, "Now God knows them" (probably עד ידעם אל for עד רד עם־אל), taking "and Judah" with the preceding clause. This version may be nothing more than an interpretation of the MT and, at the most, presupposes a text that differs from the MT in only one letter. The translation of the *RSV* and of the others entails a greater change in the Hebrew. The *LXX* concludes the line thus: "And they shall be called God's holy people." This is probably an interpretation and not a witness to a variant Hebrew text.

Verse 2 (Heb. 3). "Judah" is not parallel to "Jacob"; so, "Israel" must be read here (thus, Harper, Weiser, Brown, Mauchline, Wolff, Nötscher, Scott [p. 147], and others). Once this change has been made, the change of "Judah" to "Jacob" in 11:12 (Heb. 12:1) is obvious. It has often been concluded that the change to "Judah" was made in vs. 2 after 11:12b (in which Judah is the subject) had been inserted by a glossator into the original text (Wellhausen, Nowack, G. A. Smith, Harper, and Knight). However, according to this theory,

11:12–12:1 lacked any reference to Jacob, and the appearance of the name (which is not the equivalent of Ephraim) in the concluding threat (vs. 2) is thus anomalous. I prefer to assume that Jacob was originally mentioned in both the invective and the threat (cf., Weiser).

Verse 4 (Heb. 5). I have translated the MT quite literally but have added "*'El*" (cf., 11:12 and *'El-Bethel* in Gen. 35:7), to make the implicit irony explicit. Interpreted in this way, the line makes excellent sense. The people's localization of divine power in Bethel, whose sanctity was originally derived from the worship of a Canaanite *'el*, is manifested already in the words of the patriarch. The proper safeguard against the misappropriation of theophanic occasions is the use of the name "Yahweh" (vs. 5), but Israel has forgotten this fact. Most modern translations presuppose textual emendations, the most extensive being that of the *RSV*, which adds "God" twice, changes the pronouns, and prefixes a preposition to Bethel.

Even if the text were to be translated "*In* Bethel he will find us, . . ." the meaning is still that the angelic being over whom Jacob has prevailed will meet him once again in Bethel and submit once more to Jacob's exploitation. The god "Bethel" was actually worshipped in ancient Palestine (see, *IDB,* A–D, p. 390). The simplest reading of the MT of Hos. 12:4b (Heb. 12:5b) is: *"Bethel* will find us. . . ." This may well be correct.

Verse 6 (Heb. 7). באלהיך תשוב does not mean "return to your God" (e.g., *KJV, Chicago,* and Wolff), because ב is the wrong preposition for that. "By (the help of) your God" (*RSV,* Harper, and G. A. Smith), is conceivable. The change to "dwell in your tents" (באהליך תשב), is not radical, however, and produces the necessary judgmental conclusion to the poem, i.e., referring to a disciplinary return to the "wilderness." This reading is adopted by *Moffatt,* Sellin, Robinson, Nötscher, and H. L. Ginsberg (in *JBL* 80 (1961), 342). It conforms fully to the climactic line of the next section (vs. 9, Heb. 10). If vss. 5–6 are interpreted in this way, they need not be regarded as a pious gloss (as they have been, for example, by Wellhausen, Smith, Harper, and Lindblom [p. 104]).

Verse 7 (Heb. 8). "A 'Canaan' (כנען) with crooked scales" may be the correct nuance (thus, e.g., Harper, Brown, and Smith).

Verse 8 (Heb. 9). A translation commonly adopted is "all his gain suffices not for the guilt which it has incurred" (cf., *RSV, Chicago,* Wellhausen, Harper, Brown, and many others). Minor textual alterations are required to achieve this meaning. There is an excellent play on words in this verse: "I have found myself *'on* (wealth). . . . They will not find in me any *'awon* (crookedness). . . ."

Verse 10 (Heb. 11). The last line is literally, "gave parables by the hand of the prophets."

Verse 11 (Heb. 12). "Heap of witness" (גלעד) is otherwise the proper noun Gilead. Since the chapter is rife with allusions to the Jacob–traditions, I take this as a reference to an ancient, sacred memorial of a theophany or providential occurrence, like the one mentioned in Gen. 31:46–48, or possibly to an old covenant, like the one between Saul and Jabesh-Gilead (1 Sam. 11). "Gilgal" also means a (sacred) circle of stones. The line thus plays on the names of cultic sites whose precise identities are not stated. Since the verse is almost cryptic, it is no wonder that numerous translations have been proposed.

Verse 12 (Heb. 13). Many commentators regard this verse as an interruption between vss. 11 and 13. The *RSV* marks it off as a parenthetical gloss. Others move it: e.g., Harper, after vs. 3; Sellin, after vs. 6; and Brown and Scott, after 3a. The play on שמר ("tended") links vs. 12 to vs. 13, but this fact has been given opposite interpretations. For example, Scott (*The Message,* p. 147) concludes that the editor moved vs. 12 from its original place on the basis of the catchword association; but Ginsberg (*op. cit.,* p. 341) insists that vs. 13 only makes sense in association with vs. 12 (not that Ginsberg opposes rearranging the verses: indeed, he prefers the order 11:12; 12:7–8, 1, 2, 3–5, 12–13, 11, 9–10, 6; pp. 341–43). If a change is to be made, the simplest would seem to be moving vss. 12–13 ahead of vs. 10. The resulting poem is an invective of four lines (12, 13, 10, and 11a), plus a threat of two lines (11b and 14), thus:

IV

12   Jacob fled to the plain of Aram;
           Israel served for a wife;
           for a wife he tended (flocks).

13   But by a prophet Yahweh brought up
           Israel from Egypt,
             and by a prophet was he tended.

10   And I spoke by the prophets;
           I multiplied visions;
             I inspired prophetic signs.

11   But the heap of witness was a fraud!
       How empty it became:
          in Gilgal they sacrifice bulls!

      But their altars (will) be like piles of rock
        along the furrows of a field.
14   Ephraim has bitterly provoked His anger.
       His Lord will leave his blood upon him
       and turn his reproaches against him.

Nowhere is the text of Hosea more obscure than in chapter 12. A careful reading of the textual notes, the standard translations, and commentaries will serve as a warning to the reader to take any interpretation of these poems as a more or less interesting speculation. One impulse that comes upon the commentator as he works over these lines is to rearrange them. Few have resisted the impulse. Fewer still have agreed on the proper arrangement. I have pondered the proposals and played with new combinations of my own. In the end, I have found them all failures. With the possible exception of the minor rearrangement described in the last textual note, all of them involve private emendations of individual words (often extensive), or produce un-poems inferior to what we already have, or both. Better abandon the text altogether! The only genuine alternative to this counsel of despair is to make sense boldly of the text as it comes to us, making only those changes in detail that seem to be absolutely necessary to achieve coherence and that have also commended themselves to other scholars. Perhaps I have stared at the received text of Hos. 12 too long and have finally seen order where none exists. Nevertheless, I do see order there, in the poetic structure of the larger components if not in every line or phrase. This order becomes clearer to the reader of the Hebrew text as he finds it resisting his effort to refashion it into some other form.

Rearrangements that one is likely to make in these poems are inevitably based on patterns derived from other prophetic oracles and from assumptions as to what these ought to say. Critical categorizing makes us insensitive to the untypical poem. The great Hebrew poets were more imaginative than their commentators, and we must constantly beware lest we cut their unique creations to fit standard types. The poems of Hos. 12 are unusual. Therein lies their difficulty as well as their special appeal.

We have already encountered manifestations of Hosea's keen sense of historical continuity. It is evident once again in this chapter, but in a different form. Elsewhere he set himself to show that the falsity of Israel's major social institutions, the monarchy and the sacrificial cultus, was evident in their practice from the beginning, and must be therefore constitutional. A number of his statements suggest also that the whole orientation of Israel's culture from the time of the settlement in Palestine was idolatrous and unjust.[1] The historical analogies in the present chapter have a greater similarity with these latter passages, which are pointing to the inner crookedness of motive and understanding, than they have with the former ones, which point to specific, formal aberrations in the political structure of Israelite life.

In other respects, the poems in Hos. 12 are unique. They are the only ones in the book that allude to patriarchal traditions. Unlike Hosea's references to the exodus–wilderness traditions, in which the providential activity of God stands out, these little poems deal with the story of Jacob, without indicating any redemptive elements in the story. We are left with the impression that the patriarchal history was not a part of the history of redemption. If this inference is correct, it means that Hosea's interpretation of the pre-Mosaic period in the life of the Israelite tribes was radically different from that of the writers of Genesis.[2]

These short poems differ from Hosea's other historical allusions in yet another respect. These episodes from the past come from the

---

[1] Cf., the whole of 2:2–13 and especially 6:7; 9:10, 15, and 11:1–2.

[2] Some commentators have argued that Jacob is presented approvingly, as a man of faith, in at least parts of chapter 12, and is thus contrasted to Hosea's apostate contemporaries. Mauchline, for instance, regards 12:4–6 as commendatory, but believes it is not an original part of the poem (cf., Scott, *op. cit.*, pp. 70–73). Knight takes the reference in 12:3–6 to mean that Hosea was calling Israel to return to Yahweh, who condescended to bless even unlikeable men like Jacob. Peters sees a model of repentance in Hosea's picture of Jacob (*op. cit.*, p. 14 f.), See, also, Cheyne and Brown. Harper, Sellin, Robinson, Lindblom (*op. cit.*, pp. 101 ff.), Weiser, and Wolff, however, have interpreted the references to Jacob unfavorably. Ginsberg (*loc. cit.*) presents a refreshing modification of this view. He argues that Ephraim is depicted less as a malicious sinner than as a stupid fool. A noteworthy interpretation of the chapter has been suggested by Mrs. Roberta Chesnut (a student in my seminar at Perkins School of Theology), according to which the favorable references to Jacob (vss. 4 and 8) are popular boasts made in a debate with the prophet (i.e., the "controversy," vs. 2). The prophet's critique of Jacob's beliefs and behavior is given in the remainder (partly in the form of divine speech).

story of a man—a hero to whose personal story many memories of tribal history have adhered, perhaps, but a man nevertheless. The follies recalled by these allusions are more personal therefore and individual rather than institutional and communal. At the same time, they are employed as historical analogies to present follies that are being universally committed in Ephraim, i.e., communal evils. The line between private and corporate behavior is an indistinct one. Thus, this is a legitimate use of the Jacobean traditions; yet it gives a different tone to these analogies from that of the others in the book. It has the effect of interiorizing the evil that is described. It is here clearly a matter of personal consciousness and will.

Throughout this chapter, the subject is constantly fluctuating between the patriarchs Jacob (Israel) and Ephraim, on the one hand, and the people Israel (Ephraim) on the other. No effort has been made to keep them distinct from one another, or to present the historical episodes in chronological order.

A regular form is used in each of the five poems. It consists of two parts. The first part is an accusation, or sarcastic recollection, consisting of from two to four lines. The second part is a threat, and is always stated in a single line. This last feature of the poems is actually the clue to the structure of the chapter. It can hardly be accidental that the chapter has one-line threats occurring at such regular intervals. Each threat is logically dependent upon what precedes it. The dependence is especially close in ii and iii, where a divine asserveration introduces the threat. The recurrence of the name Yahweh at almost the same point in four of the five parts, and nowhere else in the poem, is another noteworthy stylistic feature.

The burden of these poems is not to show that the policies of seventh-century Israel were anticipated by similar ones in the life of the ancestor Jacob. Outward conditions of life had changed so much in the intervening centuries that almost nothing had remained of the old tribal society. Therefore, there was scarcely any basis left for comparison on the corporate level. The similarity between "Ephraim's" behavior in Hosea's time and Jacob's, as it is alluded to here, lay in their motives. Their deeds were analogous because they were products of similar dispositions.

Some of the ancient allusions in these oracles can be identified with episodes recorded in Genesis. This is true of Jacob's prenatal seizure of Esau's heel (12:3, cf., Gen. 25:26), his nocturnal contest with a divine being (vss. 3–4, cf., Gen. 32:24–30), and his extended servitude to Laban, in return for his daughters (vs. 12, cf., Gen. 29). The others are obscure. Vs. 4b could be a reference to Jacob's dream at Bethel (Gen. 28:10–17), but both this line and the scornful remark in 11:12b seem to be aimed at the patriarchal worship of local Palestinian deities, whom Jacob is here implicitly accused of exploiting for personal gain. In his insatiable self-seeking, he misconstrued the nature of God. Not only did the ancestors attempt to control the transcendent power of God, but they misconstrued also the moral character of their relationship to him. The post-Mosaic settler, Ephraim, is depicted in 12:7–8 as one who disregarded the deep moral requirements of his existence in the land. He regarded himself as sinless, because he had committed no crime—at least none that could be discovered. His energy was spent acquisitively, however, in the absence of a positive sense of communal dedication.

I take vs. 11 as a reference to the phase of Jacob's career east of the Jordan, which was marked by his service to Laban (vs. 12) and by such religious events as his encounter with the angel at Peniel (Gen. 32:24–30) and the covenant with Laban at Mizpah. This covenant was sealed with a "heap of witness" (Gen. 31:43–54). These sacred events were associated with sanctuaries that Hosea knew as principal scenes of Israel's later apostasy from Yahweh.

None of the sacred memories of Jacob, not even the great religious experiences that were celebrated in the Israelite sanctuaries, could compare with Yahweh's redemptive revelation mediated by Moses and other prophets (vss. 10 and 13). Israel preferred the undemanding Palestinian deities, however, to the God of the covenant (vss. 4–5, and 8–9). These did not demand the same radical obedience that Yahweh did. Therefore, Israel could promote "religion" at the ancient sanctuaries without feeling compelled to bring her "nonreligious" activities under the scrutiny of a God who claimed sovereignty over the whole of life. The religion of the Jacobean cult-places was subversive of Yahwism because it was private and atomistic whereas the latter was corporate and integrative. The "religious experiences" of Jacob, and their renewal in the cult, could easily have stood apart from the traditions and practices of the Yahwistic assembly (vs. 9), which was based upon the exodus event and the Mosaic covenant. A preoccupation with justice was inseparable from Yahwism, but it had no necessary connection with the cult-legends of Jacob. This was true, even though Yahwistic orthodoxy incorporated these legends into the Pentateuch and linked explicitly the patriarch's experiences to the Mosaic tradition (Exod. 3:15-16; 6:3).

The religion of the patriarchs was not incompatible with Mosaic Yahwism in what it affirmed. Indeed, there were at least two features that were indispensable to the latter faith. The first of these was the conviction that the deity established a personal relationship with men. The second was that the deity was a protector of the nomadic tribe, and was as free to move as the tribe itself. This notion of omnipresence, that is, of not being confined to a particular holy place or territory, was capable of extension to an idea of universal transcendence, that is, of not being confined to nature itself or to any particular people. However, this feature of nomadic, tribal religion was not memorialized in the Jacobean legends to which Hosea referred. The religion of these traditions was a devotion to local Palestinian deities. They were "personal," to be sure, but only in a limited way. They were primarily the objects of numinous feeling, projections of religious ecstasy. What happened to a man in his encounter with such a power was independent of his social relationships and had no positive implications for his social responsibilities. It left out of account therefore the most fundamental dimension of human existence.

Yahwism did not lack an awareness of the holy. The exodus and the Sinai traditions are filled with accounts of Israel's overwhelming experience of the terrifying, transcendent power of God. Yahweh was not only holy, however, and his worship was not merely the cultivation of numinous experiences. He had revealed himself to a community by changing the course of their corporate life. He had come to them as to a group and created in them a common faith and loyalty. Their "religious experience" was inseparable from the social crises of their history, and it had unavoidable implications for the conduct of their human relationships, both within Israel and without. A Yahwist's faith in God was personal and inward, and it could be associated with ecstatic experiences, such as that of Jacob in the cult legends. However, it could not be reduced to private, ecstatic events, because it was inconceivable apart from the social events in which Yahweh had made himself known. It was therefore inseparable from commitment to the community in which the faithful man stood.

This irreducible social dimension of Yahwistic faith might have meant nothing more than the exaltation of Israel's particular mores to the status of divine law. This phenomenon did indeed take place, and most of the "divine" commandments contained in the corpus of Old Testament law are Israelite laws given religious sanction. Not all, however. Some of the most basic ethical principles of covenantal Yahwism are derived explicitly from the exodus faith. The belief that God had saved Israel from slavery and extinction in Egypt and the desert imposed on the faithful an obligation to eliminate similar threats to human existence that were found in their environment. This ethic was ultimately capable of universal extension, both in the sense that it applied to every level of man's being, and in the sense that it was relevant to all men, as promise and as demand.

Israel disavowed this ethic, and the faith that supported it, in favor of the easier religion of the Palestinian sanctuaries. In doing this, however, the Israelites were unable to escape the justice of Yahweh. Their denial of his lordship did not strip him of his power. He would still execute his judgments and they would still suffer the consequences of their actions. They would be required, against their will and at a terrible cost, to surrender the bogus religion of the *'elim,* with its pathetic little rituals, and return to the "desert" (vs. 6 and 9). There, in austerity, they could atone for their guilt (vs. 14), learn again the convenantal virtues of loyalty (*ḥesed*) and justice (*mishpaṭ*), and renew their faith in the Lord, who is never controlled, but who comes to those who wait to do his will (vs. 6).

CHAPTER

14 FROM LIFE TO DEATH:

HOSEA 13

I

1   When Ephraim spoke, there was trembling;
         he was exalted in Israel.
                 But he became guilty with Baal and died.
2   So now they persist in transgression,
         and make molten images for themselves:
     Elegant idols of silver,
         each the work of an expert!
     Sacrifice to these, they say.
         Men kiss calves!

3   So they will be like a morning cloud,
         and like dew that goes early away,
     Or like chaff blown from a threshing-floor,
         or smoke from a hole in the wall.

II

4   I am Yahweh your God
         from the land of Egypt;
     And you know no God but me;
         for besides me there is no savior.
5   I shepherded you in the wilderness,
         in a land of drought.
6   As they were pastured, so they were satisfied;
         (as) they were satisfied, so they were arrogant.
                 Thus they forgot me.

7   So I have become like a lion to them;
         like a leopard I will lurk by the way.
8   I will meet them as a bear bereaved of her cubs,
         and tear them open to the heart.
     I will devour them there like a lion,
         (as) a wild beast would tear them apart.

218   :

9   It is your destruction, O Israel,
          since your help was in me!
10   I am your king.
          Where is your savior
               in all your cities, and your champions,
          Of whom you said,
               "Give me a king and princes"?
11   I give you a king in my anger!
          and take him away in my wrath!

III

12   Ephraim's guilt is wrapped up;
          his sin is hidden.
13   The pains of childbirth begin for him,
          but he is a child without sense.
     When it is time, he does not come
          to the mouth of the womb.

14   Shall I ransom them from the power of Sheol?
          Shall I deliver them from death?
     I am your pestilence, O Death!
          I am your plague, O Sheol!
               Repentance is hid from my eyes!

IV

15   Although he flourishes among his brothers,
          an east wind, a wind of Yahweh will blow,
               rising from the desert;
     And his springs will be parched,
          and his well will dry up.
     His stores will be plundered,
          all his precious things.

16   Samaria will bear her guilt,
          for she has rebelled against her God.
     They will fall by the sword;
          their babies will be dashed to death,
               and their pregnant wives slashed open.

NOTES ON THE TEXT

Verse 1. The *LXX* presupposes *toroth* (רתת) for "trembling" (תרת), and some scholars have adopted that text ("oracles," Robinson; "my torah," Sellin; cf., Peters, *Osee,* p. 29, who regards this as a reference to the Mosaic covenant). It is extremely unlikely, however, that *toroth,* even with defective spelling (instead of תורת or תורות), would have been misread as רתת, which occurs nowhere else in the OT (though, compare, רטט in Jer. 49:24 and רתת in the Qumran Hymn, IQH IV, 33). It was Ernst Sellin's interpretation of this verse (together with 12:14) as an allusion to a tradition concerning the martyrdom of Moses at the hands of his own people that led Sigmund Freud to propound his bizarre but entertaining theses concerning Yahwistic religion in *Moses and Monotheism.* See Sellin, "Hosea und das Martyrium des Mose," *ZAW* 46 (1928), 26–33.

Verse 2. The last line is obscure. The MT apparently reads (literally), "To them they are speaking sacrificers of men they kiss calves." Some such rendering is adopted by the *LXX,* Vulgate, and many ancient and modern commentators. The text I have adopted is the favorite alternative (cf., for instance, *RSV,* Brown, Nötscher, and Mauchline). It entails the minor change of זבחי to זבחו.

Verse 4. The *LXX* (and probably the Hebrew text from which it was translated) added (after "Yahweh your God"), "Who establishes the heaven and creates the earth, whose hands have created all the host of heaven. But I did not show them to you that you should go after them." This affirmation recalls Deut. 32:8–9, in its last part, and the doxologies in Amos 4:13; 5:8–9; and 9:5–6, in its first part.

Verse 5. The MT is "I knew you (ידעתיך) in the wilderness"; but the *LXX,* Syriac, Vulgate, and Targum read "shepherded" (רעתיך), which is a better parallel to the next line (which also employs רעה, though in the intransitive sense, "graze, feed"). It is adopted by Smith, Sellin, Robinson, Brown, Harper, Weiser, Wolff, and others.

Verse 6. Literally, "according to their pasturage."

Verse 7. The English versions follow the *LXX* in making the first verb future (the difference from MT lies only in the vocalization). The MT properly conveys the Hosean idea that the divine judgment has already begun, so I prefer to retain it.

Verse 9. The irony in Hosea's designation of Yahweh as Israel's help is lost if the text is emended to "Who can help you?" (*RSV, Chicago,* Brown, Weiser, Wolff, and others).

Verse 14. The radical monotheism of Hosea is nowhere more boldly or terribly expressed than in these lines. The common emendation of "I am" (אהי) to "where is?" (איה) (cf., the ancient and English versions and most modern commentators) is a bowdlerizing of the text. The ancient commentators generally followed the *LXX* in interpreting the verse as a promise of redemption (cf., Paul's allusion to it in 1 Cor. 15:55), but the moderns are almost unanimous in judging it a threat. Thus, the emended text is generally taken to mean "Bring on your pestilence, O Death!" In the context, vs. 14a is best translated as a question, although it lacks an interrogative particle (cf., *Chicago, Moffatt, RSV, G.K.* 150a, Brown, Harper, Nötscher, and Wolff, among others). It can be translated as a declaration, however: "I shall ransom them. . . . I shall deliver them. . . ." (cf., *Jerusalem,* the older English versions, Robinson, and Weiser). Although most modern commentators consider vs. 14 a threat, several interpret it as a promise of new life to Ephraim (Robinson, Weiser, and Knight). This interpretation requires the separation of the passage from its context (Robinson and Weiser). It is always possible to resort to this device, but it is not a persuasive solution to the problem. The simplest solution, by far, is to make no textual changes at all and accept vs. 14a as a question. The passage is thus consistent both internally and in relation to its context.

Verse 15. "Like a reed plant" (כאחי) should perhaps be read instead of "among brothers" (בן אחים) (cf., *Moffatt, RSV,* Robinson, Mauchline, and Wolff). The *LXX* and other ancient versions support the translation "since he will cause a division among brothers," which is adopted by some scholars (either by emending פרא to פרד, or פרע, or by interpreting פרא with G. R. Driver [*JTS* 39, 164] in the sense of Akkadian *para'u* II, "to separate"). There may be a pun on the name Ephraim (אפרים) in the verb פרא.

Verse 16 (Heb. 14:1). Instead of "bear guilt," אשם might be translated "make atonement" (Weiser) or "pay the penalty." Cf., 5:15 and 10:2.

THE MOODS of Hosea's final oracles are immoderate. Here the two realities of Hosea's prophetic life are given complete expression. On the one hand, his faith in God and his confidence in the eventual triumph of God's love give rise to the joyous song of renewal in chapter 14. On the other, the terrible fact of Israel's national disaster is given absolute expression in chapter 13. The realities described and the emotions they convey are as different as life and death, for life and death are precisely what they are about.

The death of Samaria and her kingdom is presented in chapter 13 in a scene of sheer horror. It closes with a cry of desolation over the gratuitous murder of the city's babies and pregnant women by her Assyrian captors. This last symbol of the evil of war is not the invention of an outraged prophetic imagination, but the product of military history. This was the worst of many atrocities to which ancient armies resorted and from which Hosea knew Samaria would not be spared. Modern man is of course no better than his ancestors. The very crime by which Assyria sealed the fate of Samaria is reported by T. E. Lawrence in his description of the Turkish capture of the Arab village of Tafas, Syria, in 1918:

> The village lay stilly under its slow wreaths of white smoke, as we rode near, on our guard. Some grey heaps seemed to hide in the long grass, embracing the ground in the close way of corpses. We looked from these, knowing they were dead; but from one a little figure tottered off, as if to escape us. It was a child, three or four years old, whose dirty smock was stained red over one shoulder and side, with blood from a large half-fibrous wound, perhaps a lance thrust, just where neck and body joined.
>
> The child ran a few steps, then stood and cried to us in a tone of astonishing strength (all else being very silent), "Don't hit me, Baba"; . . . dropped in a little heap, while the blood rushed out again over her clothes; then, I think, she died.
>
> We rode past the other bodies of men and women and four more dead babies, looking very soiled in the daylight, towards the village; whose loneliness we now knew meant death and horror. By the outskirts were low mud walls, sheepfolds, and on one something red and white. I looked close and saw the body of a woman folded across it, bottom upwards, nailed there by a saw bayonet whose haft stuck hideously into the air from between her naked legs. She had been pregnant, and about her lay others, perhaps twenty in all, variously killed, but set out in accord with an obscene taste.[1]

The only difference between this scene and the one in Hos. 13 is that Tafas had no military importance and was capriciously destroyed by a defeated army in retreat, whereas Samaria was the capital of a kingdom that had provoked an Assyrian invasion by political rebellion. Ancient kings, moreover, knew in advance the cost of failure in such a revolt. Therefore, king Hoshea of Israel was as guilty a butcher as Sargon II of Assyria.

[1] T. E. Lawrence, *Seven Pillars of Wisdom* (Garden City, N.Y., 1936), p. 631.

Hosea laid the guilt of Samaria's death squarely upon the kingdom itself (vs. 16). The slaughter of her people was the last death she had to die. The first had been the baalization of her religion (vs. 1). Death thus marks the beginning and end of these oracles as it did mark Ephraim's political history. Ephraim, son of Joseph, had been for centuries the chief among the ten northern tribes and still enjoyed premier status in Hosea's time.[2] As a matter of fact, the loss of the northern and eastern Israelite territories to Assyria in 733 B.C. had left Ephraim almost alone as a "flourishing" tribe (vs. 15). However, his days, too, were numbered.

What commands our attention in this chapter is not so much Hosea's ethical analysis, or his description of the end of Samaria, as his assertion that Yahweh is the Destroyer. This is the salient theological feature of the oracle. Even this is not theoretically new, because Hosea has already said repeatedly in previous oracles that Yahweh executes his justice through the terrible realities of history. Belief in the universal sovereignty of a righteous God demands that conclusion. The uniqueness of chapter 13 lies in the relentless manner in which this logic is worked out.

Yahweh is the Lord of existence, and existence is an eternal conflict between good and evil, life and death. Nevertheless, the faithful have perennially preferred to attribute the power of death (in so far as death may be spoken of as a power, rather than as the negation of power) to something other than God. Is not God the Lord of the living, after all? Is not Death God's first enemy, and is not the realm of death outside the sphere of God's life-giving spirit? Even if the second question be answered negatively, and if it be denied that Sheol (Hades, the Grave, the Pit, the Underworld) is beyond God's saving reach, is it not true, nevertheless, that death is fundamentally opposed to God? The inner necessity of affirming this conviction led Hosea's heirs in the biblical tradition to formulate a limited cosmic dualism, with Satan and his demonic legions arrayed in battle against God for possession of the world and man. These are the spiritual hosts of wickedness in the heavenly places, to which the New Testament refers, and the fallen angels of ancient speculation, whom Milton best portrays.[3]

The combatants in Hosea's cosmic battle were Israel and Yahweh,

---

2 See, Gen. 37:5–11; 48; and 49:22–26.
3 See, e.g., Eph. 6:12 and Milton, *Paradise Lost*, Book I.

with Egypt, Assyria, and Hosea playing secondary roles. No transcendent demonic force stood between God and Israel. He was the one who confronted them at every point in their history. In the beginning he had been their savior (vss. 7–9, 14). Having turned from him to seek their welfare in non-covenantal goals, they simply encountered him again, barring their way (vss. 6–8). The anarchy that attended the dynastic changes of Israel's last years was a manifestation of the wrath of Yahweh (vs. 11). Championing causes subversive of justice and Yahwistic faith, Israel's kings became entirely futile (vs. 10). Thus, disavowing their ultimate help, they turned their penultimate help to their own destruction (vs. 9).

Israel's death-struggle with God was not a blind conflict with an arbitrary power, nor with a power that unknowingly wrought havoc in the world. Hosea's divine destroyer is not be be equated with what modern man calls natural evils, and the jurists, "acts of God." Hosea may also have believed that God's hand lay directly behind natural disasters, but he did not leave us a record of the conviction. The acts he spoke about were, on the surface, "acts of men." To the prophetic eye, however, the very "pestilence of death" that swept Israel from among the kingdoms of the world, was God himself. This was the God whom Israel had known (vs. 4), the God of righteousness. Ephraim had been free to choose life or death under him, and he stupidly chose death, like a child refusing to be born (vs. 13). So, finally, the great reservoir of evil, which he had accumulated through decades of folly, burst forth upon him and he perished (vs. 12).

The reader is repelled by the terrible words Hosea speaks for God: "*I am your plague, O Sheol! Repentance is hid from my eyes!*" Yet this was the only honest conclusion to the logic of Hosea's theology of history. Hosea was not merely an observer of the tragedy, of course. He was affected by it as thoroughly as any man in Israel. The horror of his images is due precisely to his involvement. It was his tragedy, too. The indignation was his, but so was the suffering, not only the potential physical pain, but the actual realization that all the labor of his nation during three hundred years was utterly wasted, that nothing whatever would remain. "Chaff blown from a threshing-floor, or smoke from a hole in the wall." And then darkness and silence. Instead of the trumpet that warned of approaching disaster (Hos. 5:8),

"A voice was heard in Ramah,
  lamentation and bitter weeping.
Rachel was weeping for her children;
  she refused to be comforted for her children,
    because they were no more."

(Jer. 31:15)

CHAPTER

15 FROM DEATH TO LIFE:
HOSEA 14

I

1   Return, O Israel,
        to Yahweh your God;
            for you have stumbled in your guilt.

2   Take with you (only) words,
        when you return to Yahweh.
    Say to him,
        "Forgive all guilt,
    That we may receive what is good,
        and offer the fruit of our lips.

3   Asshur cannot save us;
        upon horses we will not ride.
    And we will never again say 'our gods'
        to the work of our hands;
            for the orphan finds mercy in thee."

II

4   I will heal their apostasy;
        I will love them willingly;
            for my anger has turned from them.

5   I will be like dew to Israel;
        he will blossom like a lily.
    He will send down roots like a poplar,

6   and his branches will spread forth.
    He will be as lovely as the olive
        and as fragrant as the cedar.

7   Those who would live in his shade will return;
        they will thrive like the corn;
    They will blossom like the vine,
        as fragrant as the wine of Lebanon.

8   What further need has Ephraim of idols?
        It is I who afflicted and I who watch for him.

I am like a luxuriant juniper tree;
your fruit is found in me.

9   [Whoever is wise, let him understand these things,
or prudent, let him know them;
For the ways of Yahweh are right,
that the righteous may walk in them
and the wicked stumble in them.]

NOTES ON THE TEXT

Verse 2 (Heb. 3). קַח ("accept"), as an imperative, is not exactly parallel either to תִשָּׂא ("thou dost forgive, remove") or to נְשַׁלְּמָה ("we will render"). The authorized English versions have supposed God to be the subject of קח and have therefore translated תשא as an imperative. The "good," which God is to accept, then, is the "fruit of our lips" (the "words" of vs. 2a). קח may be construed as parallel to נשלמה, however (with a great many modern commentators and translators), if וּנְקַח is read in place of וקח. The original text would then have been עֵון וּנְקַח, and in this sequence the second נ could easily have been lost. פרים is either "bulls," which is figuratively rendered "fruit," or פרי ("fruit") with an enclitic מ (thus, many recent commentators, obviating the deletion of the final מ, a practice common among earlier critics).

Verse 3 (Heb. 4). "Asshur" is Assyria, of course, but the Semitic name served for the god Asshur as well as for the city and empire. In the present context this dual meaning is particularly appropriate.

Verse 5 and 6 (Heb. 6 and 7). Read לִבְנֶה ("poplar") for לבנון ("Lebanon") in vs. 5 and take לבנון in vs. 6 as an allusion to the famous cedars of Lebanon. "As fragrant as Lebanon," however, does make sense.

Verse 7 (Heb. 8). The textual difference between the MT's "in *his* shadow" (בְצִלּוֹ) and "in *my* shadow" (בְצִלִּי) (*Moffatt, RSV,* Wellhausen, Weiser, Wolff, and others) is slight, but the ancient versions support the MT, and in the context the tree is Ephraim, not God. The emendation therefore amounts to eisegesis.

Verse 8 (Heb. 9). The MT is "Ephraim, what more have I (to do) with idols," but the simple change of לִי to לוֹ (which is supported by the *LXX*) makes much better sense. Ephraim is then referred to uniformly in the third person, and the proper contrast between idols and Yahweh as objects of his devotion is secured. This reading is adopted by many commentators, including Robinson, Weiser, Wolff, and Nötscher.

Innumerable translations of line 2 have been proposed. If the MT is retained, the first verb means either "I answer(ed), hearken(ed)" (*ASV, RSV, JPS, Jerusalem,* Wolff, and others) or "I afflict(ed), humble(ed)" (*LXX, Moffatt*), and the second, "I (will) regard, watch" (*ASV, RSV, KJV, JPS,* Brown, Wolff, and others). The *LXX* translates the second "strengthen." The slight change of שׁור to שׁוב, with the sense of "affirm," "establish," or "restore," has often been proposed (e.g., *BH*, Robinson, and Weiser). The resulting statement is eloquent: "It is I who afflict(ed) and I (shall) restore." Yet, שׁור occurs in 13:7 in a negative sense ("lurk, watch"), and its positive use here is thus especially meaningful. God, the Watcher, is both disciplinarian and benefactor. Wellhausen's suggestion, that the original was אני ענתו ואשׁרתו, "I am his 'Anath and his 'Asherah," was described by Harper as a "freak of the imagination," but Duhm, Gressmann, Sellin, Nyberg (*Studien,* p. 115), Fohrer (*op. cit.,* p. 171), and *Chicago,* have been less squeamish and have adopted it. Köhler's minor emendation of ואשׁורנו to וַאֲאַשְּׁרֶנּוּ (*sic*) (II אשׁר Pi.) yields a good line: "I have afflicted and I will lead him in the straight way" (*Lexicon,* p. 95).

Verse 9 (Heb. 10). This appendage in the style of the wisdom literature is universally acknowledged as an editorial comment. It is an appropriate comment, however, on a book that concludes with oracles on the way of death (chap. 13) and the way of life (chap. 14). Its easy piety is somewhat offensive, perhaps, coming as it does after the turmoil of Hosea's oracles.

H OSEA'S AGE was an age of wrath. His contemporaries in the two decades after the death of Jeroboam II (742 B.C.) would probably have evaluated it differently, but their criteria would also have differed from his. Although they were partly frustrated in the fulfilment of their hopes, they probably did not believe them futile or sterile. They discovered their futility too late, at the very end of the era. It was their descendants, therefore, who first became fully conscious of their own existence in wrath. In this sense, then, Hosea shared the age of wrath with the generations that followed Israel's loss of independence. We do not know what happened to the Israelite population after 721 B.C. The account in 2 Kings 17 pictures their being absorbed into the hybrid culture of the Assyrian Empire, through the assimilation of the exiles abroad and the syncretism of those who remained at home.

The Books of Kings are highly tendentious history, however, and the cultural destiny of the people of Israel may not have been as bleak and anonymous as this account declares. There are other indications in the Old Testament that descendants of the Ten Tribes continued to believe in the God of their fathers and to maintain the worship of Yahweh.[1] Many of the survivors of the Assyrian invasion of 724–21 B.C. undoubtedly fled to Judah. Curiously, their destiny there as men of Yahweh was hardly less problematic than that of the exiles, or that of the remnant in Assyrian Israel; for Judah suffered the same ravages of syncretism during most of the following century that had plagued her northern sister.

Nevertheless, Judah did provide the minimal conditions necessary for the survival of a covenantal community. I believe that Yahwism would have survived the simultaneous destruction of both Israel and Judah in the eighth century, and that forms for maintaining a community of faith would have been found at that time, similar to those created after the eventual collapse of Judah. However, until Judah actually fell, the Judean cultus was the chief means of continuity for the people of Yahweh. There may also have been an unbroken line of prophets during this period, although it is impossible to reconstruct one out of the few whom we know from the biblical records. These few contributed immeasurably, of course, to the task of maintaining a genuine Yahwism. Thus, the cult, although it was a poor thing by prophetic standards, together with the witness of the prophets themselves, provided the context within which the presence of God could be made known and faith in him affirmed from generation to generation.

Even in an age of wrath, God's presence and purpose can be proclaimed, and faith in him affirmed. Hosea's oracles spoke to such an

---

[1] See the discussion of this subject in A. C. Welch, *Post-Exilic Judaism* (Edinburgh and London, 1935), pp. 17–61. Working from such materials as Deut. 7; 28:27–37, 45–57; Jer. 3:21–4:1; 2 Chron. 30; Neh. 9; and Pss. 44 and 80, he attempts to show that Yahwism did not die in Israel after 721 B.C., but that a substantial contribution was made to post-exilic Judaism by survivors of the northern kingdom.

age. We assume that they were not really heard by the men of Israel before the fall of Samaria, although there may have been some who were influenced by his words. From the fact that his oracles were collected and transmitted into the main stream of the Judean literary tradition we conclude that they were heard more especially by subsequent generations—at first perhaps by only a few, in the prophetic circle itself, but ultimately by many more. The theological affinities that exist among Hosea, Deuteronomy, and Jeremiah suggest that Hosea was one of the prime contributors to the traditional Yahwistic minority that lived during the black half-century of Manasseh's reign and that fostered the reform in the reign of Josiah.[2] If this was so, then Hosea's oracles were indirectly proclaimed again during the final decades of the Judean kingdom; proclaimed once again, that is, in an age of wrath, when Judah followed Israel to her death.

By whatever route we follow the Book of Hosea, therefore—and all are hypothetical, because the Bible is silent on matters of literary history—we come at last to the post-exilic era, post-721 B.C. and post-587 B.C. The national state of Judah proved to be as impotent a vehicle of the covenant of God as Israel had been, and the hope of Hosea that God would create a faithful people after the fall of Samaria was not to be realized through the agency of the monarchy. The editor who wrote Hos. 1:7 and 1:11–2:1 seems to have believed that the kingdom of David would be the rallying point for a great revival of all the tribes of Israel; but he was wrong. Hosea himself tied none of his hopes to the Judean state nor to any other political institution. His hopes were founded entirely upon God. He believed God to be Lord of history, and he was certain that God would come again, as he had in the past, to create for himself an obedient people. Israel, the people of Yahweh, was not destroyed with the kingdom of Israel, or later with the kingdom of Judah. Yahweh could use the shattered fragments of the old people with which to begin again.

---

[2] On the Ephraimite origin of the Deuteronomic tradition, which influenced the Judean revival of Yahwism in the late seventh century, see A. C. Welch, *The Code of Deuteronomy* (London, 1924), and G. von Rad, *Studies in Deuteronomy (Studies in Biblical Theology* No. 9, London, 1953). The relationship between Jeremiah and Hosea can be seen especially in Jer. 1–6. A simple reading of Jer. 2–3, for instance, by one who has carefully read Hosea, will demonstrate the remarkable affinity in idea and image. For details, of course, any standard commentary on Jeremiah will be helpful. I have called attention in Additional Note C to the evidence that supports a seventh-century date for the (initial) Judean revision of the Book of Hosea.

In chapter 14, as in chapters 2–3 and 11, Hosea addressed his promises of renewal to those who were already Yahwists. The new community, therefore, was to be created out of them or out of their descendants. The chances are very slight that he reflected upon the prospects of the future conversion of non-Israelites to Yahwistic faith. There is no positive hint of that idea in his oracles. Yet who are the people of Israel whom he addresses here? What are their distinguishing marks? There is only one, faith in Yahweh, inherent in which is the disavowal of idolatry (14:3), the acknowledgment of the need of forgiveness (vs. 2), and the grateful acceptance of his gifts (vss. 4–8). The new people of the covenant would be those who worshipped Yahweh with these words of faithful confession (vs. 2). However wide Hosea's imagination may have been at this point, his words cannot be used in any narrower sense than this. The meaning of Hos. 14 to subsequent readers can only be that whoever serves Yahweh in faithful obedience belongs to Israel. Israel consists of those who serve him in faith.

The original covenantal people had been made up of diverse elements of highly uncertain pedigree, few of whom could seriously have "claimed Abraham as their father." Throughout the centuries, countless Israelites after the flesh refused service to Yahweh, while countless others became participants in the worshipping community. There was no rigid birthright to a place in that assembly. To be sure, many early conversions were probably tribal and therefore superficial. Others came about by intermarriage, military conquest, and the acquisition of slaves. The individual "sojourners," i.e., the resident aliens, were permitted to become full covenanters, and large numbers surely did. Much of this change of religion was probably nothing more than an exchange of divine names and the adoption of a new set of rituals. On the other hand, birthright membership in Israel was certainly no guarantee of true knowledge, faith, or righteousness! If the cultic community of Yahweh had always been open to anyone who accepted the cultic prescriptions, how much more open (or was it less open, since it was a "circumcision of the heart"?) was Hosea's new people of God.

Pre-exilic Israel had not been merely a cultic community, of course. It was also a civil society whose life was regulated by law. Although Israelite law was in many respects not unlike that of other ancient societies, there was, nevertheless, an Israelite legal tradition that defined the community as effectively as its cultus did. The convert to Yahwism took upon himself an obligation, therefore, to the civil law as well as to the law of the sanctuary. Hosea's oracles of renewal, however, say nothing about the role of that legal tradition in the life of the future people of God, just as they say nothing about the role of the old cultus in their life. Because of Hosea's profoundly critical attitude toward the sacrificial cult, I am inclined to take his silence at this point as a denial of its future usefulness. On the other hand, no permanent religious community is possible without a cultus of some sort. Is it possible that Hosea imagined a new ritual of the word? Vss. 14:2–3 may not have been written with any specific act in mind, but it is perfectly appropriate to the ritual of the word that was actually developed in the later synagogue.

Hosea was also silent, both in his promises and in his denunciations, about civil law. This silence is not surprising, however. Civil law in Israel was as fluid as everywhere else. The laws themselves were constantly changing and few of them could be considered absolute norms of covenantal life. Those that could, that is, those that were fundamental principles of Yahwism, such as respect for human life, property, and dignity were unequivocally endorsed by Hosea. This is clear in his denunciation of the absence of such virtues in Israel (e.g., 4:1–2), and is explicit in his promise of a new covenant (2:19). It could be assumed that the specific laws of the people of God would be applications of these principles in the changing conditions of their existence, but not that a paradise would ever exist in which laws would be unnecessary.

Hosea's great promises of restoration are not predicated upon the continuation or construction of any particular political or ecclesiastical institutions, but only upon confession, forgiveness, the healing of the apostate will, and faith (14:1–4). Several reasons may be advanced to explain why he should have framed only these conditions and no others. One is that he was too close to the ruin of the old community to have any inkling of the forms that reconstruction might take. This limitation was not peculiar to Hosea, of course, but applied to all prophets. It is simply one instance of the general human ignorance of the future. Incidentally, the absence from this poem of any concrete suggestions concerning the structure or setting of the restored community points away from a post-exilic (i.e., post-587

B.C.) date for this oracle. The further away from Hosea himself one moves in seeking a composer for it, the harder it is to account for this basic feature of the promise.

Hosea's promise to Israel had both immediate and perennial significance. The immediate truth of his word was that Ephraim's destruction was a new opportunity. God the Destroyer was, first and last, God the Creator. The fulfilment of his covenantal purpose was completely dependent upon the faithful response of men, for his purpose was to create a community of free, righteous, and faithful persons; but, his purpose was not to be frustrated by Ephraim's recent (and ancient) failure. Yahweh would come again to those of Ephraim who would hear. This promise was as true for the remnant of Israel on the day after the fall of Samaria as it was for any later generation.

At the same time, Hosea's promise is perennially true. God is forever coming to his people, and to those who are not yet his people, so as to re-create them in obedience and trust. The conditions are always the same, confession, forgiveness, the healing of the apostate will, and faith. Of course, it is always a community of men to whom he comes, and part of their response to God's merciful and loyal love (*hesed*) is to show *hesed* to each other and to establish justice. In saying this about Hos. 14, I do not mean to imply that he offered a vague, romantic wish. Not at all. He was no romantic. The renewal he promised was not merely for those few individuals who, disregarding the hell in which they actually lived, could rise to serenity in the world of their imagination. It was a promise to every sort of man, one that could transform his personal existence in the very hell where he lived, as well as all his human relationships, including even the corporate structures of his society. That the promise was never perfectly fulfilled among sinful men, or never long maintained, did not make it untrue or irrelevant. It was always capable of renewal, and was so at the most mundane level of human experience.

Since the truth of this oracle does not depend on its being Hosea's, the simple question of authorship is not of great importance. However, the relationship of this promise to Hosea's oracles of doom is an important issue. Hölscher put the sentiment of two generations of scholars very well when he said that Hosea had no hope beyond the fall of the nation because he did not, like Amos, individualize and universalize his conception of religion.[3] To this argument one must reply, first of all, that it proposes false alternatives. While Hosea's oracles are all addressed to individuals as moral agents, the oracles presuppose at the same time the covenant-community within which these individuals stand. Further, and even more decisive is the fact that the community presupposed by Hosea's promise is not the monarchial state but the people of the covenant. These people, in their long history, had survived many changes of political organization, economy, geography, and cult. Neither the extant state nor the extant cult was necessary for the preservation of the community of the faithful. They were actually detriments, as has been thoroughly established in our study of Hosea's oracles of denunciation. Once this point has been accepted, it becomes clear that chapter 14 is not a contradiction to chapter 13, and the main objection to the Hosean authorship of the final promise falls away.

Other objections that have often been raised are that chapter 14 presupposes the fall of Samaria and that it could not have been written therefore by Hosea; that the allusion to "horses" (vs. 3) as a symbol of Egyptian alliance is dependent upon Isa. 31:1 (cf., 30:16) and upon 31:9–21; that the picture of fulfilment through natural blessings is un-Hosean; that the demand for mere words contrasts with Hosea's demand for deeds; that an alliance with Egypt (vs. 3) was impossible in Hosea's time; and, that Hosea could not have spoken of Yahweh's wrath as having departed from Israel.[4]

The affinity between Hos. 14 and Isa. 31 hardly demonstrates dependence in either direction. If there be any, nevertheless, then Hos. 14 is probably the prior term. The allusion in 14:3 to Egyptian horses is matched by numerous references to Egypt in other parts of Hosea and is therefore no anachronism, whether or not it implies

---

[3] Die Propheten (Leipzig, 1914), p. 220.

[4] Most of these are listed, with approval, by Harper, though some have been taken from Wellhausen and Hölscher (loc. cit.). Similar arguments will be found in most of the standard commentaries and manuals written between 1890 and 1940. In the 1920's, Scott in the United States and Sellin and Kittel in Germany were almost alone among so-called liberal scholars in defending the genuineness of the hopeful parts of Hosea. In the 1930's, there were, in addition, Brown, Bewer, Oesterley, Robinson, and Eissfeldt. After World War II, the balance of opinion shifted the other way, as indicated by the works of Bentzen, Weiser, Procksch, Snaith, Nötscher, and H. W. Robinson; and today it is nearing a consensus. One hopes it will not be an uncritical consensus.

operation of retributive justice. God's holiness transcends any human standard of justice. His love also transcends any human love. It is, among other things, the motive of divine wrath. So much is implied by chapters 2, 3, and 11. Yet wrath is more than the disciplinary agent of a love that seeks to educate. Wrath is a destructive power, the evil effect of which on human life cannot be rationalized away with pious words about the "ultimate" love of God.

The actual destruction of the Israelite kingdom was an event of wrath. Terrible evils came to pass in this event, which continued to plague the survivors of 721 B.C. They were children of wrath as much as their compatriots who perished in the Assyrian invasion. They had not died, to be sure, but dying is not the only kind of suffering. The pain suffered by the survivors must have been manifold and prolonged. Indeed, there was no end to the age of wrath for the men of the old order, in whom the memory of that order continued to contrast with the outward circumstances of the new era of "Egyptian slavery." They were all orphans (14:3) of the deceased Ephraim.

Hosea promised the new life of faith to these very orphans, the children of wrath. He declared that God's anger had passed away and that God watched for their return, ready to heal their apostasy (vss. 4 and 8). The Destroyer had become the Redeemer. On the one hand, the precondition of their loving acceptance by Yahweh was their return to him (vs. 1), that is, the contrite renewal of their faith in him. On the other hand, the very promise that he was eager to love them and heal their turning away (vs. 4) was the foundation of their repentance. They could know already, if they would believe the prophet, that they were accepted into a renewed covenant with the Lord. His love, therefore, freely offered, was the precondition of their obedience, freely rendered. The promise of God's future readiness to love was in fact the expression of a love already at work. The knowledge of that love created the possibility of contrition and the occasion for faith.

God's love did not momentarily transform the political and economic conditions of Israel's existence. From the perspective of the old royal and ecclesiastical orders, the effects of wrath remained fully evident. Covenantal renewal took place within the conditions of wrath. Hosea promised the eventual fulfilment of Israel's natural life (14:5-7), by which was implied the whole order of creation, but he gave no assurance of an immediate perfection of that order or the

any diplomatic ties between Israel and Egypt. Israel had bc
horses from Egypt from the time of Solomon (1 Kings 10:28

The reference to Assyria certainly gives contemporaneity tc
confession in 14:2–3. The denial made here recalls the earlier fo
of the Israelite kings. On the other hand, many survivors of the 1
dom undoubtedly sought salvation through Assyria. This confe:
is relevant in principle to any man of faith, however, and not m
to those who lived through the destruction of Samaria and the fol
ing period of Assyrian mastery. The mention of Assyria, and pos
Egypt, does not prove that Hosea wrote this passage. Howeve
does tie it to the rest of the book.

The "mere words" called for in this oracle are not to be
against Hosea's demand for total obedience. Although this p
does not explicitly say so, the words of confession it contains are
very foundation of such obedience. Confession of guilt and fait
God are no substitutes for "deeds" of justice and love, but cha
14 does not imply that they are. They are demanded here i
substitute for Israel's old performance of material sacrifice. In fut
these words of faith are to be the only ritual offering that Is
presents to Yahweh.

Two objections from the list given above demand fuller comn
and provide the occasion for discussing the significance of the or
itself. The objection that the oracle presupposes the fall of Sam
is only logically but not chronologically true. For Hosea to h
spoken of its aftermath, the event need not have happened. A si
lar cavil, that Hosea could not have spoken of Yahweh's wrath a
a thing of the past, is no more serious. However, the question of
relationship between wrath and love is not merely a matter of t
poral succession. This point is important for a proper understanc
of the relevance of chapter 14.

God's wrath and love can exist simultaneously and can be m;
fested in the same circumstances of a people's life. When Hosea sp
of God as experiencing anthropopathically feelings of anger ;
love, he had to speak of one feeling displacing the other, because
is the way with human feelings. But God is not man, and div
wrath and love are not merely feelings. We have already seen
chapter 11 that Hosea refused to limit the holiness of God to

[5] According to the writer of 2 Kings 18, Judah relied on Egypt for char:
and horsemen in the eighth century B.C. (vs. 24; cf., Isa. 36:9).

removal of the conditions of wrath. Yahweh's natural blessing upon Israel was eschatological in the sense that his purpose as Lord of nature was to bring harmony and blessedness to Israel within the natural order, just as it was his purpose as Lord of the covenant to bring about justice and faith. This natural blessing was ultimately assured, but it was not immediately available in its fullness.

It has bothered some commentators, as I have noted, that the imagery of 14:5–8 should be drawn from nature. It is no embarrassment to Hosea's theology of grace, however. The entire second chapter of the book is devoted to the theme of Yahweh's simultaneous lordship over Israel's historical destiny and over the natural order. Hosea's quarrel with the baalized cultus was not over the question whether God was involved with nature. Of course, God was involved. The issue was whether God himself was a part of the natural order and, therefore, subject to manipulation by cultic means, or whether he was essentially outside the natural order and, hence, cultically approachable only as the free giver of natural blessings. This issue was central to Hosea's entire proclamation, and it would have been surprising and disappointing if his oracles of fulfilment had not affirmed his faith in Yahweh's sovereignty over nature and his free bestowal of natural gifts.

This last affirmation is actually only implicit in the imagery of chapter 14, for the terms of this promise may be interpreted as figuratively applying to the ethical rather than to the material realm. However, the explicit terms of chapter 2 make it clear that the promise comprehends both realms. Indeed, there is no suggestion of a separation between the two. Both belong to the unity of the redeemed creation. The final unity remains to be achieved. The faithful in Israel can live as if it were already achieved, provided the love of God is appropriated in the confession of guilt and in the renewal of covenantal obedience. Hosea's promise was true for the men of his age as well as for their heirs among the unlimited community of the people of God.

ADDITIONAL NOTE A:
THE DESIGNATIONS OF
HOSEA'S AUDIENCE

"Samaria," as capital of the northern kingdom, was the embodiment of the two great aberrations of Israelite history, the paganizing of worship (8:4–6; 10:5) and the misappropriation of political power (13:9–14:1). Its history was entirely bound up with the monarchy, since it had been built by Omri, chief architect of the royal Israelite state. Monarchy and capital city would rightly fall together (10:7).

"Ephraim" is used flexibly in Hosea and more often than in any other book of the Old Testament (thirty-five times). It is Hosea's favorite designation of the northern Israelite state (4:7; 5:3, 5, 9, 11, 12, 13, 14; 6:4, 10; 7:1, 8, 11; 8:9, 11; 9:3, 11, 13, 16; 10:6, 11, 11; 11:12; 12:1, 9, 15; 13:1; 14:8).[1] Nevertheless, the tradi-

[1] It is far from clear why he focused upon Ephraim alone among the northern tribes and referred only occasionally to Jacob (10:11; 12:3, 12) or to the "tribes" of Israel (5:9). Perhaps the oracles that designate the state as "Ephraim" were uttered after Assyria had annexed Galilee and the trans-Jordanian territories (732 B.C.) and after the kingdom had shrunk to what was later called Samaria, i.e., roughly the traditional portion of Ephraim (so, G. Hölscher, *Die Propheten,* pp. 212 f., and A. Alt, "Hosea 5, 8—6, 6, Ein Krieg und seine Folgen in prophetischer Beleuchtung," *Neue kirchliche Zeitschrift* 30 [1919], pp. 544 f., = *Kleine Schriften* II, Munich, 1953, p. 176). Such a possibility depends upon whether Hosea had prophesied after 735 B.C. Scholars formerly resisted this assumption on the ground that the important Syro–Ephraimite conflict that began in 735 B.C. was not mentioned in the book (cf., for instance, Smith and Harper). In the article cited, Alt has argued, however, that Hos. 5:8–6:6 describes a phase of that war, and many other critics have subsequently shown a willingness to carry Hosea's ministry below 735 B.C. (cf., A. Weiser, *The OT: Its Formation and Development,* New York, 1961, p. 233 [English tr. of *Einleitung in das Alte Testament,* 4th ed., Göttingen, 1948]). Hosea's preference for the name "Ephraim" may reflect nothing more than the locale of his prophetic activity, or, again, the place of his own origin. Most recent commentators have accepted Alt's theory that Hosea's usage reflects Israel's territorial losses in 733 B.C., but the word of caution written by Budde in 1934 (*JPOS* 14, pp. 8–9) is a good one. He considered it inconceivable that a nation should call itself by a new name like this immediately after such a loss. National pride would have precluded

tional tribal character of the name persists in the prophet's recollection of covenantal history (11:3; cf., 13:1). In 9:3, "Ephraim" means the people rather than the state or the ancestral tradition, but in 9:13 this ambiguous usage is avoided and the people are called "sons of Ephraim." In 9:8, the Hebrew text reads, "The prophet is the watchman of Ephraim with ('im) my God," or something like it. The RSV emends to, "The prophet is the watchman of Ephraim, the people ('am) of my God." Numerous other interpretations have been proposed for this difficult line. In proximity to 9:3 and 9:13, the RSV rendering is a reasonable one. It makes the prophet primarily responsible to the covenant people rather than to the Israelite state. In connection with the tribal memory of 11:3, the divine question, "How can I give you up, O Ephraim," presumably refers to the people. God's determination never again to destroy Ephraim (11:9), then, refers to the people as a community of the covenant.

The last passage is confusing at first sight. In so far as Ephraim is truly destroyed, it is destroyed as the Israelite state. Yet, for Ephraim to continue, one whom God "will not again destroy," Ephraim must be the people. The perplexity is dispelled, however, by the recognition that all occurrences of the name "Ephraim" as a reference to the people are in contexts where the subject is not the kingdom but the tribal antecedents of the monarchy (11:3; 12:8 f., 13 f.), or, alternatively, the future survivors of its fall (9:3, 13, cf., 9:8; 11:8–9; 14:8). Elsewhere, by contrast, the political character of the name is highlighted by its association with the kingdom of Judah (5:5, 10, 12, 13, 14; 6:4; 10:11; 11:12). Hosea's use of the synonymous parallelism "Ephraim"// "House of Israel" in a passage where the subject is an institution of the kingdom (11:12) strongly suggests that the latter phrase denotes the state and its instruments (including, of course, the official cultus). This comment also applies to the MT of 6:10, although I have emended "Beth ('House of')-Israel" there to read "Bethel." See the textual note.

---

it. It is far more likely, he said, that the usage was ancient, dating from a time when the kingdom was small, and that it continued in vogue after the nation's territories were expanded. He also noted the use of "Ephraim" for the kingdom in 5:3 ff., a passage he dated *prior* to 735 B.C. See, also, J. Lindblom, *A Study of the Immanuel Section in Isaiah* (Lund, 1958), p. 28.

"House of Israel" appears once more in Hosea in a highly instructive passage. In 5:1 it occurs at the head of a series of brief oracles dealing with the cultic and political follies of the kingdom, in which "Ephraim" is used eight times for the Israelite state (5:1–14). "Hear this, O priests! Take heed, O House of Israel! Hearken, O house of the king! For the judgment concerns you: you have been a trap at Mizpah, a net spread upon Tabor." The prophet is addressing the officials, whom he regards as deceivers of the people. The House of Israel here is not the covenant-community but its official representatives in palace and temple.

What is true of all four occurrences of the phrase "House of Israel" is sometimes true of the name "Israel" as well. In this unmodified form it appears thirty times in the Book of Hosea. Its specific connotation varies, as we might expect, since this is the most comprehensive term of all. Often it means the northern kingdom (4:5, 16; 5:3, 3, 5; 6:10; 7:10; 8:2, 3, 5, 8; 9:1, 7; 10:1, 6, 8, 9, 15; 13:9). This meaning is especially clear where it is associated with the king (10:15; 13:9) or with the kingdom of Judah (8:14), or is identified with Ephraim as the Israelite state (4:6; 5:3, 5; 6:10; 7:10 [cf. 7:8]; 8:8 [cf., 8:9]; 9:1 [cf., 9:3]; 10:6 [cf., 10:7], 8, 9; [10:11]). Alternatively, the term is used to designate the people of God. The passage 6:11b–7:1a is notable: "When I would reverse the captivity of my *people*, when I would heal *Israel*, then *Ephraim's* guilt becomes clear, and the evils of *Samaria*." The first term is in synonymous parallelism with the second, and so is the third with the fourth. The first pair might also be synonymous with the second pair. However, if all these terms denote the people, in distinction from the royal institutions, it is clear from what follows (7:3, 5, 7, 8, 11) that what corrupts Ephraim–Samaria are the international policies and ritual practices of the monarchy. The two pairs of terms are probably not synonymous, however, but synthetic. Each successive term overlaps its predecessor but is not identical with it. Ephraim and Samaria, then, designate the northern kingdom, a part of the larger entity, Israel, the people of God. There are other passages where the term "Israel" is used also in a comprehensive sense for the covenant-people. It carries this meaning in reference to the patriarchal (12:12; 13:1) and exodus traditions (11:1; 12:13), and to Hosea's ultimate hope (11:8; 14:1, 5).[2]

By comparison with "Ephraim" and "Israel," "my people" occurs only occasionally in the Book of Hosea. It seems to mean the covenant-community. This community of the faithful is not identical with the northern kingdom, even though members of the one are subjects of the other. The distinction between the people of the covenant and the institutions that are supposed to serve them is clearly made in chapter 4 (cf., vss. 4, 6, 8, 9, 12, and 14).[3]

God's people are not only the individual, living persons who participate in the life of the sacral community at a given time. They are also that enduring company of faithful men that transcends each particular generation. In Hosea's time this company consisted of a people "bent on turning way" from God (11:7) and was prevented by national corruption from being divinely healed (6:11). This is to say, it was "Not-My-People" (1:9, 11). Nevertheless, there was always the possibility that God would give this community new life and make it again "My-People" (1:11; 2:1, 23).[4]

[2] A detailed analysis of the meaning of the term "Israel" is presented in G. A. Danell, *op. cit.*, pp. 136–145. Danell's purpose is to determine the instances where the term means the northern kingdom, in distinction to the kingdom of Judah, and the instances where it means the totality of the twelve tribes. In those cases where the northern kingdom is meant, he does not seek to establish whether it indicates the people or the state. His results, therefore, neither confirm nor refute those of the present study.

[3] On the difficult problem of 4:4, see the textual note to this verse.

[4] "My people" occurs in 1:9, 11; 2:1, 23; 4:6, 8, 12; 6:11; and 11:7; "a people," in 4:9; and "the people," in 4:14.

ADDITIONAL NOTE B:
HOSEA 4:2 AND THE
DECALOGUE

Does Hos. 4:2 show a knowledge of the Ten Commandments? Well-hausen and Marti reflected the general nineteenth-century opinion of the lateness of the Pentateuch, especially of its codes of law, when they denied that Hosea had any knowledge of the Decalogue in its present form. In recent decades, scholars have been almost universally willing to date the Decalogue in the period from the thirteenth to the ninth century B.C., and commentators on Hosea have been corespondingly willing to attribute probable knowledge of it to Hosea.

The comparison often made between the first two terms of vs. 4:2 (כחש, אלה) and the ninth commandment is imprecise, since the latter deals with the giving of false legal testimony against another man, whereas the former deals with the uttering of curses and false oaths of indeterminate kind. The third commandment of the Decalogue is closer to Hos. 4:2a, but its wording is quite different. Hos. 4:2b has nothing to do with the injunctions of the Decalogue. This leaves 4:2ab, "murdering, and stealing, and committing adultery" (רצח, גנב, נאף), the terms of which are identical with the sixth, eighth, and seventh commandments (Exod. 20:13–15; Deut. 5:17–19), both in their juxtaposition and in their absolute form. Jer. 7:9 lists the same three, also as absolutes, though in a different order (stealing, murdering, committing adultery). This passage is even closer to the Decalogue than Hos. 4:2, however, for it lists, in addition, violation of the first commandment (going after "other gods"), as well as false swearing (שבע לשקר). This phrase differs in wording from both Hos. 4:2 and the third and ninth commandments. Jeremiah's familiarity with the oracles of Hosea and his affinity with the Deuteronomic tradition are well-known, as is the northern prophetic influence upon both the Elohistic source of the Pentateuch (in which Exod. 20 stands) and the Book of Deuteronomy. The a priori probability that Hosea's work came from the same circles as these other traditions reinforces the evidence provided by 4:2.

Nevertheless, the case is not nearly so clear-cut as the scholarly consensus implies. Hos. 4:2 is at least as close to Lev. 19 as it is to the Decalogue. Lev. 19 lists prohibitions against stealing (גנב, vs. 11), dealing falsely (כחש, vs. 11), lying, and swearing falsely (vss. 11–12). It enjoins the fear of God (vs. 14), with which the knowledge of God in Hos. 4:1 can be compared. The oppression (עשק) and blood threats prohibited here (vss. 13, 16) are reminiscent of Hos. 4:2b. Love of the neighbor (אהב, vs. 19) recalls Hosea's ḥesed (4:1), and the verb in the admonition to reason with the neighbors (vs. 17) is the same word Hosea uses in 4:4ab (יכח). The recurrent prohibition of various kinds of divination (vss. 26, 31) parallels Hos. 4:12; and the warning in vs. 29 against making a harlot (להזנותה) of one's daughter, lest the land become harlotrous (ולא־תזנה הארץ), is astonishingly close to Hos. 4:13–15. Lev. 19 does not mention adultery, but it is surrounded by enumerations of sexual crimes, including adultery (18:6–23; 20:10 ff.). Finally, the threat of expulsion from the land as a punishment for violation of these commandments (18:24–30), reinforced by a recollection of the similar fate of the Canaanites, corresponds well to threats uttered by Hosea, though not specifically in chapter 4 (though the defilement of the land in Lev. 18:25, 28 may be compared to its desolation in Hos. 4:3).

Lev. 19 belongs to the Holiness Code (Lev. 17–26), the date and origin of which are indeterminate. It was presumably incorporated into the Judean collection of priestly traditions after the Babylonian exile. It is improbable that Hosea had any knowledge of this literary tradition, either in oral or written form. The fact that the literary parallels between Lev. 18–20 and Hos. 4 are on the whole as close as those between Hos. 4 and the Decalogue, makes it extremely hazardous to conclude that Hos. 4 shows direct acqaintance with the Decalogue. Weiser's casual statement that the Decalogue was well-established in the public liturgy of Israel in Hosea's time is in fact highly problematic (see his commentary on Hos. 4:2).

Rather than think of the Decalogue as *the* definitive epitome of Yahwistic ethical instruction, north and south, from early times on, we are forced to assume a wide variety of traditions, all incorporating some of the same fundamental teachings, but phrasing and epitomizing them in different ways. The three great crimes of murder, robbery, and adultery appear to have constituted an especially memorable and significant triplicity, not only among prophetic and priestly circles, but also among the sages of Israel. Job 24:14–15 lists the three in the same absolute form (i.e., without the specification of particular objects or circumstances) as that used in Jer. 7:9, Hos. 4:2, Exod. 20:13–15, and Deut. 5:17–19, and in the same order as that in Hos. 4:2 (6, 8, 7—using the enumeration of the Decalogue; Jeremiah's order is 8, 6, 7).

ADDITIONAL NOTE C:
REFERENCES TO JUDAH IN
THE BOOK OF HOSEA

Chapters 4–14 contain no favorable references to Judah and none to
the sole legitimacy of the Judean state. The references to Judah in
5:5, 10, 12, 13, 14; 6:4, 11; 8:14; 10:11; and 12:2 are strictures,
though most of them appear to be redactional. If vs. 4:15 is correct,
it is not an endorsement of Judean practice but a mere warning to
keep away from Israel's sanctuaries. Vs. 11:12 (Heb. 12:1) has
been translated by the *LXX* and others (e.g., *RSV*) as a favorable
comment about Judah, but it is probably a jibe: "Judah (Jacob?)
again strays with 'El, and is faithful with 'holy ones' " (similarly,
Weiser and Sellin; cf., *Moffatt* and the *Westminster Study Edition of
the Holy Bible,* footnote). See the textual note to this verse. Many
of these statements about Judah are too bland to be Hosea's and
certainly do not affect our judgment about his theology.

In chapters 1–3, the references to Judah are wholly favorable and
occur chiefly in the poems of promise. The critical consensus still
stands solidly against vs. 1:7 and the phrase "and David their king"
in 3:5. On the other hand, defenders of the Hosean origin of vs. 1:11
are now numerous (e.g., Mauchline, Weiser, and Wolff). Vs. 1:7 presupposes the events of 701 B.C. (see the textual note) but must have
been written before 587 B.C. Who could have taken comfort in the
deliverance of 701 B.C. if he had experienced the events of 587 B.C.
and those of the following years? Again, the Davidic insertion in
vs. 3:5 is a bit too casual for the post-exilic period, i.e., it sounds
like something added while the dynasty was still in power. Contrast
the markedly post-exilic character of Jer. 23:5; 30:9; 33:15–26;
Ezek. 34:23 f.; 37:24 f.; and Zech. 12:7–13:1. Hos. 3:5 is closer
to Isa. 9:6, which is probably pre-exilic, even if not Isaianic. Conversely, vs. 1:11 appears to presuppose the exile of both Israel and
Judah (it has a close affinity to Ezek. 34:24 f., incidentally, though
so does Hos. 2:18–23 to Ezek. 34:25–31). If vss. 1:7 and 3:5a
are seventh-century additions, chapters 1 and 3 must be generally

older, i.e., these chapters may be dated in their written form close to the eighth century, on relatively objective grounds. The Judean editing of chapters 4–14 is also best dated between the times of Hezekiah and Josiah, for the interpolations in these chapters were clearly made when the Judean kingdom was still flourishing. This is now the practically established opinion (cf., R. E. Wolfe, *op. cit.,* pp. 91 ff.; Wolff, pp. xxvi f.; and Weiser, on 4:15).

The following critics regard all references to Judah in the Book of Hosea as secondary: Marti, Nowack, Robinson, Pfeiffer (*op. cit.,* p. 567, although he does not explicitly reject Alt's view of 5:8–6:6), and R. E. Wolfe (*op. cit.,* pp. 91–93). Since Alt's interpretation of 5:8–6:6 has been so widely accepted, other Judah-references in Hosea have also been defended. Mauchline retains the references to Judah in 1:11; 5:10 (?); and 6:4; Weiser, in 1:11; Wolff, in 1:11; 8:14; 10:11; and 11:12; and Knight in 4:15; 6:11; and 12:2. But notice that each list is different from the others! Danell (*op. cit.,* p. 139) accepts all occurrences of "Judah" as probably original.

Hos. 5:5c and 6:11a are obviously marginal comments that have crept into the text. Both are outside the poetic parallelism to which they have been appended. Vs. 5:15 is the most suspect passage of all. "Judah" is a poor parallel to "Jacob" in 12:2 (read, therefore, "Israel"). The same is true in 8:4. Hos. 10:11 is impossibly confused. "Judah" may have displaced "Israel" here also, though the entire clause is perhaps superfluous. Older commentators generally changed "Judah" to "Israel" in 5:10–14 and 6:4, and several scholars since Alt have continued to do so (Robinson, R. E. Wolfe, and, with reservations, Mauchline and Pfeiffer). See the textual notes to the several passages.

SELECTED BIBLIOGRAPHY

1. COMMENTARIES ON HOSEA

I listed only those commentaries that I have found to be most thorough or helpful, or most representative of important phases of the modern criticism of Hosea. The books by Lindblom and Nyberg in list 3A, below, are also important critical studies.

The opinions of commentators who wrote prior to 1905 are fully catalogued in Harper. There is no comparable treatment of the work done between 1905 and the present, although full bibliographies are provided in Wolff's commentary.

Brown, Sydney L. *The Book of Hosea* (*Westminster Commentaries*), London, 1932.

Cheyne, T. K. *Hosea* (*The Cambridge Bible for Schools and Colleges*), Cambridge, 1889.

Harper, W. R. *Amos and Hosea* (*The International Critical Commentary*), Edinburgh and New York, 1905.

Knight, G. A. F. *Hosea* (*Torch Bible Commentaries*), London, 1960.

Marti, Karl. *Das Dodekapropheton* (*Kurzer Hand-Commentar zum A. T.* XIII), Tübingen, 1904.

Mauchline, John. "The Book of Hosea: Introduction and Exegesis," *The Interpreter's Bible,* Vol. 6, pp. 553–725. New York and Nashville, 1956.

Nötscher, Friedrich. *Zwölfprophetenbuch oder kleine propheten* (*Echter Bibel*), Würzburg, 1954.

Nowack, W. *Die kleinen Propheten* (*Handkommentar zum A. T.* III, 4), Göttingen, 1903.

Robinson, T. H., and Horst F. *Die zwölf kleinen Propheten* (*Handbuch zum A. T.* XIV), 2nd ed. Tübingen, 1954.

Sellin, Ernst. *Das Zwölfprophetenbuch* (*Kommentar zum A. T.* XII), Leipzig, 1922.

Smith, G. A. *The Book of the Twelve Prophets.* Vol. I, *Amos, Hosea, and Micah* (*The Expositor's Bible*), London, 1896.

Weiser, Artur. *Das Buch der zwölf kleinen Propheten* (*Das Alte Testament Deutsch,* XXIV, 1), Göttingen, 1949.

Wellhausen, Julius. *Die kleinen Propheten übersetzt mit Noten* (*Skizzen und Vorarbeiten,* Vol. 5), Berlin, 1892.

Wolff, H. W. *Dodekaprophten 1: Hosea* (*Biblischer Kommentar* XIV/1), Neukirchen, Kreis Moers, 1961.

2. THE THEOLOGY OF HOSEA

The following works are among the most useful for the interpretation of Hosea's oracles:

Buber, Martin. *The Prophetic Faith*. New York, 1949.
Eichrodt, Walther. "The Holy One in Your Midst: the Theology of Hosea," *Interpretation* 15 (1961), 259–73.
Fohrer, Georg. "Umkehr und Erlösung beim Propheten Hosea," *TZ* 11 (1955), 161–185.
Procksch, Otto. *Theologie des Alten Testaments*. Gütersloh, 1950.
Ritschl, Dietrich. "God's Conversion: An Exposition of Hosea 11," *Interpretation* 15 (1961), 286–303.
Scott, Melville. *The Message of Hosea*. New York and London, 1921.
Snaith, N. H. *Mercy and Sacrifice*. London, 1953.
Welch, A. C. *Kings and Prophets of Israel*. London, 1952.
Wolff, H. W. " 'Wissen um Gott' bei Hosea als Urform von Theologie," *Ev. Theol.* 12 (1952/53), 533–54.

3. OTHER WORKS

A. GENERAL

There are scores of books on the prophets that contain chapters on Hosea. Since most of these deal very briefly with the several aspects of Hosea's thought and do not attempt to give original interpretations, I omitted most of them. Those of W. R. Smith, Cornill, Lods, Hölscher, and J. M. P. Smith (W. A. Irwin's revision) have been included as representative studies from various periods in the past seventy-five years of prophetic criticism.

Ackroyd, P. R. "Hosea," *Peake's Commentary on the Bible*, M. Black and H. H. Rowley, eds., pp. 603–13. London, 1962.
Anderson, B. W. "Studia Biblica XXVI. The Book of Hosea," *Interpretation* 8 (1954), 290–303.
Baumann, E. " 'Wissen um Gott' bei Hosea als Urform der Theologie?" *Ev. Theol.* 15 (1955), 416–25.
Bentzen, Aage. *Introduction to the Old Testament*. 2 vols. 2nd ed. Copenhagen, 1952.
Böhmer, J. "Die Grundgedanken der Predigt Hoseas," *Zeitschrift für Wissenschaftliche Theologie* 45 (1902), 1–24.
Buck, F. *Die Liebe Gottes beim Propheten Osee*. Rome, 1953.
Buss, M. J. *A Form-Critical Study in the Book of Hosea with Special Attention to Method* (Dissertation), Yale University, New Haven, 1958.

Cornill, Carl. *The Prophets of Israel.* 10th ed. Chicago, 1913.

Danell, G. A. *Studies in the Name Israel in the Old Testament.* Uppsala, 1946.

Day, Edward. "Is the Book of Hosea Exilic?" *AJSL* 26 (1909/1910), 105–32.

Eissfeldt, Otto. *Einleitung in das Alte Testament.* 3rd ed. Tübingen, 1964.

Farr, George. "The Concept of Grace in the Book of Hosea," *ZAW* 70 (1958), 98–107.

Gemser, B. "The *rib*-or controversy-pattern in Hebrew mentality," *Wisdom in Israel and the Ancient Near East* (*H. H. Rowley Festschrift*), M. Noth and D. W. Thomas, eds., pp. 120–37. (*Supplements to Vetus Testamentum* Vol. III), Leiden, 1955.

Gottwald, Norman K. *All the Kingdoms of the Earth. Israelite Prophecy and International Relations in the Ancient Near East.* New York, 1964.

Harper, Wm. R. *The Structure of the Text of the Book of Hosea.* Chicago, 1905.

Hölscher, Gustav. *Die Propheten.* Leipzig. 1914.

Kaufmann, Yehezkel. *The Religion of Israel.* Chicago, 1950.

Lindblom, Johannes. *Hosea, Literarisch Untersucht.* (Acta Academiae Aboensis: Humaniora V), Abo, 1927.

———. *Prophecy in Ancient Israel.* Oxford, 1962.

Lods, Adolphe. *The Prophets and the Rise of Judaism.* London, 1937.

McKenzie, J. L. "Divine Passion in Osee," *CBQ* 17 (1955), 287–99.

———. "Knowledge of God in Hosea," *JBL* 74 (1955), 22–27.

Maly, E. H. "Messianism in Osee," *CBQ* 19 (1957), 213–25.

May, H. G. "The Fertility Cult in Hosea," *AJSL* 48 (1931/32), 73–98.

Mowinckel, S. *Prophecy and Tradition.* Oslo, 1946.

Muilenburg, James. "The History of the Religion of Israel," *The Interpreter's Bible,* Vol. 1, pp. 292–348. New York and Nashville, 1952.

Noth, M. *The History of Israel.* 2nd ed. New York, 1960.

Nyberg, H. S. *Studien zum Hoseabuche* (*Uppsala Universitets Årsskrift* 1935:6), Uppsala, 1935.

Östborn, Gunnar. *Yahweh and Baal: Studies in the Book of Hosea and Related Documents.* Lund, 1956.

Owens, J. J. "Exegetical Study of Hosea," *Review and Expositor* 54 (1957), 522–43.

Peters, Norbert. *Osee und die Geschichte.* Paderborn, 1924.

Pfeiffer, R. H. *Introduction to the Old Testament.* New York, 1948.

Rad, Gerhard von. *Theologie des Alten Testaments.* Band II. *Die Theologie der prophetischen Überlieferungen Israels.* Munich, 1961.

Rieger, J. *Die Bedeutung der Geschichte für die Verkündigung des Amos und Hosea.* Giessen, 1929.

Robinson, H. W. *Two Hebrew Prophets.* London, 1948. The section on Hosea was published also separately as *The Cross of Hosea.* Philadelphia, 1949.

Rowley, H. H., ed. *The Old Testament and Modern Study.* Oxford, 1951.

Rust, E. C. "The Theology of Hosea," *Review and Expositor* 54 (1957), 510–21.

Schumpp, P. M. *Das Buch der zwolf Propheten (Herders Bibelkommentar)*, Frieburg, 1950.

Smart, J. D. "Hosea (Man and Book)," *The Interpreter's Dictionary of the Bible*. New York and Nashville, 1962.

Smith, J. M. P. *The Prophets and Their Times*. Rev. ed. by W. A. Irwin. Chicago, 1941.

Vuilleumier, R. *La tradition cultuelle d'Israël dans la prophétie d'Amos et d'Osee*. (*Cahiers Theologiques* 45). Neuchâtel, 1960.

Weiser, Artur. *The Old Testament: Its Formation and Development*. New York, 1961.

Wolfe, R. E. *Meet Amos and Hosea*. New York, 1945.

Wolff, H. W. "Guilt and Salvation: A Study of the Prophecy of Hosea," *Interpretation* 15 (1961), 274–85.

———. "Erkenntnis Gottes im Alten Testament," *Ev. Theol.* 15 (1955), 426–31.

———. "Hoseas geistige Heimat," *Theologische Literaturzeitung* 81 (1956), 83–94.

B. SPECIAL

Ackroyd, P. R. "Hosea and Jacob," *VT* 13 (1963), 245–59.

Allegro, J. M. "A Recently Discovered Fragment of a Commentary on Hosea from Qumran's Fourth Cave," *JBL* 78 (1959), 142–48.

Alt, Albrecht. "Hosea 5:8–6:6. Ein Krieg und seine Folgen in prophetischer Beleuchtung," *Kleine Schriften zur Geschichte des Volkes Israel* II, pp. 163–87. Munich, 1953.

Batten, L. W. "Hosea's Message and Marriage," *JBL* 48 (1929), 257–73.

Bentzen, A. "The Weeping of Jacob, Hos. XII 5A," *VT* 1 (1951), 58 f.

Budde, Karl. "Der Abschnitt Hosea 1–3," *Theologische Studien und Kritiken* 96/97 (1925), 1–89.

———. "Zu Text und Auslegung des Buches Hosea," *JBL* 45 (1926), 280–97.

———. "Zu Text und Auslegung des Buches Hosea. 3. Kap. 5:1–6:6. Falscher und rechter Jahwedienst," *JPOS* 14 (1943), 1–41.

Cazelles, Henri. "The Problem of the Kings in Osee 8:4," *CBQ* 11 (1949), 14–25.

Dobbie, R. "The Text of Hosea IX 8," *VT* 5 (1955), 199–203.

Driver, G. R. "Difficult Words in the Hebrew Prophets," *Studies in Old Testament Prophecy*, H. H. Rowley, ed., pp. 52–72. London, 1950.

———. "Linguistic and Textual Problems. Minor Prophets. I," *JTS* 39 (1938), 154–66.

———. "Studies in the Vocabulary of the Old Testament. IV," *JTS* 33 (1932), 38–47.

Elliger, K. "Eine verkannte Kunstform bei Hosea," *ZAW* 69 (1957), 151–60.

Gaster, T. H. "Hosea VII 3–6, 8–9," *VT* 4 (1954), 78–79.

Gertner, M. "The Masorah and the Levites. Appendix: An Attempt at an Interpretation of Hosea XII," *VT* 10 (1960), 272–84.

Ginsberg, H. L. "Hosea's Ephraim, More Fool than Knave," *JBL* 80 (1961), 339–47.

———. "Studies in Hosea 1–3," *Yehezkel Kaufmann Jubilee Volume,* M. Haran, ed., pp. 50–69. Jerusalem, 1960.

Gordis, R. "Hosea's Marriage and Message: A New Approach," *HUCA* 25 (1954), 9–35.

———. "The Text Meaning of Hosea XIV 3," *VT* 5 (1955), 88–90.

Gordon, C. H. "Hosea 2:4–5 in the Light of New Semitic Inscriptions," *ZAW* 54 (1936), 277–80.

Junker, H. "Textkritische, formkritische und traditionsgeschichtliche Untersuchung zu Os. 4:1–10," *BZ* N.F. 4/2 (1960), 165–73.

König, Franz. "Die Auferstehungshoffnung bei Osee 6:1–3," *Zeitschrift für katholische Theologie* 70 (1948), 94–100.

Kuhl, C. "Neue Dokumente zum Verständnis von Hosea 2:4–15," *ZAW* 52 (1934), 102–9.

Lohfink, Norbert. "Zu Text und Form von Os. 4:4–6," *Biblica* 42 (1961), 303–32.

May, H. G. "An Interpretation of the Names of Hosea's Children," *JBL* 55 (1936), 285–91.

Nötscher, F. "Zur Auferstehung nach drei Tagen," *Biblica* 35 (1954), 313–19.

Robertson, Edw. "Textual Criticism of Hosea X 11," *Transactions of the Glasgow Univ. Oriental Soc.* 8 (1936/37), 16–17.

Rost, Leonhard. "Erwägungen zu Hosea 4:13 f.," *Festschrift für A. Bertholet,* pp. 451–60. Tübingen, 1950.

Rowley, H. H., "The Marriage of Hosea," *Bulletin of the John Rylands Library* 39 (1956/57), 200–33.

Schmidt, Hans. "Die Ehe des Hosea," *ZAW* 42 (1924), 245–72.

———. "Hosea 6:1–6," *Sellin-Festschrift. Beiträge zur Religionsgeschichte und Archäologie Palästinas,* pp. 111–26. Leipzig, 1927.

Sellin, E. "Hosea und das Martyrium des Mose," *ZAW* 46 (1928), 26–33.

Smith, W. R. *The Prophets of Israel.* Rev. by T. K. Cheyne. London, 1895.

Spiegel, S. "A Prophetic Attestation of the Decalogue: Hosea 6:5 . . . ," *Harvard Theological Review* 27 (1934), 105–44.

Stamm, J. J. "Eine Erwägung zu Hosea 6:1–2," *ZAW* 57 (1939), 266–68.

Stinespring, W. "Hosea, Prophet of Doom," *Crozer Quarterly* 27 (1950), 200–7.

Testuz, Michel. "Deux fragments inédits des manuscrits de la Mer Morte," *Semitica* 5 (1955), 37–38.

Torczyner, Harry. "Dunkel Bibelstellen," *BZAW* 41 (1925), 274–80.

Tushingham, A. D. "A Reconsideration of Hosea, Chapters 1–3," *JNES* 12 (1953), 150–59.

Waterman, L. "Hosea, Chs. 1–3, in Retrospect and Prospect," *JNES* 14 (1955), 22–27.

Wolff, H. W. "Der grosse Jesreeltag (Hosea 2:1–3)," *Ev. Theol.* 12 (1952/53), 78–104.

Zolli, J. "Hosea 4:17–18," *ZAW* 56 (1938), 175.

————. "Note on Hosea 6:5," *Jewish Quarterly Review* 31 (1940/41), 79–82.

Index of Biblical References

The list of references to the Book of Hosea includes only passages referred to out of context.

Index of Subjects and Authors